직독직해로 읽는
오즈의 마법사
The Wonderful Wizard of Oz

직독직해로 읽는
오즈의 마법사
The Wonderful Wizard of Oz

개정판 2쇄 발행　2020년　3월　20일
초판 1쇄 발행　　2012년　6월　5일

원작	라이먼 프랭크 바움
역주	이현구
디자인	IndigoBlue
일러스트	정은수
발행인	조경아
발행처	랭귀지북스
주소	서울시 마포구 포은로2나길 31 벨라비스타 208호
전화	02.406.0047　　**팩스**　　02.406.0042
이메일	languagebooks@hanmail.net
홈페이지	www.languagebooks.co.kr
등록번호	101-90-85278　　**등록일자**　　2008년 7월 10일
ISBN	979-11-5635-042-2 (13740)
가격	13,000원

ⓒ LanguageBooks 2012

잘못된 책은 구입한 서점에서 바꿔 드립니다.
blog.naver.com/languagebook에서 MP3 파일을 다운로드할 수 있습니다.

「이 도서의 국립중앙도서관 출판예정도서목록(CIP)은 서지정보유통지원시스템 홈페이지(http://seoji.nl.go.kr)와 국가자료공동목록시스템(http://www.nl.go.kr/kolisnet)에서 이용하실 수 있습니다.(CIP제어번호: CIP2016006148)」

직독직해로 읽는
오즈의 마법사
The Wonderful Wizard of Oz

라이먼 프랭크 바움 원작
이현구 역주

Language Books

머리말

요즈음 원서 읽기의 열기는 굳이 설명하지 않아도 누구나 알 것입니다. 수많은 학습자들은 여러 가지 방법을 시도해보지만, 효과적인 학습법을 찾지 못하는 분이 많습니다.

이런 분들이 원서를 읽으면 효율적으로 읽기, 듣기, 말하기 능력을 향상시킬 수 있습니다. 원서를 빠르게 읽고, 어휘력과 표현력을 늘리고, 회화와 쓰기 능력을 효과적으로 준비할 수 있습니다. 그러나 원어민들이 즐겨 읽는 원서나 고전 작품에는 어려운 표현과 어휘 때문에 쉽게 도전하기 힘든 경우도 있습니다.

이렇게 자신에게 맞는 공부법을 찾는 데 어려움을 겪고 있는 분들과, 높은 수준의 원서를 혼자 공부하기 힘들어하는 분들을 위해 이 책을 쓰게 되었습니다. 다시 말하여 영어 학습에 도움이 될 만한 작품들을 여러분이 쉽게 이해할 수 있도록 직독직해로 설명해 놓았습니다. 또한 원작의 내용을 이해하는데 아무런 문제가 없도록 글의 구성에 정성을 기울였습니다. 직독직해로 읽는 습관에 익숙해지면, 읽기 속도가 모국어 수준에 가까워집니다.

세계명작 작품에는 대화체 표현이 풍부합니다. 그래서 본 교재로 듣기와 말하기를 연습할 수 있도록, 원어민 성우가 녹음한 MP3 파일을 다운로드 할 수 있습니다.

PREFACE

거기다 고교 영어 수준으로 원서의 난이도를 조정했습니다. 실제로 본 책에서 설명된 대부분의 어휘와 숙어는 고교 영어 수준에 속합니다. 또한 중요 문법을 설명하여 독자가 공부하는데 어려움이 없도록 하였습니다.

분명 유창하고 높은 수준의 영어를 자유자재로 사용할 수 있으려면, 장기간 공부해야 됩니다. 그 시간을 최대한 단축시키려면 원어민 수준으로 빠르게 영어를 읽고(직독직해), 자신의 생각을 표현하는 능력(동시통역연습)을 키워야 합니다. 그리고 영어 실력을 높이는데 무엇보다 중요한 것은 열정적이고 성실한 학습자의 마음가짐입니다. 부디 이 책과 여러분의 성실함을 무기로 큰 성과를 올리길 기대해 봅니다.

본 책이 출판되도록 물심양면으로 전폭적인 지지와 성원을 보내준 아내와 가족에게 감사의 뜻을 전합니다. 또한 여식이 가족의 사랑 속에서 항상 밝고 건강하게 자라길 기원합니다.

이현구

저자 소개

라이먼 프랭크 바움에 대하여

L. Frank Baum

- 1856년 미국 뉴욕 주에서 태어남
- 배우, 점원, 외판원, 신문기자, 잡지사 편집장, 작가로 활동
- 미국 동화작가로 소설 55편, 단편 82편 외에 다수의 작품을 집필
- 비평가와 독자들로부터 동시에 호평 받은 대표작은 『오즈의 마법사』임
- 여성 참정권을 주장한 페미니스트
- 40대부터 작품 활동에 몰입
- 『오즈의 마법사』는 1939년에 뮤지컬 영화로 제작
- 1986년 만화영화로 제작

작품 소개

『오즈의 마법사 The Wonderful Wizard of Oz』 중에 사람들에게 널리 알려진 명대사를 소개합니다.

"People would rather live in homes regardless of its grayness.
"사람들은 특별한 매력이 없을 지라도 집에서 살길 원해.

There is no place like home."
집만큼 좋은 곳은 없으니까."

"You have plenty of courage, I am sure," answered Oz.
"분명히 너는 용기가 많아" 오즈가 대답했다.

"All you need is confidence in yourself.
"네가 필요한 것은 단지 자신을 믿는 거야.

There is no living thing that is not afraid when it faces danger.
위험에 부딪쳤을 때 두려워하지 않는 존재는 없어.

The true courage is in facing danger when you are afraid,
두렵지만 위험에 부딪치는 것이 진정한 용기야,

and that kind of courage you have in plenty."
그리고 너는 그럴 용기가 충분해."

INTRODUCTION

"I think you are wrong to want a heart.
"심장을 갖길 원하는 건 옳지 않아.

It makes most people unhappy.
심장 때문에 대부분 사람들이 불행하니까.

If you only knew it, you are in luck not to have a heart."
네가 그런 것을 알면, 심장이 없는 게 다행이야."

"A baby has brains, but it doesn't know much.
"아기도 두뇌가 있지만 아는 것이 많지 않아.

Experience is the only thing that brings knowledge,
경험으로만 지식을 얻을 수 있어.

and the longer you are on earth the more experience you are sure to get."
네가 이 세상에 오래 살수록 분명히 더 많은 경험을 얻을 거야."

"I shall take the heart.
"나는 심장을 원해.

For brains do not make one happy,
두뇌는 사람을 행복하게 해주지 않으니까,

and happiness is the best thing in the world."
그리고 행복이 세상에서 최고니까."

"My people have been wearing green glasses on their eyes for so long
"내 백성들은 초록색 안경을 너무나 오랫동안 착용해서

that most of them think this really is an Emerald City."
대부분의 사람들은 이 도시가 정말로 에메랄드 도시라고 생각하지."

직독직해 가이드

직독직해로 읽어야 영어소설을 감각적으로 즐길 수 있다.

　직독직해로 영어를 빠르게 이해하려면, 영어 문장의 순서에 따라 앞에 있는 말과 다음에 나오는 말과 어떤 관계인지 자연스럽게 느낄 수 있어야 합니다. 즉 영어의 어순대로 문장의 의미를 파악하는 훈련을 해야 합니다. 게다가 직독직해로 영어를 이해하려면, 문장구조를 파악하면서 기본 문법 지식을 활용해야 합니다.

　하지만 길고 복잡한 문장을 이해할 때, 더 많은 문법 지식이 필요한 것은 아닙니다. 이런 문장을 쉽게 이해하는 방법은 매우 간단합니다. 그것은 어려운 문법을 따져가며 문장을 분석하기보다 영어의 언어 논리를 익히는 것입니다.

　아래에 있는 문장은 『마지막 잎새』에 나옵니다. 직독직해에 익숙하지 않은 사람이라면, 영어 문장을 앞뒤로 읽으며 해석합니다.

In one corner　was　a blank canvas　on an easel
　　1　　　　　 2　　　　3　　　　　　 4

that had been waiting there for twenty-five years　to receive
　　　　　　　　　5　　　　　　　　　　　　　　　 6

the first line of the masterpiece.
　　　　　7

앞에 있는 문장을 우리말 어순에 따라 해석하면, 다음과 같습니다.

> 한쪽 구석에는(1) / 아무 그림도 없는 캔버스가(3) / 이젤 위에(4) / 있었는데(2) / 명작의 첫 번째 대열에 속하는(7) / 대우를 받으려고(6) / 25년 동안 거기에 있었던 것이다.(5)

다시 말하여 영어 문장은 1-2-3-4-5-6-7 순서이지만, 우리말 어순에 맞게 해석해보면, 1-3-4-2-7-6-5 순으로 이해할 수 있습니다. 이런 순서로 이해하려면, 한 문장을 이해하는데 많은 시간이 걸립니다. 이런 방식으로 읽기를 지속하면, 긴 문장을 듣자마자 이해하는 것은 매우 어렵습니다. 또한 회화와 영작을 할 때, 영어로 유창하게 표현하는 능력이 개발되지 않습니다.

같은 문장을 영어 어순대로 이해하려면, 직독직해로 문장을 이해해야 합니다. 아래에 있는 설명처럼 이해할 수 있습니다.

> In one corner → 한쪽 구석에는
> was → 있었다.
> a blank canvas → (무엇이 있었는가?) 아무 그림도 없는 캔버스가
> on an easel → (캔버스는 어디에 있는가?) 이젤 위에
> that had been waiting there for twenty-five years →
> (그 그림 없는 캔버스는 어떤 것일까?) 25년 동안 거기에 있었던
> to receive → (왜 기다리고 있었을까?) 대우를 받으려고
> the first line of the masterpiece. → (어떤 대우를 받으려고 기다리는가?) 명작의 첫 번째 대열에 속하는

GUIDE

앞의 설명에서 알 수 있듯이 영어는 우리말과 어순이 매우 다릅니다. 그래서 영어 어순대로 이해하는 연습을 해야 합니다. 이것이 직독직해를 익히는 첫 번째 단계일 뿐입니다. 그리고 앞에 나오는 단어나 표현을 보면, 다음에 어떤 내용이 올지 예측할 수 있는 힌트가 있습니다. 예를 들어 앞의 문장을 보면, 'was'라는 'be'동사가 '~이 있다, 존재하다'라는 의미로 쓰였습니다. '존재하다'라는 의미로 쓰인 'was'를 보자마자 '어떤 물건'이 '어디에' 있는지 예측할 수 있어야 합니다. 그래서 문장의 의미가 연결되는 힌트를 감각적으로 알아보려면, 영어의 언어논리를 익혀야 합니다.

영어의 논리를 쉽게 익히려면,

첫째, 주어, 동사, 목적어, 보어를 보고, 문장의 핵심 내용을 감각적으로 파악해야 합니다.
둘째, 동사의 종류에 따라 다음에 어떤 내용이 올지 예측할 수 있어야 합니다. 그래서 다양한 동사의 쓰임새에 익숙해져야 합니다.
셋째, 보통 관계 대명사나 부정사 앞에 나오는 내용을 보면, 다음에 어떤 내용이 올지 예측할 수 있어야 합니다. 즉 부정사와 관계대명사는 상황을 더 자세히 설명합니다.

넷째, 접속사를 보면서, 글에 나타나는 논리관계를 이해할 수 있어야 합니다.
다섯째, 대명사와 같은 기초 문법을 활용할 줄 알아야 합니다.
마지막으로 문법 학습에 지나치게 얽매이지 않도록 주의해야 합니다.

영어 문장을 읽자마자 이해하는 습관이 형성되면, 더 빠르게 읽고 이해할 수 있습니다. 이런 훈련을 하면, 스토리를 듣자마자 이해할 수 있습니다. 마지막 단계로 입으로 영작하는 연습을 게을리 하지 않습니다. 입으로 영어 문장을 유창하게 구사할 수 있다면, 회화와 영작이 즐거워집니다. 이런 입체적인 방법으로 공부하면, 원서를 읽고, 회화를 하는 것은 즐겁고 신나는 일이 됩니다.

읽기 가이드

영어를 공부할 때 흥미로운 이야기를 읽으며, 읽기, 듣기, 말하기를
동시에 할 수 있습니다. 그래서 『오즈의 마법사』를 읽으면서
최대 효과를 낼 수 있는 공부 방법을 소개합니다.
그것은 읽기 능력을 토대로, 듣기 연습을 하고,
듣기 능력을 토대로, 말하기 연습까지 하는 것입니다.

첫째, 직독직해로 읽는 연습을 하여, 원어민 속도로 읽는 능력을 키웁니다.
둘째, 본문을 빠른 속도로 읽고 이해할 수 있으면,
읽은 내용으로 듣기 연습을 합니다.
마지막으로, 동시통역 연습을 하여, 유창하게 말하는 연습을 합니다.

이와 같은 능력을 개발하려면, 원어민과 비슷한 속도로 영어를 이해하고, 영어로 표현하는 훈련(동시통역 연습)을 해야 합니다. 다시 말하여 영어를 직독직해로 빠르게 읽는 연습을 하고, 직독직해로 해석한 내용을 보면서 영어로 말하는 연습(동시통역 연습)을 꾸준히 실천해야 합니다. 이런 목적을 성취하도록 『오즈의 마법사』를 직독직해로 읽고, 연습문제에서 동시통역 연습을 할 수 있도록 교재를 구성했습니다. 아래에 자세히 설명한 단계에 따라 공부하면, 영어 실력이 빠르게 향상됩니다.

Step 1 영어 어순대로 이해하기

원서를 직독직해로 읽는 능력을 키우려면, 영어 어순대로 읽는 능력과 풍부한 어휘력이 필요합니다. 먼저 『오즈의 마법사』를 직독직해로 읽으면서 영어 어순대로 읽고 이해하는 연습을 합니다. 이야기를 읽는 동안 모르는 어휘나 이해하기 어려운 문장이 나오면, 중요한 의미만 파악하고, 빠르게 읽고 이해해야 합니다. 본 교재를 두 번째로 읽을 때는 모르는 어휘를 익히고, 어려운 문장을 좀 더 정확히 이해해야 합니다. 때로는 모르는 어휘와 문장을 단번에 모두 익히겠다고 지나치게 욕심을 부리면, 오히려 학습에 흥미가 떨어지고 지속적으로 공부할 수 없게 됩니다. 개인에 따라 차이가 있지만, 본 교재를 세 번 또는 네 번 읽으면서 모르는 어휘와 문장과 친숙해지면, 몰랐던 단어를 쉽게 익힐 수 있습니다. 또한 어렵게 느껴졌던 문장도 쉽게 이해할 수 있습니다.

Step 2 원어민 속도로 읽기

　직독직해로 읽는 연습을 한 다음 원어민과 비슷한 속도로 읽을 수 있을 때까지 본 교재를 반복하여 읽는 연습을 권합니다. 속독 연습을 하려면 해설을 보지 않고 『오즈의 마법사』를 빠르게 읽는 연습을 합니다. 빠르게 읽는 연습을 권장하는 이유는 두 가지가 있습니다. 첫째 영어 어순대로 이해하는 능력을 키워야 원어민과 비슷한 속도로 읽고 이해할 수 있기 때문입니다. 둘째 읽기 속도가 빨라져야 듣기가 즐겁고 편해지기 때문입니다.

Step 3 원어민 수준으로 듣고 이해하기

　듣기 연습은 녹음을 들으면서 원어민처럼 소설을 이해하는 것입니다. 영어로 쓰인 이야기를 빠른 속도로 읽고 이해할 수 있을 때 듣기 연습에 들어갑니다. 그래야 듣기 연습이 매우 즐거운 일이 됩니다. 이런 연습을 꾸준히 하면, 원어민이 빠르게 말해도 듣자마자 이해할 수 있습니다. 이렇게 듣자마자 이해하는 능력을 키워야 유창하게 회화를 할 수 있는 기반이 마련됩니다.

READING GUIDE

Step 4 동시통역 연습

연습문제 중 동시통역을 연습할 수 있는 부분을 만들어 놓았습니다. 간단히 말하면 동시통역이란 입으로 영작하는 것입니다. 즉 직독직해로 해석된 문장을 보자마자 영어로 유창하게 말하는 것입니다. 동시통역을 꾸준히 연습하면, 유창하게 영어로 말하는 능력을 키울 수 있습니다. 혼자서 영어회화를 공부하는 사람들에게는 매우 효과적인 방법입니다.

하지만 동시통역 연습을 할 때, 주의할 사항이 있습니다. 첫째 영어 문장을 만들 때 필요한 단어를 뜸들이지 않고 말하는 것입니다. 둘째 문장을 만드는데 필요한 기초 문법을 제대로 활용하는 것입니다. 즉 문법을 실용적으로 이용할 수 있는 사람은 문장을 만들 때 문법을 의식하지 않아도 문법을 이용할 수 있습니다. 셋째 자연스럽고 유창하게 발음하는 것입니다. 동시통역 연습을 꾸준히 실천하면, 읽기 속도가 **빨라지고**, **빠르게** 듣고 이해할 수 있으며, 유창하게 말할 수 있습니다.

퀴즈 가이드

『오즈의 마법사』를 읽으면서 동시에 복습할 수 있도록 퀴즈를 만들었습니다.
각 퀴즈는 모두 3개의 파트(A. 단어, B. 직독직해, C. 동시통역)로
구성되어 있습니다. 이야기를 읽고 주요 단어를 복습합니다.
그리고 퀴즈에 나온 직독직해 연습문제를 풀어보고
최종적으로 동시통역 연습을 합니다. 동시통역을 연습할 때 주의할 점은
문장을 영어로 말하는 연습을 해야 한다는 겁니다.

* 어떻게 퀴즈를 활용할까?

A. 단어

영어로 설명된 정의에 어울리는 단어를 찾는 것입니다. 적당한 단어를 보기에서 선택합니다. 이런 연습을 하는 목적은 영어로 풀이된 단어의 정의에 익숙해져야 단어를 영어로 설명할 수 있기 때문입니다. 이런 능력을 키워야 빠르게 읽고 유창하게 말할 수 있습니다.

QUIZ GUIDE

B. 직독직해

퀴즈의 직독직해 연습을 해보면, 영어 문장을 스스로 읽자마자 얼마나 이해할 수 있는지 체크해볼 수 있습니다. 본문에 나오는 문장 중에서 약간 까다롭거나 구조가 복잡한 문장을 골랐습니다. 퀴즈의 직독직해 연습을 통하여 스스로 영어의 어순대로 읽고 이해하는 훈련을 할 수 있습니다.

C. 동시통역

영어의 어순대로 한글로 제시하고, 한글 해석을 보자마자 영어로 말하는(동시통역) 파트입니다. 이런 연습을 하면, 듣기능력과 회화 능력을 단기간에 향상시킬 수 있습니다. 동시통역을 연습할 때, 최대한 원어민처럼 유창하게 발음하고 빠르게 말하면 더 효과적입니다. 처음에는 생소하고 힘들겠지만 꾸준히 연습하길 바랍니다.

목차

CONTENTS

Chapter 1. The Cyclone — 22

Chapter 2. The Council with the Munchkins — 32

    Quiz 1 — 50

Chapter 3. How Dorothy Saved the Scarecrow — 52

    Quiz 2 — 70

Chapter 4. The Road Through the Forest — 72

Chapter 5. The Rescue of the Tin Woodman — 74

    Quiz 3 — 92

Chapter 6. The Cowardly Lion — 94

Chapter 7. The Journey to the Great Oz — 108

    Quiz 4 — 126

Chapter 8. The Deadly Poppy Field — 128

Chapter 9. The Queen of the Field Mice — 130

Chapter 10. The Guardian of the Gates — 132

Chapter 11. The Wonderful City of Oz — 134

    Quiz 5 — 164

Chapter 12. The Search for the Wicked Witch — 166

    Quiz 6 — 196

Chapter 13. The Rescue — 198

Chapter 14. The Winged Monkeys — 199

Chapter 15. The Discovery of Oz, the Terrible — 200

    Quiz 7 — 224

CONTENTS

Chapter 16. The Magic Art of the Great Humbug 226

Chapter 17. How the Balloon Was Launched 236

   Quiz 8 248

Chapter 18. Away to the South 250

Chapter 19. Attacked by the Fighting Tree 251

Chapter 20. The Dainty China Country 252

Chapter 21. The Lion becomes the King of Beasts 254

Chapter 22. The Country of Quadlings 256

Chapter 23. Glinda The Good Witch Grants Dorothy's Wish 258

Chapter 24. Home Again 269

   Quiz 9 270

The Wonderful Wizard of Oz를 다시 읽어 보세요. 272

Chapter 1. The Cyclone
회오리바람

Dorothy lived / in the midst of the great Kansas prairies,
도로시는 살았다 / 캔자스 대초원 중앙에 /

/ with Uncle Henry, / who was a farmer, /
헨리 삼촌과 / 농부인 /

and Aunt Em, / who was the farmer's wife.
그리고 엠 숙모와 함께 (살았다) / 농부의 아내인

Their house was small, / for the lumber to build it /
그들의 집은 작았다 / 왜냐하면 집을 짓기 위한 나무들을 /

had to be carried / by wagon / many miles.
가져와야 했기에 / 마차로 / 멀리서

There were four walls, / a floor and a roof, /
네 개의 벽이 있었고, / 바닥과 지붕이 하나씩 있었다 /

which made one room; and this room contained /
그래서 방이 하나뿐이었다; / 그리고 이 방에는 있었다 /

a rusty looking cookstove, / a cupboard for the dishes, /
녹슬어 보이는 난로와 / 그릇을 넣어두는 찬장 하나, /

a table, / three or four chairs, / and the beds.
식탁 하나, / 서너 개의 의자와, / 침대 몇 개가.

Uncle Henry and Aunt Em had a big bed / in one corner,
헨리 삼촌과 엠 숙모는 큰 침대를 썼고 / 한쪽 구석에 있는 /

/ and Dorothy a little bed / in another corner.
도로시는 작은 침대를 썼다 / 반대쪽에 있는

There was no garret at all, / and no cellar / --except a
다락방도 없었고, / 지하실도 없었다 / 작은 구덩이 말고는 /

small hole dug / in the ground, / called a cyclone cellar, /
바닥에 파 놓은 / '회오리바람' 지하실이라 불리는 /

where the family could go / in case one of those great
가족들은 그곳으로 갔다 / 강한 회오리바람이 불 경우에 /

whirlwinds arose, / mighty enough to crush any building
건물도 쓰러뜨릴 만큼 강한 (회오리바람이) /

/ in its path.
지나갈 때면.

It was reached by a trap door / in the middle of the floor, /
구덩이는 뚜껑 문으로 들어갔다 / 바닥 중간에 있는 /

from which a ladder led down / into the small, dark hole.
그 문으로부터 사다리가 걸쳐져 있었다 / 작고 어두운 구멍까지.

When Dorothy stood in the doorway / and looked around,
도로시가 문가에 서서 / 주위를 둘러보면, /
/ she could see / nothing but the great gray prairie /
그녀는 볼 수 있었다 / 단지 거대한 회색 빛 평원만을 /

on every side. Not a tree nor a house broke /
사방으로 펼쳐진. 나무 한 그루나 집 한 채도 가로막지 않았고 /

the broad sweep of flat country / that reached to the
넓고 길게 펼쳐진 평평한 시골 들판을 / 들판은 하늘 끝까지 펼쳐져 있었다 /

edge of the sky / in all directions. The sun had baked
사방으로. 태양이 경작지를 뜨겁게 달궈놓았고 /

the plowed land / into a gray mass, / with little cracks
회색빛으로 / 경작지는 갈라져 작은 금이 갔다.

running through it. Even the grass was not green, /
심지어 풀도 초록색이 아니었다 /

for the sun had burned the tops of the long blades /
햇볕이 긴 풀잎의 끝을 말려버렸기 때문에 /

until they were the same gray color / to be seen
똑같은 회색빛이 될 때까지 / 사방에 보이는 (회색빛이)

everywhere. Once the house had been painted, /
한때 집에 페인트칠을 했다 /

but the sun blistered the paint / and the rains washed
하지만 햇볕 때문에 페인트칠은 부풀어 터지고 / 빗물에 씻겨서 /

it away, / and now the house was as dull and gray as
이제 집은 다른 것들처럼 흐릿한 회색빛이 되었다.

everything else.

in the midst of ~ 한 가운데, 중앙에 lumber 목재, 나무 rusty looking 녹슬어 보이는 garret 다락방
cellar 지하실 in case ~할 경우에 trap door 뚜껑 문 nothing but 단지(오로지) ~일뿐
the broad sweep of 넓고 길게 펼쳐진 edge 끝, 가장자리 crack 금, 틈 blade 풀잎
blister 부풀어 터지게 하다, 부풀어 오르게 하다

When Aunt Em came there to live / she was a young,
엠 숙모가 그곳에 살러 왔을 때 /   그녀는 젊고 예쁜 부인이었다.

pretty wife. The sun and wind had changed her, too.
태양과 바람이 그녀도 바꿔 놓았다.

They had taken the sparkle / from her eyes /
태양과 바람은 생기를 빼앗고 /   그녀의 눈에서 /

and left them a sober gray; / they had taken the red /
눈에 어두운 회색빛을 남겨놓았다 / 태양과 바람은 또한 발그레한 빛을 빼앗아 /

from her cheeks and lips, / and they were gray also.
뺨과 입술에서 /   회색빛이 되었다.

She was thin and gaunt, / and never smiled now.
숙모는 마르고 수척했고 /   이제는 미소도 사라졌다.

When Dorothy, who was an orphan, first came to her, /
고아인 도로시가   처음 왔을 때 /

Aunt Em had been so startled / by the child's laughter /
엠 숙모는 너무 놀라서 /   아이의 웃음 소리에 /

that she would scream and press her hand upon her heart
그녀는 비명을 지르고 손으로 가슴을 쓸곤 했다 /

/ whenever Dorothy's merry voice reached her ears; and
도로시의 즐거운 웃음 소리가 귓가에 들려올 때마다;

she still looked at the little girl / with wonder /
숙모는 여전히 아이를 바라보았다 /   놀라면서 /

that she could find anything to laugh at.
아이가 웃을 거리를 찾을 수 있다는 것에.

---

sparkle 광채, 생기 gaunt 수척한, 여윈 startle 깜작 놀라게 하다 merry 즐거운

Uncle Henry never laughed. He worked hard / from
헨리 삼촌은 결코 웃지 않았다. 열심히 일했고 /

morning till night / and did not know / what joy was.
아침부터 밤까지 / 몰랐다 / 즐거움이 무엇인지.

He was gray also, / from his long beard / to his rough
그 또한 회색빛이었고, / 긴 턱수염에서 낡은 장화까지, /

boots, / and he looked stern and solemn, / and rarely spoke.
 무뚝뚝하고 근엄해 보였으며 / 거의 말이 없었다.

It was Toto / that made Dorothy laugh, / and saved her /
바로 토토가 / 도로시를 웃게 만들고 / 그녀를 구해주었다 /

from growing as gray / as her other surroundings.
회색빛으로 변하지 않도록 / 다른 주변 환경처럼.

Toto was not gray; he was a little black dog, /
토토는 회색이 아니었다 / 그는 검은 강아지였다 /

with long silky hair and small black eyes / that twinkled
길고 윤이 나는 털과 작고 검은 눈을 가진 / 그리고 그 눈은 유쾌하

merrily / on either side of his funny, wee nose.
게 반짝였다 / 우스꽝스럽게 생긴 작은 코의 양쪽에서.

Toto played all day long, / and Dorothy played with him, /
토토는 하루 종일 놀았고 / 도로시는 토토와 놀았으며 /

and loved him dearly.
토토를 끔찍이 좋아했다.

Today, / however, / they were not playing. Uncle Henry
이 날 / 하지만 / 둘은 놀지 않았다. 헨리 삼촌은

sat upon the doorstep / and looked anxiously at the sky, /
현관 계단에 앉아서 / 걱정스런 표정으로 하늘을 쳐다봤다 /

which was even grayer than usual. Dorothy stood in the
하늘은 평소보다 더 컴컴했다. 도로시도 문가에 서서 /

door / with Toto in her arms, / and looked at the sky too.
 토토를 팔에 안고 / 역시 하늘을 쳐다보았다.

Aunt Em was washing the dishes.
엠 숙모는 설거지를 하고 있었다.

stern 무뚝뚝한, 엄격한 solemn 근엄한, 엄숙한 rarely 거의 ~않다, 좀처럼 ~않다 surrounding 주변 환경
twinkle 반짝이다 wee 작은 dearly 끔찍이

From the far north / they heard a low wail of the wind, /
북쪽 먼 곳에서 / 낮게 윙윙거리는 바람소리가 들렸고 /

and Uncle Henry and Dorothy could see / where the long
헨리 삼촌과 도로시는 볼 수 있었다 / 긴 풀들이 바람 속에 파

grass bowed in waves / before the coming storm.
도처럼 쓰러지는 곳을 / 다가오는 폭풍 앞에.

There now came a sharp whistling in the air /
이번에는 날카롭고 휘파람 같은 바람소리가 들렸다 /

from the south, / and as they turned their eyes that way
남쪽에서 / 그리고 그들이 그 쪽으로 눈을 돌렸을 때 /

/ they saw ripples in the grass / coming from that
그들은 보았다 / 풀의 물결모양을 / 남쪽 방향에서도 다가오는

direction also.

Suddenly Uncle Henry stood up.
갑자기 헨리 삼촌이 일어섰다.

"There's a cyclone coming, / Em," he called to his wife.
"회오리바람이, 오고 있어, / 엠" 삼촌이 숙모를 불렀다.

"I'll go look after the stock." Then he ran toward the
"가축을 돌보러 갈게." 그리고는 헛간으로 달려갔다 /

sheds / where the cows and horses were kept.
소와 말이 있는.

Aunt Em dropped her work / and came to the door.
엠 숙모는 하던 일을 멈추고 / 문 쪽으로 왔다.

One glance told her / of the danger close at hand.
한눈에 알아차렸다 / 가까이 다가온 위험을

"Quick, Dorothy!" she screamed. "Run for the cellar!"
"서둘러, 도로시!" 숙모가 외쳤다. "지하실(구덩이)로 달려가!"

Toto jumped out of Dorothy's arms / and hid under the
토토가 도로시의 품을 빠져 나와 / 침대 밑에 숨어 버려서 /

bed, / and the girl started to get him.
도로시가 잡으러 갔다.

Aunt Em, / badly frightened, / threw open the trap door /
엠 숙모는 / 무척 놀란 / 구멍이 문을 열고 /

in the floor / and climbed down the ladder / into the
마루에 있는 / 사다리로 내려갔다 / 좁고 어두운 구덩이로.

small, dark hole.

Dorothy caught Toto / at last / and started to follow her
도로시는 토토를 잡았고 / 마침내 / 숙모를 따라가려고 했다.

aunt. When she was halfway across the room /
그녀가 방을 반쯤 지나갔을 때 /

there came a great shriek from the wind, /
엄청나게 날카로운 바람 소리가 들려왔고, /

and the house shook so hard / that she lost her footing /
집이 심하게 흔들려서 / 도로시는 균형을 잃고 /

and sat down suddenly / upon the floor.
갑자기 주저앉아 버렸다 / 바닥에.

Key Expression

관계대명사 that은 주격으로 사용되고, 앞에 나온 명사(eyes)를 더 자세히 설명한다. 그래서 that을 "그리고 그 눈은"이라고 해석한다.

he was a little black dog, / with long silky hair and small black eyes /
그는 검은 강아지였다 / 길고 윤이 나는 털과 작고 검은 눈을 가진 /
that twinkled merrily / on either side of his funny, wee nose.
그리고 그 눈은 유쾌하게 반짝였다 / 우스꽝스럽게 생긴 작은 코의 양쪽에서.

---

wail 울부짖는 소리 ripple 물결(모양) stock 가축 shed 헛간 drop one's work 하던 일을 멈추다
shriek 날카로운 소리, 비명소리 lose one's footing 균형을 잃다

Then a strange thing happened.
그러고 나서 신기한 일이 벌어졌다.

The house whirled around / two or three times /
집이 빙글빙글 돌더니 / 두세 번 /

and rose slowly / through the air. Dorothy felt /
천천히 떠올랐다 / 공중으로. 도로시는 느꼈다 /

as if she were going up / in a balloon.
자신이 떠오르고 있는 것처럼 / 풍선을 타고.

The north and south winds met / where the house stood,
북풍과 남풍이 충돌해서 / 바로 집이 있던 곳에서 /

and made it the exact center of the cyclone.
집이 회오리바람의 한 가운데가 되었다.

In the middle of a cyclone / the air is generally still, /
회오리바람의 중심은 / 보통 바람이 잔잔했다 /

but the great pressure of the wind / on every side of the
하지만 바람의 엄청난 압력이 / 집의 사방에 /

house / raised it up higher and higher, / until it was at the
집을 점점 더 높이 띄워 올렸다 / 집이 회오리바람의 꼭대기까지

very top of the cyclone; and there it remained /
올라갈 때까지; 그곳에 머무르더니 /

and was carried / miles and miles away /
날아갔다 / 아주 멀리까지 /

as easily as you could carry a feather.
여러분들이 깃털을 움직이는 것처럼 쉽게.

It was very dark, / and the wind howled horribly /
매우 어두웠고 / 바람이 심하게 큰소리를 내며 불었다 /

around her, / but Dorothy found / she was riding quite
도로시 주변에서 / 하지만 도로시는 알아차렸다 / 자신이 꽤 편하게 바람을 타고 있다는

easily. After the first few whirls around, /
것을. 처음에 몇 번 빙글빙글 돈 후에 /

and one other time / when the house tipped badly, /
다음 순간 / 집이 심하게 기울었을 때 /

she felt / as if she were being rocked gently, /
도로시는 느꼈다 / 마치 자신이 부드럽게 흔들리고 있는 것처럼 /

like a baby in a cradle.
요람에 누운 아기같이.

Toto did not like it. He ran about the room, / now here,
토토는 좋아하지 않았다. 그는 방안을 뛰어다녔다 / 이곳으로 저곳으로 /

now there, / barking loudly; but Dorothy sat quite still /
크게 짖어대면서; 하지만 도로시는 꼼짝 않고 앉아서 /

on the floor / and waited to see / what would happen.
바닥에 / 알아보려고 기다렸다 / 무슨 일이 일어날지.

Once Toto got too near the open trap door, / and fell in;
한 번은 토토가 열려있던 뚜껑 문에 너무 가까이 가서 / 떨어졌다 /

and at first / the little girl thought / she had lost him.
처음에 / 도로시는 생각했다 / 토토를 잃어버렸다고.

But soon she saw / one of his ears sticking up /
하지만 곧 그녀는 보았다 / 토토의 귀 한 쪽이 삐죽 나온 것을 /

through the hole, / for the strong pressure of the air /
구멍으로 / 공기의 강한 압력이 /

was keeping him up / so that he could not fall.
토토를 받쳐주어서 / 그는 떨어지지 않았던 것이다.

She crept to the hole, / caught Toto by the ear, /
도로시는 구멍으로 기어가 / 토토의 귀를 잡고 /

and dragged him into the room again, / afterward closing
그를 방으로 다시 끌어당기고 / 그 다음 문을 닫았다 /

the trap door / so that no more accidents could happen.
그래서 더 이상 사고가 일어날 수 없었다.

Key Expression

"be 동사+being+과거분사"의 패턴은 진행형 수동태문장이다. 그래서 "as if she was being rocked gently"를 "마치 자신이 부드럽게 흔들리고 있는 것처럼"이라고 해석한다.

she felt / as if she were being rocked gently, / like a baby in a cradle.
그녀는 느꼈다 / 마치 자신이 부드럽게 흔들리고 있는 것처럼 / 요람에 누운 아기같이.

---

whirl 빙빙 돌다, 회전하다 howl (바람이) 큰소리를 내며 불다, 울부짖다 horribly 심하게, 아주 tip 기울다
rock 흔들다 cradle 요람

Hour after hour passed away, / and slowly /
몇 시간이 흘렀고 / 서서히 /

Dorothy got over her fright; but she felt quite lonely, /
도로시는 두려움을 이겨냈다; 하지만 그녀는 외로워졌고 /

and the wind shrieked so loudly / all about her /
바람이 너무 세차게 불었다 / 주위에서 /

that she nearly became deaf.
그래서 도로시는 귀가 먹먹해졌다.

At first / she had wondered / if she would be dashed
처음에 / 도로시는 궁금했다 / 자신이 산산조각이 나지 않을지 /

to pieces / when the house fell again; but as the hours
집이 다시 떨어진다면; 하지만 시간이 흐르고 /

passed / and nothing terrible happened, / she stopped
아무 일도 일어나지 않았기에 / 도로시는 걱정을 멈추고 /

worrying / and resolved / to wait calmly and see /
결심했다 / 조용히 기다리며 지켜보기로 /

what the future would bring.
어떤 미래가 펼쳐질 지.

At last / she crawled over the swaying floor / to her bed, /
마침내 / 도로시는 흔들리는 바닥을 기어가서 / 침대로 갔고 /

and lay down upon it; and Toto followed and lay down
그 위에 누웠다; 토토가 따라와 누웠다 /

beside her.
도로시 옆에.

In spite of the swaying of the house and the wailing of
집이 흔들리고 바람이 구슬픈 소리를 냈어도 /

the wind, / Dorothy soon closed her eyes / and fell fast
도로시는 곧 눈을 감고 / 깊이 잠들었다.

asleep.

get over 극복하다, 이겨내다 fright 공포, 두려움 be dashed to pieces 산산조각이 나다 resolve 결심하다
sway 흔들리다

Chapter 2. The Council with the Munchkins

먼치킨들과의 만남

She was awakened / by a shock, / so sudden and severe /
도로시는 잠에서 깼다 / 충격으로 / 너무 갑작스럽고 심한 (충격으로) /

that if Dorothy had not been lying / on the soft bed /
도로시가 누워있지 않았다면 / 부드러운 침대에 /

she might have been hurt. As it was, / the jar made her
그녀는 상처를 입었을지도 모른다. 사실은 / 그 충격으로 도로시는 숨을 죽

catch her breath / and wonder what had happened;
이고 / 무슨 일이 일어난 걸까 궁금해 했다;

and Toto put his cold little nose into her face /
토토는 도로시의 얼굴에 작고 차가운 코를 갖다 대고 /

and whined dismally.
우울하게 낑낑거렸다.

Dorothy sat up and noticed / that the house was not
도로시는 바로 앉으면서 알아챘다 / 집이 흔들리지 않는다는 사실을;

moving; nor was it dark, / for the bright sunshine came
또 어둡지도 않았다 / 밝은 햇빛이 들어와 /

in / at the window, / flooding the little room.
창문으로 / 작은 방에 쏟아져 들어왔다.

She sprang from her bed / and with Toto at her heels /
그녀는 침대에서 벌떡 일어나 / 토토가 뒤를 따르고 /

ran and opened the door.
달려가서 문을 열었다.

The little girl gave a cry of amazement / and looked
도로시는 깜짝 놀라 소리를 지르고 / 주변을 보고 /

about her, / her eyes growing bigger and bigger /
눈은 점점 더 커졌다 /

at the wonderful sights she saw.
엄청난 광경을 보고.

The cyclone had set the house down / very gently /
회오리바람은 집을 내려놓았다 /   살짝 /

--for a cyclone-- / in the midst of a country of marvelous
회오리바람 치고는 /   매우 아름다운 마을 한가운데에.

beauty. There were lovely patches of greensward /
아름다운 잔디밭이 있었고 /

all about, / with stately trees bearing rich and luscious
온 사방에 /   위엄이 있어 보이는 나무에 풍성하고 잘 익은 과일이 매달려 있었다.

fruits. Banks of gorgeous flowers were on every hand,
사방에 여러 줄로 늘어선 화려한 꽃들이 활짝 피어 있었고 /

/ and birds with rare and brilliant plumage / sang and
진귀하고 반짝이는 깃털을 가진 새들이 /   지저귀며 날아다녔다

fluttered / in the trees and bushes.
/   나무와 풀숲에서.

A little way off / was a small brook, / rushing and
약간 떨어진 곳에 / 작은 시내가 있었고 /   반짝이며 흘렀고 /

sparkling along / between green banks, / and murmuring
푸른 강둑 사이에서 /   속삭이는 듯했다 /

/ in a voice very grateful / to a little girl / who had
매우 기분 좋은 소리로 /   도로시에게는 /   오랫동안 살았던 /

lived so long / on the dry, gray prairies.
              건조한 회색 빛 초원에서.

Key Expression

"so sudden and severe"는 앞에 나온 명사인 "shock"을 수식한다. 그리고 that 다음에 오는 가정법 과거완료형태를 이용하여 과거에 일어난 사건에 반대되는 상황을 가정한다.

She was awakened / by a shock, / so sudden and severe / that if Dorothy
그녀는 잠에서 깼다 / 충격으로 / 너무 갑작스럽고 심한 (충격으로) / 도로시가

had not been lying / on the soft bed / she might have been hurt.
누워있지 않았다면 /   부드러운 침대에 / 그녀는 상처를 입었을지도 모른다.

---

severe (충격이) 심한, 격심한 as it is 사실은 jar 충격 whine (개가) 낑낑거리다 dismally 우울하게
flood (빛이) 쏟아져 들어오다 at one's heels ~의 뒤를 따르는, 뒤에
give a cry of amazement 깜짝 놀라 소리를 지르다 amazement 깜짝 놀람, 경악 in the midst of ~의 한가운데
patch 밭 greensward 잔디 stately 당당한, 위엄 있는 luscious 잘 익은, 맛있는 gorgeous 화려한, 눈부신
plumage 깃털 flutter (새가) 날아다니다 brook 시내 murmur 속삭이다 grateful 기분 좋은, 유쾌한

While she stood / looking eagerly / at the strange and
도로시가 서있을 때 / 열심히 바라보며 / 낯설고 아름다운 광경을 /

beautiful sights, / she noticed coming toward her /
자신에게 다가오는 것을 발견했다 /

a group of the queerest people / she had ever seen.
가장 독특한 사람들이 무리를 지어 / 여태껏 본 사람 중에.

They were not as big as the grown folk / she had always
그들은 어른만큼 크진 않았다 / 도로시에게 익숙한

been used to; but neither were they very small.
그렇다고 아주 작지도 않았다.

In fact, / they seemed about as tall as Dorothy, /
사실 / 그들은 도로시의 키와 거의 비슷했고 /

who was a well-grown child for her age, / although they
도로시는 나이에 비해 큰 편이었다 / 비록 그들은 /

were, / so far as looks go, / many years older.
겉보기에 / 훨씬 나이 들어 보였지만.

Three were men and one a woman, / and all were oddly
남자 셋과 여자 하나였으며 / 모두 이상한 옷을 입고 있었다.

dressed. They wore round hats / that rose to a small point
그들은 둥근 모자를 썼으며 / 그 모자는 뾰족하게 솟아올라 있었고 /

/ a foot above their heads, / with little bells around the
머리위로 30센티미터 정도 / 모자의 테두리에는 작은 종이 매달려 있었고 /

brims / that tinkled sweetly / as they moved.
좋은 맑은 소리를 냈다 / 움직일 때마다.

queer 이상한, 독특한 brim (모자의) 테, 가장자리

The hats of the men were blue; the little woman's hat was
남자의 모자는 파란색이고; 체구가 작은 여자의 모자는 흰색이었는데, /

white, / and she wore a white gown / that hung in pleats
그녀는 흰 옷을 입고 있었다 / 어깨부터 주름이 잡혀 있는,

from her shoulders.

Over it / were sprinkled little stars / that glistened in the
옷 위에는 / 작은 별이 박혀 있었고 / 햇빛 속에서 반짝이고 있었다 /

sun / like diamonds. The men were dressed in blue, /
다이아몬드처럼. 남자는 파란색 옷을 입고 있었고 /

of the same shade as their hats, / and wore well-polished
모자와 같은 색깔의 / 잘 닦여진 장화를 신고 있었으며 /

boots / with a deep roll of blue at the tops.
푸른색의 장화의 앞코가 살짝 말려 있었다.

The men, / Dorothy thought, / were about as old as
남자들은 / 도로시 생각에 / 헨리 삼촌 또래처럼 보였다 /

Uncle Henry, / for two of them had beards.
그들 중 두 사람이 턱수염이 있어.

But the little woman was doubtless much older.
체구가 작은 여자는 틀림없이 남자보다 나이가 훨씬 들어 보였다.

Her face was covered with wrinkles, / her hair was
여자의 얼굴에는 주름이 가득했고 / 머리는 거의 백발이었으며 /

nearly white, / and she walked rather stiffly.
약간 부자연스럽게 걸었다.

When these people drew near the house /
사람들이 집 가까이 다가왔을 때 /

where Dorothy was standing in the doorway, /
도로시는 문간에 서 있던 (집에) /

they paused / and whispered among themselves, /
사람들이 걸음을 멈추고 / 소곤거리기 시작했다 /

as if afraid to come farther.
마치 더 이상 다가오길 두려워하는 듯.

---

pleat (스커트 따위의) 주름 sprinkle ~을 뿌리다, 산재시키다 shade 색조, 색깔 well-polished 잘 닦여진
doubtless 틀림없이 wrinkle 주름 whisper 속삭이다, 소곤거리다

But the little old woman walked up to Dorothy, /
그러나 체구가 작은 여인이 도로시에게 다가와 /

made a low bow and said, / in a sweet voice:
허리 숙여 절을 하고 말을 걸었다 / 부드러운 목소리로:

"You are welcome, / most noble Sorceress, /
"환영합니다 / 대단히 고귀하신 마법사님 /

to the land of the Munchkins. We are so grateful to you /
먼치킨의 나라에 오신 것을. 매우 고맙게 생각합니다 /

for having killed the Wicked Witch of the East, /
동쪽 마녀를 처치해주셨고 /

and for setting our people free from bondage."
사람들을 속박에서 해방시켜 주신 것에."

Dorothy listened to this speech / with wonder.
도로시는 이 말을 들었다 / 깜짝 놀라며.

What could the little woman possibly mean /
이 체구가 작은 여인이 무슨 말을 하는 거지 /

by calling her a sorceress, / and saying / she had killed
자신을 마법사라고 부르고 / 얘기하는 것이 / 자신이 동쪽 마녀를

the Wicked Witch of the East? Dorothy was an innocent,
처치했다고? 도로시는 순진하고, /

/ harmless little girl, / who had been carried by a cyclone
남을 해칠 줄 모르는 아이였다 / 회오리바람에 휩쓸려 날아온 /

/ many miles from home; and she had never killed
집에서 멀리 떨어진 곳으로; 그녀는 뭔가를 죽여본 적이 없었다 /

anything / in all her life.
평생 동안.

But the little woman evidently expected her to answer;
하지만 체구가 작은 여인은 분명히 도로시의 대답을 기다렸다;

so Dorothy said, / with hesitation,
그래서 도로시는 말했다 / 머뭇거리며, /

"You are very kind, / but there must be some mistake.
"정말 친절하시네요, / 하지만 뭔가 오해가 있었나 봐요.

I have not killed anything."
전 아무도 죽이지 않았어요."

"Your house did, anyway," replied the little old woman, /
"어쨌든 네 집이 죽였어" 체구가 작은 여인이 대답했다 /

with a laugh, / "and that is the same thing. See!"
웃으며 / "그러니 요정님이 한 거나 마찬가지죠. 보세요!"

she continued, / pointing to the corner of the house.
그녀는 말을 이었다 / 집 모퉁이를 가리키며.

"There are her two feet, / still sticking out from /
"발이 보이죠 / 삐죽 튀어나온 /

under a block of wood."
집의 목재 밑에."

Key Expression

"grateful(고맙게 생각하는)" 다음에 for가 오면, 무엇 때문에 고마워하는지 그 이유를 설명하고 동명사구가 사용된다.

We are so grateful to you / for having killed the Wicked Witch of the East, /
매우 고맙게 생각합니다 / 동쪽 마녀를 처치해주셨고 /
and for setting our people free from bondage.
사람들을 속박에서 해방시켜 주신 것에.

Sorceress 마법사(여성형) bondage 구속, 속박 with hesitation 머뭇거리며, 망설이며 stick out 튀어나오다

Dorothy looked, / and gave a little cry of fright.
도로시는 돌아보고, / 깜짝 놀라 작은 소리로 비명을 질렀다.

There, / indeed, / just under the corner of the great beam
그곳에 / 정말로 / 커다란 대들보 모퉁이 바로 아래에 /

/ the house rested on, / two feet were sticking out, /
집이 놓여있던 / 두 개의 발이 튀어나와 있었다 /

shod in silver shoes with pointed toes.
앞코가 뾰족한 은 구두를 신은 (발이).

"Oh, dear! Oh, dear!" cried Dorothy, / clasping her hands
"어머나! 이럴 수가!" 도로시가 외쳤다 / 손뼉을 치며 /

together / in dismay. "The house must have fallen on her.
당황하여. "우리 집이 저 사람 위에 떨어졌나 보군요.

Whatever shall we do?" "There is nothing to be done,"
어떻게 해야 하죠?" "아무 것도 할 필요 없어요,"

said the little woman calmly.
체구가 작은 여인이 차분하게 대답했다.

"But who was she?" asked Dorothy.
"그런데 저 사람은 누구죠?" 도로시가 물었다.

"She was the Wicked Witch of the East, / as I said,"
"서쪽 사악한 마녀예요 / 말씀 드렸듯이"

answered the little woman. "She has held all the
체구가 작은 여인이 대답했다. "마녀는 모든 먼치킨 사람들을 노예로 만들었고 /

Munchkins in bondage / for many years, / making them
오랜 세월동안 / 혹사시켰어요 /

slave / for her night and day. Now they are all set free, /
밤낮으로. 이제 모두가 자유를 찾았어요 /

and are grateful to you for the favor."
호의에 감사드립니다."

"Who are the Munchkins?" inquired Dorothy.
"먼치킨 사람들이 누구죠?" 도로시가 물었다.

"They are the people / who live in this land of the East /
"사람들이에요 / 동쪽 땅에 사는 /

where the Wicked Witch ruled."
사악한 마녀가 다스리던"

"Are you a Munchkin?" asked Dorothy.
"할머니도 먼치킨 사람인가요?" 도로시가 물었다.

"No, / but I am their friend, / although I live in the land
"아니에요, / 그들의 친구죠 / 전 북쪽 땅에 살고 있어요.

of the North. When they saw the Witch of the East was
먼치킨 사람들이 동쪽 마녀가 죽은 걸 보고 /

dead / the Munchkins sent a swift messenger to me, /
그들은 제게 신속하게 소식을 전했고

and I came at once. I am the Witch of the North."
그래서 즉시 달려왔지요. 저는 북쪽 마녀예요."

"Oh, gracious!" cried Dorothy. "Are you a real witch?"
"어머나!" 도로시가 소리쳤다. "진짜 마녀라고요?"

"Yes, indeed," answered the little woman.
"그래요" 체구가 작은 여인이 대답했다.

"But I am a good witch, / and the people love me.
"하지만 저는 착한 마녀예요 / 그래서 사람들이 저를 좋아하죠.

Key Expression

"comma(쉼표)" 다음에 오는 making은 계속적 용법으로 사용되는 현재분사다. 간단하게 "그리고 ~하다"라고 해석하면 된다.

~for many years, / making them slave / for her night and day.
~오랜 세월동안 / 그리고 그들을 혹사시켰다 / 밤낮으로.

give a little cry of fright 깜짝 놀라 작은 소리로 비명을 지르다 beam 대들보 shod 신은 (shoe의 과거분사)
shoe 신발을 신기다 clasp one's hands together 손뼉을 치다 dismay 당황, 당혹 wicked 사악한, 나쁜
bondage 노예(신분) make one slave 노예처럼 혹사시키다 inquire 묻다

I am not as powerful / as the Wicked Witch was / who
힘이 세지 못해요 /　　　　　　사악한 마녀만큼 /

ruled here, / or I should have set the people free myself."
이곳을 통치하던 /　그렇지 않았다면 제가 직접 사람들을 구해 주었을 거예요."

"But I thought all witches were wicked," said the girl, /
"하지만 마녀들은 모두 나쁘다고 생각했어요."　　　　　도로시가 말했다 /

who was half frightened / at facing a real witch.
약간 겁먹은 채 /　　　　　　진짜 마녀를 만나서.

"Oh, no, / that is a great mistake.
"아니에요 /　　그것은 오해예요.

There were only four witches / in all the Land of Oz, /
네 명의 마녀가 있어요 /　　　　　오즈의 나라에는 /

and two of them, / those who live in the North and the
그들 중 두 명은 /　　　　북쪽과 남쪽에 사는 /

South, / are good witches. I know this is true, /
　　　　착한 마녀예요.　　　제 말은 사실이에요.

for I am one of them myself, / and cannot be mistaken.
저도 착한 마녀 중 한 명이고, /　　　　분명한 사실이니까요.

Those who dwelt in the East and the West were, /
동쪽과 서쪽에 사는 마녀들은 /

indeed, / wicked witches; but now that you have killed
정말로 /　　사악한 마녀예요;　　하지만 당신이 그중 하나를 죽여주셨으니 /

one of them, / there is but one Wicked Witch /
　　　　　　　사악한 마녀는 한 명 밖에 안 남았어요 /

in all the Land of Oz / --the one who lives in the West."
오즈 전체에 /　　　　　바로 서쪽 마녀죠."

"But," said Dorothy, / after a moment's thought,
"하지만" 도로시가 말했다, /　　잠시 생각한 후,

"Aunt Em has told me / that the witches were all dead /
"엠 숙모가 저에게 말했어요 /　　마녀는 모두 죽었다고 /

--years and years ago."
　아주 오래 전에."

half frightened 약간 겁먹은 cannot be mistaken 잘못되었을 리가 없다, 분명한 사실이다 dwell 살다, 거주하다

"Who is Aunt Em?" inquired the little old woman.
"엠 숙모가 누구죠?" 체구가 작은 여인이 물었다.

"She is my aunt / who lives in Kansas, /
"숙모예요 / 캔자스에 사는 /

where I came from."
제가 그곳에서 왔지요."

The Witch of the North seemed to think / for a time,
북쪽 마녀는 생각에 잠긴 듯 했다 / 잠시 /

/ with her head bowed and her eyes upon the ground.
고개를 숙이고 땅을 쳐다보며.

Then she looked up and said, / "I do not know /
그리고 나서 고개를 들고 말했다 / "모르겠네요 /

where Kansas is, / for I have never heard /
캔자스가 어디에 있는지 / 들어본 적이 없기에 /

that country mentioned before.
(누군가) 그런 곳을 전에 말하는 것을.

But tell me, / is it a civilized country?"
말해주세요 / 캔자스는 문명국인가요?"

"Oh, yes," replied Dorothy.
"그럼요," 도로시가 대답했다.

"Then that accounts for it. In the civilized countries /
"그럼 이해가 되는군요. 문명국에는 /

I believe there are no witches left, / nor wizards, /
남아있는 마녀가 없을 거예요 / 마법사도 /

nor sorceresses, / nor magicians.
여자 마법사도 / 마술사도.

---

mention ~을 언급하다, 말하다 civilized 문명화된 reply 대답하다 that accounts for it. 이해가 된다.
wizard 마법사

But, / you see, / the Land of Oz has never been civilized,
하지만 / 알다시피 / 오즈는 문명국이 아니에요 /

/ for we are cut off / from all the rest of the world.
우리는 단절되어 있기 때문에 / 다른 세상과.

Therefore / we still have witches and wizards /
그래서 / 마녀와 마법사가 아직 있어요 /

amongst us."
우리나라에는"

"Who are the wizards?" asked Dorothy.
"마법사는 누가 있어요?" 도로시가 물었다.

"Oz himself is the Great Wizard," answered the Witch, /
"오즈, 그분이 가장 위대한 마법사죠," 마녀가 대답했다 /

sinking her voice to a whisper.
목소리를 낮춰 속삭이며.

"He is more powerful than all the rest of us together.
"그분은 우리 마녀와 마법사들 중에 가장 힘이 세요.

He lives / in the City of Emeralds."
그분은 살고 있지요 / 에메랄드 시에."

Dorothy was going to ask another question, / but just
도로시는 다시 질문하려 했다 /

then the Munchkins, / who had been standing silently
하지만 바로 그때 먼치킨 사람들이 / 입을 다물고 서 있던 /

by, / gave a loud shout / and pointed to the corner of the
큰 소리로 비명을 지르며 / 집 모퉁이를 가리켰다 /

house / where the Wicked Witch had been lying.
마녀가 깔려 있던.

"What is it?" asked the little old woman, /
"무슨 일이지?" 체구가 작은 여인은 묻고 /

and looked, / and began to laugh.
쳐다보더니 / 웃음을 터뜨리기 시작했다.

The feet of the dead Witch had disappeared entirely, /
죽은 마녀의 발이 완전히 사라져버리고 /

and nothing was left / but the silver shoes.
아무 것도 남아있지 않았다 / 은색 구두 말고는.

"She was so old," / explained the Witch of the North, /
"마녀는 너무 늙었다." / 북쪽 마녀가 설명했다 /

"that she dried up quickly / in the sun.
"그래서 그녀는 금방 말라버린 거예요 / 햇볕에.

That is the end of her. But the silver shoes are yours, /
마녀의 최후네요. 하지만 은 구두는 당신 거예요 /

and you shall have them to wear."
당신이 그것들을 신도록 해요."

She reached down / and picked up the shoes, / and after
마녀는 몸을 굽히고 / 구두를 집어 들고 /

shaking the dust out of them / handed them to Dorothy.
구두의 먼지를 털어내더니 / 도로시에게 건넸다.

"The Witch of the East was proud of those silver shoes,"
"동쪽 마녀는 이 은 구두를 자랑스럽게 생각했지요."

said one of the Munchkins, "and there is some charm
먼치킨 사람들이 말했다 / "구두와 연관된 마법의 힘이 있지요;

connected with them; but what it is we never knew."
하지만 그게 무엇인지는 모르겠어요."

> ### Key Expression
>
> "so 형용사 that"의 문장은 "너무 ~해서 ~하다", 또는 "너무 ~하다, 그래서 ~하다"라고 해석할 수 있다. 즉 so는 형용사를 강조하는 말이고, that 앞에 사건의 결과를 설명하기 위해 사용된다.
>
> "She was so old," explained the Witch of the North, /
> "마녀는 너무 늙었다." 북쪽 마녀가 설명했다 /
> "that she dried up quickly / in the sun.
> "그래서 그녀는 금방 말라버린 거예요 / 햇볕에

sink one's voice to a whisper 목소리를 낮춰 속삭이다 sink 가라앉히다, 낮추다 entirely 완전히
reach down 몸을 아래로 뻗다, 몸을 굽히다 charm 마력, 마법의 힘

Dorothy carried the shoes into the house / and placed
도로시는 구두를 들고 집안으로 들어가 / 탁자 위에 구두를 올려

them on the table.
놓았다.

Then she came out again to the Munchkins / and said:
그리고 다시 밖으로 나와 먼치킨 사람들에게 / 말했다:

"I am anxious to get back / to my aunt and uncle, /
"돌아가고 싶어요 / 삼촌과 숙모에게 /

for I am sure / they will worry about me.
틀림없이 / 그분들은 저를 걱정하고 있을 거예요.

Can you help me find my way?"
돌아가는 길을 찾도록 도와주시겠어요?"

The Munchkins and the Witch first looked at one another,
먼치킨 사람들과 마녀가 서로를 쳐다보더니 /

/ and then at Dorothy, / and then shook their heads.
도로시를 바라보고 / 고개를 가로저었다.

"At the East, / not far from here," said one, /
"동쪽에, / 그리 멀지 않은 곳에" 한 사람이 말했다 /

"there is a great desert, / and none could live to cross it."
"넓은 사막이 있어요 / 하지만 아무도 살아서 그곳을 건너가지 못했어요."

"It is the same at the South," said another,
"남쪽도 마찬가지예요." / 다른 사람이 말했다

"for I have been there / and seen it.
"가본 적이 있거든요 / 직접 보았지요.

The South is the country of the Quadlings."
남쪽은 쿼들링의 나라고요."

"I am told," said the third man, "that it is the same at the
"들었어요," 또 다른 사람이 말했다 / "서쪽도 마찬가지래요.

44 The Wonderful Wizard of Oz

West. And that country, / where the Winkies live, /
그곳은 / 윙키 사람들이 사는 곳인데 /

is ruled by the Wicked Witch of the West, / who would
나쁜 서쪽 마녀가 다스리지요 / 당신도 노예로 만들어

make you her slave / if you passed her way."
버릴 거예요 / 그곳을 지나간다면."

"The North is my home," said the old lady,
"북쪽은 제가 사는 곳이죠." 할머니(체구가 작은 여인)가 말했다.

"and at its edge / is the same great desert /
"그런데 그 끝에는 / 똑같이 거대한 사막이 있어요 /

that surrounds this Land of Oz.
오즈 전체를 감싸고 있는.

I'm afraid, my dear, / you will have to live with us."
유감이지만 / 우리와 함께 살아야겠군요."

Dorothy began to sob at this, / for she felt lonely / among
도로시는 이 말에 흐느껴 울기 시작했다 / 외로워졌기 때문에 /

all these strange people. Her tears seemed to grieve the
낯선 사람들 속에 있으니. 도로시의 눈물은 아프게 한 것 같았다 /

kind-hearted Munchkins, / for they immediately took out
착한 먼치킨 사람들의 마음을 / 왜냐하면 그들은 곧 손수건을 꺼내 들고는 /

their handkerchiefs / and began to weep also.
그들도 또한 흐느껴 울기 시작했다.

As for the little old woman, / she took off her cap /
체구가 작은 노파에 대해 말하면 / 그녀는 모자를 벗고 /

and balanced the point / on the end of her nose, /
모자 끝의 균형을 잡았다 / 코끝에서 /

while she counted "One, two, three" / in a solemn voice.
"하나, 둘, 셋"이라고 숫자를 세는 동안에 / 엄숙한 목소리로.

At once / the cap changed to a slate, / on which was
갑자기 / 모자가 필기용 석판으로 변하더니 / 그 위에 글씨가 적혔다 /

written / in big, white chalk marks:
크고 하얀 분필로:

anxious ~하고 싶어 하는 edge 끝, 테두리 surround 둘러싸다, 에워싸다 sob 흐느껴 울다
grieve (마음을) 아프게 하다 weep 눈물을 흘리다, 울다 solemn 엄숙한, 근엄한 at once 갑자기 slate (필기용) 석판

"LET DOROTHY GO TO THE CITY OF EMERALDS"
"도로시는 에메랄드 시로 가게 해라"

The little old woman took the slate from her nose, /
노파는 칠판을 코끝에서 내리고 /

and having read the words on it, / asked,
그 위에 적힌 글을 읽고 나서 / 물었다,

"Is your name Dorothy, my dear?"
"이름이 도로시인가요?"

"Yes," answered the child, / looking up /
"네," 도로시가 대답했다 / 올려다보며 /

and drying her tears.
눈물을 닦고.

"Then you must go to the City of Emeralds.
"그럼 당신은 에메랄드 시로 가야 해요.

Perhaps Oz will help you."
아마 마법사 오즈가 도와줄 거예요."

"Where is this city?" asked Dorothy.
"어디에 있는데요?" 도로시가 물었다.

Key Expression

"as for"는 전에 말하던 것과 연관된 사람이나 사건에 대해 말하기 시작할 때 사용하며, "~는 어떤가하면, ~에 관해서는, ~에 대해 말하면"이라고 해석한다.

As for the little old woman, / she took off her cap /
체구가 작은 노파에 대해 말하면 / (그녀는) 모자를 벗고 /
and balanced the point on the end of her nose, ~.
코끝에서 모자 끝의 균형을 잡았다

"It is exactly in the center of the country, / and is ruled
"에메랄드 시는 오즈 나라의 한 가운데에 있고 / 오즈가 다스려요 /

by Oz, / the Great Wizard / I told you of."
위대한 마법사인 / 제가 말씀 드렸던."

"Is he a good man?" inquired the girl anxiously.
"착한 사람인가요?" 도로시가 걱정스러운 표정으로 물었다.

"He is a good Wizard. Whether he is a man or not /
"그는 착한 마법사예요. 사람인지 아닌지는 /

I cannot tell, / for I have never seen him."
잘 모르겠어요 / 한 번도 본 적이 없으니까요."

"How can I get there?" asked Dorothy.
"그곳에 어떻게 가나요?" 도로시가 물었다.

"You must walk. It is a long journey, / through a country
"걸어가야 해요. 긴 여행이 될 거예요 / 때로는 즐거운 마을을 지나고 /

that is sometimes pleasant / and sometimes dark and
때로는 어둡고 끔찍한 (여행이 될 거예요).

terrible. However, / I will use all the magic arts /
하지만, / 모든 마법을 사용할 거예요 /

I know of / to keep you from harm."
내가 알고 있는 / 당신을 위험에서 구해주기 위해."

"Won't you go with me?" pleaded the girl, /
"저랑 같이 가지 않나요?" 도로시가 애원했다 /

who had begun to look upon the little old woman /
체구가 작은 노파를 여기기 시작한 (도로시가) /

as her only friend.
자신의 유일한 친구로.

plead 애원하다 look upon as ~라고 생각하다, 여기다

47

"No, I cannot do that," she replied, "but I will give you my kiss, / and no one will dare injure / a person who has been kissed / by the Witch of the North."

She came close to Dorothy / and kissed her gently on the forehead. Where her lips touched the girl / they left a round, shining mark, / as Dorothy found out soon after.

"The road to the City of Emeralds / is paved with yellow brick," said the Witch, "so you cannot miss it. When you get to Oz / do not be afraid of him, / but tell your story / and ask him to help you. Good-bye, / my dear."

The three Munchkins bowed low to her / and wished her a pleasant journey, / after which they walked away / through the trees.

The Witch gave Dorothy a friendly little nod, / whirled around on her left heel / three times, /

and straightway disappeared, / much to the surprise of
곧 사라져버렸다 / (그러자) 작은 토토는 몹시 놀랐다 /

little Toto, / who barked after her / loudly enough /
짖어대던 (토토는) / 매우 큰 소리로 /

when she had gone, / because he had been afraid even to
마녀가 사라지자 / 으르렁 거리는 소리를 내는 것조차도 두려워했기 때문에 /

growl / while she stood by.
마녀가 옆에 있는 동안에는.

But Dorothy, / knowing her to be a witch, /
하지만 도로시는 / 그녀가 마녀임을 알았기 때문에 /

had expected her to disappear / in just that way, /
사라질 거라고 생각했다 / 그런 방식으로 /

and was not surprised / in the least.
그래서 놀라지 않았다 / 조금도.

Key Expression

아래 예문의 관계대명사 which가 계속적 용법으로 사용되고 앞에 나온 내용을 가리키므로, after which를 "그(그 사건) 후에"라고 해석한다. which가 계속적 용법으로 사용되면, 앞에 나온 구, 절을 수식한다.

The three Munchkins bowed low to her / and wished her a pleasant journey, /
세 명의 먼치킨 사람들도 허리 숙여 인사하며 / 즐거운 여행이 되길 빌었다 /
after which they walked away / through the trees.
그 후에 그들은 떠나갔다 / 나무 사이로.

---

forehead 이마 pave (도로를) 포장하다, 덮다 whirl 빙빙 돌다, 빙그르 돌다 straightaway 곧 disappear 사라지다
bark (개가) 짖다 growl (개가) 으르렁 거리는 소리를 내다 expect ~할 것이라고 생각하다, 예상하다

Quiz 1

A. 단어

다음 단어의 설명을 읽고, 어떤 단어를 설명하는지 아래의 박스에서 알맞은 단어를 고르세요.

1. to ask for something in an urgent way
2. to believe something will happen
3. feeling strongly that you want to do something
4. to say something as an answer
5. a small line in the skin caused by old age
6. to say something very quietly, using your breath rather than your voice
7. to move through the air with short, quick, light movements
8. small or little
9. a small bed for a baby
10. to move slowly from side to side

wrinkle	expect	cradle	reply	flutter	plead
sway	anxious	wee	whisper		

B. 직독직해

아래에 제시된 문장을 직독직해로 해석해보세요.

1. Aunt Em had been so startled / by the child's laughter / that she would scream / and press her hand upon her heart.

   →

2. Just then the Munchkins, / who had been standing silently by, / gave a loud shout / and pointed to the corner of the house / where the Wicked Witch had been lying.

   →

Answer
A. 단어 1. plead 2. expect 3. anxious 4. reply 5. wrinkle 6. whisper 7. flutter 8. wee 9. cradle 10. sway
B. 직독직해 1. 엠 숙모는 너무 놀라서 / 아이의 웃음소리에 / 그녀는 비명을 지르고 / 손으로 가슴을 쓸곤 했다.
2. 바로 그 때 먼치킨 사람들이 / 입을 다물고 옆에 서 있던 / 큰 소리로 비명을 지르며 / 집 모퉁이를 가리켰다 / 마녀의 깔려 누워있는 (집 모퉁이를)

3. "She was so old," / explained the Witch of the North, / "that she dried up quickly / in the sun."

   →

4. At once / the cap changed to a slate, / on which was written / in big, white chalk marks.

   →

5. Whether he is a man or not / I cannot tell, / for I have never seen him.

   →

C. 동시통역

아래에 제시된 직독직해를 보고, 영어로 말해보세요.

1. 토토가 도로시의 품을 빠져 나와 / 침대 밑에 숨어 버려서 / 도로시가 잡으러 갔다.

   →

2. 그들의 집은 작았다 / 왜냐하면 집을 지기 위한 나무들을 / 가져와야 했기에 / 마차로 / 멀리서.

   →

3. "남쪽도 마찬가지예요." / 다른 사람이 말했다. "가본 적이 있거든요 / 직접 보았지요."

   →

4. 그럼 당신은 가야 해요 / 에메랄드 시로. 아마 / 마법사 오즈가 도와줄 거예요.

   →

5. 세 명의 먼치킨 사람들도 허리 숙여 인사하며 / 그녀에게 즐거운 여행이 되길 빌었다.

   →

Answer

3. "마녀는 너무 늙었다." / 북쪽 마녀가 설명했다 / "그래서 그녀는 금방 말라버린 거예요 / 햇볕에."
4. 갑자기 / 모자가 필기용 석판으로 변하더니 / 그 위에 글씨가 적혔다 / 크고 하얀 분필로.
5. 그가 사람인지 아닌지는 / 나는 모르겠어요 / 나는 그를 한 번도 본 적이 없으니까요.

C. 동시통역 1. Toto jumped out of Dorothy's arms / and hid under the bed, / and the girl started to get him.
2. Their house was small, / for the lumber to build it / had to be carried / by wagon / many miles.
3. "It is the same at the South," said another, "for I have been there / and seen it."
4. Then you must go / to the City of Emeralds. Perhaps / Oz will help you.
5. The three Munchkins bowed low to her / and wished her a pleasant journey.

Chapter 3. How Dorothy Saved the Scarecrow
도로시는 어떻게 허수아비를 구했는가

When Dorothy was left alone / she began to feel hungry.
혼자 남게 되자 / 도로시는 배가 고파졌다.

So she went to the cupboard / and cut herself some
그래서 찬장으로 가서 / 빵을 좀 자르고 /

bread, / which she spread with butter.
빵에 버터를 발랐다.

She gave some to Toto, / and taking a pail from the shelf
토토에게 빵을 조금 주고 / 선반에서 양동이 하나를 꺼내 /

/ she carried it down to the little brook / and filled it /
시냇가로 가지고 가서 / 양동이에 채웠다 /

with clear, sparkling water. Toto ran over to the trees /
맑고 반짝이는 물로. 토토는 나무로 달려가 /

and began to bark / at the birds sitting there.
짖기 시작했다 / 나무 위에 앉아있는 새를 향해

Dorothy went to get him, / and saw such delicious fruit
도로시는 토토를 데리러 가서 / 맛있어 보이는 열매를 보고 /

/ hanging from the branches / that she gathered some
나뭇가지에 매달린 / 열매를 따기 시작했다 /

of it, / finding it just what she wanted to help out her
아침식사로 딱 원하던 것이라고 생각하며.

breakfast.

Then she went back to the house, / and having helped
그러고 나서 집으로 다시 돌아와 / 토토와 마음껏 마신 후 /

herself and Toto / to a good drink of the cool, clear
시원하고 맑은 물을 /

water, / she set out making ready for the journey /
여행을 떠날 준비를 시작했다 /

to the City of Emeralds.
에메랄드 시로.

Dorothy had only one other dress, / but that happened to
도로시는 옷이 한 벌 밖에 없었다 / 하지만 그 옷은 우연히 깨끗하고 /

be clean / and was hanging on a peg / beside her bed.
고리에 걸려 있었다 / 침대 옆에 있는.

It was gingham, / with checks of white and blue;
그건 면으로 된 옷이었는데 / 흰색과 푸른색 체크무늬가 있는;

and although the blue was somewhat faded /
푸른색이 좀 바랬지만 /

with many washings, / it was still a pretty frock.
여러 번 빨아서 / 그래도 예쁜 드레스였다.

The girl washed herself carefully, / dressed herself in the
도로시는 조심스럽게 세수를 하고 / 깨끗한 옷으로 갈아입고 /

clean gingham, / and tied her pink sunbonnet /
분홍색 보닛 모자를 썼다 /

on her head. She took a little basket / and filled it /
머리에. 작은 바구니를 가져와 / 채웠고 /

with bread from the cupboard, / laying a white cloth over
천장에서 꺼낸 빵으로 / 바구니 윗부분을 흰색 천으로 덮었다.

the top. Then she looked down at her feet / and noticed /
그리고 나서 자신의 발을 쳐다보고 / 알아챘다 /

how old and worn her shoes were.
신발이 너무 오래 되어 낡아버린 것을.

"They surely will never do / for a long journey, / Toto,"
"틀림없이 이 신발로는 충분하지 않아 / 긴 여행에 / 토토"

she said. And Toto looked up into her face /
도로시가 말했다. 토토는 도로시를 올려다보며 /

with his little black eyes / and wagged his tail /
작고 검은 눈으로 / 꼬리를 흔들었다 /

to show he knew / what she meant.
알아차렸다는 것을 보여주듯 / 도로시가 하는 말을.

At that moment / Dorothy saw / lying on the table the
그 순간 / 도로시는 보았다 / 탁자 위에 은 구두가 놓여 있는 것을 /

shelf 선반 set out 시작하다 peg 고리 gingham 체크무늬가 있는 면 fade (색이) 바래다 frock 여성복, 드레스
sunbonnet 보닛모자, 햇빛가리는 모자 wag (꼬리를) 흔들다

silver shoes / that had belonged to the Witch of the East.
동쪽 마녀가 신었던.

"I wonder if they will fit me," she said to Toto.
"나한테 맞을지 모르겠어" 토토에게 말했다.

"They would be just the thing / to take a long walk in, /
"이 구두가 딱 맞을 거야 / 오랫동안 걷는 데 /

for they could not wear out."
은 구두는 닳지 않을 것이니까."

She took off her old leather shoes / and tried on the silver
도로시는 오래된 가죽 구두를 벗고 / 은 구두를 신어보았다 /

ones, / which fitted her as well / as if they had been made
그것은 아주 꼭 맞았다 / 마치 도로시를 위해 은 구두가 만들어진

for her.
것처럼.

Finally she picked up her basket.
마침내 도로시는 바구니를 집어 들었다.

"Come along, Toto," she said.
"이리와, 토토" 도로시가 말했다.

"We will go to the Emerald City / and ask the Great Oz /
"에메랄드 시로 가서 / 위대한 오즈에게 물어볼 거야 /

how to get back to Kansas again."
캔자스로 돌아가는 방법을."

Key Expression 🔑

전치사 at은 "목표, 대상"을 의미하면 "~을 향해"라고 해석한다.

Toto ran over to the trees / and began to bark / at the birds sitting there.
토토는 나무로 달려가 / 짖기 시작했다 / 나무 위에 앉아있는 새를 향해

wear out 닳다

She closed the door, / locked it, / and put the key
도로시는 문을 닫고 / 잠그고 / 조심스럽게 열쇠를 넣었다 /

carefully / in the pocket of her dress.
드레스 주머니에.

And so, / with Toto trotting along soberly behind her, /
그리고 / 뒤에서 진지하게 빠른 걸음으로 따라오는 토토와 함께 /

she started on her journey.
그녀는 여행을 떠났다.

There were several roads near by, / but it did not take her
근처에 여러 갈래의 길이 있었다 / 하지만 오래 걸리지 않았다 /

long / to find the one paved with yellow bricks.
노란 벽돌이 깔린 길을 찾는 데에는.

Within a short time / she was walking briskly / toward
잠시 후 / 그녀는 활기차게 걷고 있었다 /

the Emerald City, / her silver shoes tinkling merrily /
에메랄드 시를 향해 / 은 구두는 딸랑딸랑 소리를 내면서 /

on the hard, yellow road-bed. The sun shone bright /
딱딱한 노란 길바닥에서. 태양은 밝게 빛났고 /

and the birds sang sweetly, / and Dorothy did not feel
새들은 즐겁게 노래했으며 / 도로시는 그다지 슬프지 않았다 /

nearly so bad / as you might think / a little girl would /
사람들이 생각하는 것처럼 / 여자아이라면 그럴 거라고 /

who had been suddenly whisked away / from her own
갑자기 (회오리바람에) 실려 가서 / 고향으로부터 /

country / and set down in the midst of a strange land.
낯선 땅 한가운데 떨어지게 된 (여자아이)

She was surprised, / as she walked along, /
도로시는 놀랐다 / 걸어갈 때 /

to see how pretty the country was about her.
매우 아름다운 주변 지역의 모습을 보고

---

trot 빠른 걸음으로 가다 soberly 진지하게 briskly 활기차게 tinkle 딸랑딸랑 소리를 내다 road-bed 길바닥, 노상

There were neat fences / at the sides of the road, /
깔끔한 울타리가 있었고 / 도로 양 옆에는 /

painted a dainty blue color / and beyond them /
푸른색으로 우아하게 칠해 놓은 / 그 너머로 /

were fields of grain and vegetables / in abundance.
곡식과 채소밭이 있었다 / 많이

Evidently / the Munchkins were good farmers /
분명했다 / 먼치킨 사람들은 훌륭한 농부들이고 /

and able to raise large crops. Once in a while /
많은 곡식을 수확할 수 있다는 것이. 이따금 /

she would pass a house, / and the people came out /
그녀는 집을 지나면 / 사람들이 밖으로 나왔다 /

to look at her and bow low / as she went by;
그녀를 보고 허리 굽혀 인사하려고 / 그녀가 지나갈 때;

for everyone knew / she had been the means of
모두가 알고 있기 때문이었다 / 그녀의 도움으로 사악한 마녀를 처치하여 /

destroying the Wicked Witch / and setting them free
자신들을 자유롭게 해 주었다는 것을.

from bondage. The houses of the Munchkins /
먼치킨의 집은 /

were odd-looking dwellings, / for each was round, /
독특한 모습을 했다 / 각자의 집은 둥글었기 때문에 /

with a big dome for a roof. All were painted blue, / for in
지붕으로 원형지붕이 있어. 모두 파란색으로 칠했다 /

this country of the East / blue was the favorite color.
이 동쪽 나라에서 / 파란색은 가장 좋아하는 색이었기에.

Toward evening, / when Dorothy was tired / with her
저녁 무렵에 / 도로시는 지쳐서 / 오래 걸은 탓에 /

long walk / and began to wonder / where she should pass
생각하기 시작했을 때 / 어디서 밤을 보내야 할지 /

the night, / she came to a house / rather larger than the
(그때) 그녀는 한 집으로 갔다 / 다른 집보다 아주 큰.

rest. On the green lawn before it / many men and
집 앞에 있는 초록 풀밭에서 / 많은 남자 여자들이 춤을 추고 있었다.

women were dancing. Five little fiddlers played /
다섯 명의 작은 사람들이 바이올린을 연주하고 /

as loudly as possible, / and the people were laughing and
매우 큰 소리로 / 사람들은 웃으며 노래를 부르고 있었다 /

singing, / while a big table near by / was loaded /
근처에 있는 큰 식탁은 / 가득 차 있었다 /

with delicious fruits and nuts, pies and cakes, /
맛있는 과일과 견과류, 파이와 케이크와 /

and many other good things to eat.
그 외에 많은 먹을 것으로.

Key Expression

to 동사원형이 앞에 오는 감정을 표현하는 형용사를 수식하면, 왜 그런 감정을 느끼게 되었는지 이유를 설명하는 경우가 있다. 즉 "to see"를 이용해 도로시가 놀라게 된 이유를 설명한다.

She was surprised, / as she walked along, / to see how pretty the country was about her.
그녀는 놀랐다 / 자신이 걸어갈 때 / 주변 지역의 매우 아름다운 모습을 보고

---

in abundance 넓게, 풍부하게, 많이 crop 곡식 destroy 죽이다, 처치하다
set ~ free from bondage 구속으로부터 해방시키다 odd-looking 이상해 보이는 dwelling 거주지, 주택
fiddler 바이올린 연주자 loaded 가득 찬

The people greeted Dorothy kindly, / and invited her /
사람들은 도로시를 친절하게 맞이하고 / 그녀를 초대했다 /

to supper and to pass the night with them; for this was
저녁식사를 먹고 그들과 함께 밤을 보내자고; 이 집은 가장 부유한

the home of one of the richest Munchkins / in the land, /
먼치킨 사람의 집이었고 / 이 나라에서 /

and his friends were gathered with him / to celebrate their
그리고 그의 친구들은 모여 있기에 / 해방을 축하하기 위해 /

freedom / from the bondage of the Wicked Witch.
사악한 마녀의 구속으로부터

Dorothy ate a hearty supper / and was waited upon /
도로시는 저녁을 배부르게 먹었고 / 시중을 받았다 /

by the rich Munchkin himself, / whose name was Boq.
부자 먼치킨 사람으로부터 직접 / 그의 이름은 보크였다.

Then she sat upon a settee / and watched the people dance.
그러고 나서 긴 의자에 앉아 / 사람들이 춤추는 모습을 지켜보았다

When Boq saw her silver shoes / he said,
보크는 도로시의 은 구두를 보자 / 그는 말했다,

"You must be a great sorceress."
"당신은 굉장한 마법사임에 틀림없군요."

"Why?" asked the girl.
"왜요?" 도로시가 물었다.

"Because you wear silver shoes / and have killed the
"구두를 신고 있고 / 나쁜 마녀도 죽였으니까요.

Wicked Witch. Besides, / you have white in your frock, /
게다가 / 흰색 옷을 입고 있잖아요 /

and only witches and sorceresses wear white."
마녀나 마법사만 흰색 옷을 입지요."

"My dress is blue and white checked," said Dorothy, /
"내 옷에는 파란색과 흰색 체크무늬가 있어요"   도로시가 말했다 /

smoothing out the wrinkles in it.
옷에 주름을 펴면서."

"It is kind of you / to wear that," said Boq.
"친절하군요 /   그런 옷을 입다니"   보크가 말했다.

"Blue is the color of the Munchkins, / and white is the
"파란색은 먼치킨의 색이고 /   흰색은 마녀의 색이예요.

witch color. So we know / you are a friendly witch."
    그러니 우리는 알아요 / 당신이 친절한 마녀라는 것을"

Dorothy did not know / what to say to this, / for all the
도로시는 몰랐다 /   뭐라고 말해야 할지 /   모든 사람들이

people seemed to think her a witch, / and she knew very
자신을 마녀라고 생각하는 것 같고 /   그녀는 잘 알고 있었기 때문에 /

well / she was only an ordinary little girl / who had come
    자신이 그저 평범한 여자아이일 뿐임을 /

by the chance of a cyclone / into a strange land.
우연히 회오리바람에 휩쓸려 오게 된 /   낯선 곳으로.

When she had tired / watching the dancing, /
도로시가 싫증이 났을 때 /   춤을 구경하는데 /

Boq led her into the house, / where he gave her a room /
보크는 그녀를 집안으로 데려가서 /   방을 내주었다 /

with a pretty bed in it. The sheets were made of blue
예쁜 침대가 놓여있는.   이불은 파란색 천으로 만들어져 있었고 /

cloth, / and Dorothy slept soundly in them / till morning,
    도로시는 그 속에서 잠을 깊게 잤다 /   아침까지 /

/ with Toto curled up / on the blue rug beside her.
토토는 몸을 웅크리고 있었다 /   그 옆에 깔린 파란색 카펫에서.

freedom 해방, 자유 bondage 구속, 속박 hearty 배부른, 많은 settee 등받이가 있는 긴 의자 smooth out (주름을)
펴다 wrinkle 주름 ordinary 평범한 chance 우연, 뜻밖의 사건 cyclone 회오리바람 soundly (잠을) 깊게, 푹

59

She ate a hearty breakfast, / and watched a wee
도로시는 아침을 배부르게 먹고 / 조그만 먼치킨 아기를 지켜보았다 /

Munchkin baby, / who played with Toto / and pulled
그 아기는 토토와 놀며 / 그의 꼬리를 잡아당기고 /

his tail / and crowed and laughed / in a way that greatly
까르르 소리치며 웃었다 / 도로시를 매우 즐겁게.

amused Dorothy. Toto was a fine curiosity /
토토는 멋진 호기심의 대상이었다 /

to all the people, / for they had never seen a dog before.
모든 사람들에게 / 그들이 강아지를 본 적이 없기 때문에.

"How far is it / to the Emerald City?" the girl asked.
"얼마나 먼가요 / 에메랄드 시 까지는?" 도로시가 물었다.

"I do not know," answered Boq gravely, / "for I have
"모릅니다," 보크가 심각한 표정으로 대답했다 / "가본 적이 없으니까요.

never been there. It is better / for people to keep away
낫거든요 / 사람들은 오즈를 멀리 하는 것이 /

from Oz, / unless they have business with him.
뭔가 일이 있지 않으면

But it is a long way to the Emerald City, / and it will take
하지만 긴 여행이고 에메랄드 시 까지 가려면 / 여러 날 걸릴 거예요.

you many days. The country here is rich and pleasant, /
이 마을은 부유하고 즐거운 곳입니다 /

but you must pass / through rough and dangerous places
하지만 지나야 해요 / 거칠고 위험한 마을을 /

/ before you reach the end of your journey."
여행의 목적지에 도달하기 전에."

Key Expression

지각동사(see, watch, hear, feel)나 사역동사(have, let, make) 다음에 목적격보어로 사용되는 동사는 to 없는 동사원형으로 사용된다. 아래 예문의 dance는 목적어(people)의 보어로 동사원형으로 사용된다.

Then she sat upon a settee / and watched the people dance.
그리고 나서 그녀는 긴 의자에 앉아서 / 사람들이 춤추는 것을 지켜보았다

wee 조그만 crow 까르르 소리치다 curiosity 호기심의 대상

This worried Dorothy a little, / but she knew /
이 말은 도로시를 좀 걱정하게 했다 / 하지만 알고 있었다 /

that only the Great Oz could help her / get to Kansas
위대한 오즈만이 자신을 도울 수 있다는 것을 / 캔자스로 다시 돌아가도록 /

again, / so she bravely resolved / not to turn back.
그래서 용감하게 결심했다 / 돌아가지 않겠다고.

She bade her friends good-bye, / and again started /
도로시는 친구들에게 작별인사를 하고 / 다시 출발했다 /

along the road of yellow brick. When she had gone
노란색 벽돌 길을 따라. 도로시가 수마일 쯤 갔을 때 /

several miles / she thought she would stop to rest, /
그녀는 쉬어야겠다고 생각하고 /

and so climbed to the top of the fence / beside the road /
울타리 위로 올라가 / 길 옆에 있는 /

and sat down. There was a great cornfield / beyond the
그 위에 앉았다. 넓은 옥수수 밭이 있었고 / 울타리 너머에 /

fence, / and not far away / she saw a Scarecrow, / placed
그리 멀지 않은 곳에서 / 그녀는 허수아비를 보았다 /

high on a pole / to keep the birds / from the ripe corn.
장대 위에 걸려 있는 / 새를 쫓기 위해 / 익은 옥수수에서.

Dorothy leaned her chin upon her hand /
도로시는 손으로 턱을 괴고 /

and gazed thoughtfully / at the Scarecrow.
생각에 잠긴 채 바라보았다 / 허수아비를.

Its head was a small sack / stuffed with straw, / with
허수아비의 머리는 작은 자루였다 / 짚을 가득 채워 넣은 (자루) /

eyes, nose, and mouth painted on it / to represent a face.
게다가 눈과 코와 입이 그 위에 그려져 있는 (자루였다) / 얼굴을 표시하기 위해.

---

resolve 결심하다 bid (bid-bade-bidden) (작별을) 고하다. (인사를) 하다 ripe 익은
lean one's chin upon one's hand 손으로 턱을 괴다 gaze 바라보다, 응시하다 thoughtfully 생각에 잠겨
stuff 채워 넣다. 채우다 represent 묘사하다, 그리다

An old, pointed blue hat, / that had belonged to some
낡고 뾰족한 파란색 모자가 / 먼치킨 사람의 것인 /

Munchkin, / was perched on his head, / and the rest of
머리에 놓여 있었고 / 나머지 모습은 /

the figure / was a blue suit of clothes, / worn and faded, /
푸른 색 옷이었다 / 낡고 빛바랜 /

which had also been stuffed with straw.
그 옷은 역시 짚이 가득 채워져 있었다.

On the feet / were some old boots with blue tops, /
발에 / 앞코가 파란색인 낡은 장화가 신겨져 있었고 /

such as every man wore in this country, /
이곳의 모든 먼치킨 사람들이 신는 /

and the figure was raised above the stalks of corn /
허수아비는 옥수숫대 보다 높이 솟아 있었다 /

by means of the pole / stuck up its back.
장대를 이용해 / 등 뒤에 꽂힌.

While Dorothy was looking earnestly / into the queer,
도로시는 열심히 쳐다보는 동안에 / 이상하게 그려진

painted face of the Scarecrow, / she was surprised /
허수아비의 얼굴을 / 그녀는 깜짝 놀랐다 /

to see / one of the eyes slowly wink at her.
보고 / 허수아비의 한 눈이 천천히 윙크하는 것을.

She thought she must have been mistaken / at first, /
잘못 본 게 분명하다고 생각했다 / 처음에 /

for none of the scarecrows in Kansas ever wink;
캔자스에 있던 허수아비는 윙크한 적이 없으니까;

but presently / the figure nodded its head to her /
하지만 곧 / 허수아비가 그녀를 향해 고개를 끄덕였다 /

in a friendly way. Then she climbed down from the fence
다정하게. 그러자 도로시는 울타리에서 내려와 /

/ and walked up to it, / while Toto ran around the pole
허수아비에게 걸어갔다 / 토토는 장대 주위를 뛰어다니며 짖어대는 동안에.

and barked.

"Good day," said the Scarecrow, / in a rather husky
"안녕," 허수아비가 말했다 / 약간 쉰 목소리로.
voice.

"Did you speak?" asked the girl, / in wonder.
"네가 말한 거야?" 도로시가 물었다 / 놀라서.

"Certainly," answered the Scarecrow. "How do you do?"
"물론이지," 허수아비가 대답했다. "안녕하세요?"

"I'm pretty well, / thank you," replied Dorothy politely.
"난 잘 지내 / 고마워" 도로시가 공손하게 대답했다.

"How do you do?"
"안녕하세요?"

"I'm not feeling well," said the Scarecrow, / with a smile,
"난 기분이 좋지 않아" 허수아비가 말했다 / 미소를 지으며 /
/ "for it is very tedious / being perched up here /
"무척 지루하거든 / 여기에 있는 것은 /
night and day / to scare away crows."
밤낮으로 / 까마귀를 쫓기 위해서."

Key Expression

"with 목적어 + 과거분사, 현재분사, 부사구, 전치사구"의 패턴으로 주절의 문장과 동시에 일어나는 사건을 표현한다. 그래서 "게다가, 그리고 ~하다"라고 해석한다.

Its head was a small sack / stuffed with straw, /
허수아비의 머리는 작은 자루였다 / 짚을 가득 채워 넣은 (자루) /
with eyes, nose, and mouth painted on it / to represent a face.
게다가 눈과 코와 입이 그 위에 그려져 있는 (자루였다) / 얼굴을 표시하기 위해.

perch 놓다, 앉히다 figure 모습, 형체 by means of ~을 써서, ~의 도움으로 queer 이상한 husky (목소리가) 쉰
in wonder 놀라서 tedious 지루한

"Can't you get down?" asked Dorothy.
"내려올 수 없어?" 도로시가 물었다.

"No, / for this pole is stuck up my back. If you will please
"안 돼 / 이 장대는 내 등에 걸려 있기 때문에. 네가 장대를 빼 준다면 /

take away the pole / I shall be greatly obliged to you."
정말 고맙게 여길 거야."

Dorothy reached up both arms / and lifted the figure off
도로시는 두 팔을 뻗고 / 허수아비를 장대에서 빼주었다 /

the pole, / for, / being stuffed with straw, / it was quite light.
왜냐하면 / 짚으로 채워져 있어서 / 허수아비는 매우 가벼웠다.

"Thank you very much," said the Scarecrow, /
"정말 고마워." 허수아비가 말했다 /

when he had been set down / on the ground.
내려왔을 때 / 땅 위에.

"I feel like a new man."
"새 사람이 된 것 같아."

Dorothy was puzzled / at this, / for it sounded queer /
도로시는 당황했다 / 이 광경에 / 이상하게 들렸기 때문에 /

to hear a stuffed man speak, / and to see /
짚으로 만든 허수아비가 말하는 것을 듣고 / 보는 것이 /

him bow and walk along beside her.
그가 절을 하며 옆에서 걸어가는 것을.

"Who are you?" asked the Scarecrow / when he had
"너는 누구니?" 허수아비가 물었다 / 기지개를 켜고 /

stretched himself / and yawned.
하품을 하면서.

"And where are you going?"
"또 어디로 가는 거니?"

"My name is Dorothy," said the girl, / "and I am going to
"내 이름은 도로시야" 도로시가 말했다 / "에메랄드 시로 가는 길이야 /

the Emerald City, / to ask the Great Oz / to send me back
 위대한 오즈에게 부탁하려고 / 나를 캔자스로 돌려보내

to Kansas."
달라고."

"Where is the Emerald City?" he inquired.
"에메랄드 시가 어디니?" 허수아비가 물었다.

"And who is Oz?"
"또 오즈는 누구니?"

"Why, don't you know?" she returned, / in surprise.
"어머, 넌 모르니?" 도로시가 대답했다 / 놀라서.

"No, indeed. I don't know anything. You see, / I am
"정말 몰라. 난 아무 것도 몰라. 보다시피 / 난 짚으로

stuffed, / so I have no brains at all," he answered sadly.
채워져서 / 두뇌가 없거든" 허수아비가 슬프게 대답했다.

"Oh," said Dorothy, / "I'm awfully sorry for you."
"어머" 도로시가 말했다 / "정말 안됐구나."

"Do you think," he asked, / "if I go to the Emerald City
"생각하니," 허수아비가 물었다 / "내가 너와 함께 에메랄드 시에 가면 /

with you, / that Oz would give me some brains?"
 그 오즈란 사람이 내게 두뇌를 줄 것이라고?"

> ### Key Expression ❗
>
> 아래 예문의 to 부정사구 "to ask"와 "to send"는 부사적 용법으로 사용되어 목적을 표현한다.
> 즉 에메랄드 시로 가는 목적으로 나타낸다.
>
> I am going to the Emerald City, / to ask the Great Oz / to send me back to Kansas.
> 나는 에메랄드 시로 가는 길이야 / 위대한 오즈에게 부탁하려고 / 나를 캔자스로 돌려보내 달라고.

be obliged to 고맙게 여기다, 고마워하다 stretch oneself 기지개를 켜다 yawn 하품을 하다

"I cannot tell," she returned, / "but you may come with me, / if you like. If Oz will not give you any brains / you will be no worse off / than you are now."

"That is true," said the Scarecrow. "You see," he continued confidentially, / "I don't mind / my legs and arms and body being stuffed, / because I cannot get hurt. If anyone treads on my toes / or sticks a pin into me, / it doesn't matter, / for I can't feel it. But I do not want / people to call me a fool, / and if my head stays stuffed with straw / instead of with brains, / as yours is, / how am I ever to know anything?"

"I understand / how you feel," said the little girl, / who was truly sorry for him. "If you will come with me / I'll ask Oz / to do all he can / for you."

"Thank you," he answered gratefully.

---

continue 말을 계속하다 confidentially 마음을 터놓고 tread 밟다 gratefully 고마워하며

They walked back to the road. Dorothy helped /
그들은 길로 돌아왔다. 도로시는 도와주었고 /

him over the fence, / and they started along the path of
허수아비가 울타리를 넘는 것을 / 그들은 노란 벽돌 길을 따라 걷기 시작했다 /

yellow brick / for the Emerald City.
에메랄드 시를 향해.

Toto did not like / this addition to the party / at first.
토토는 싫어했다 / (허수아비가) 일행에 추가된 것을 / 처음에.

He smelled around the stuffed man / as if he suspected /
그는 허수아비 주위를 냄새 맡았다 / 마치 의심하는 듯 /

there might be a nest of rats / in the straw, / and he often
쥐떼가 있다고 / 짚 속에 / 그리고 때때로

growled / in an unfriendly way / at the Scarecrow.
으르렁거렸다 / 쌀쌀한 태도로 / 허수아비를 향해.

"Don't mind Toto," said Dorothy to her new friend.
"토토는 신경 쓰지 마," 도로시가 새 친구에게 말했다.

"He never bites."
"물지 않으니까"

"Oh, I'm not afraid," replied the Scarecrow.
"무섭지 않아" 허수아비가 대답했다.

"He can't hurt the straw.
"지푸라기를 다치게 할 순 없으니.

Do let me carry that basket for you.
내가 바구니를 들게.

I shall not mind it, / for I can't get tired.
나는 괜찮아 / 지치는 법이 없거든.

I'll tell you a secret," he continued, / as he walked along.
비밀을 말해 줄게" / 그가 말을 이었다 / 걸으면서.

suspect 의심하다   growl 으르렁거리다   lighted match 불붙은 성냥

The Wonderful Wizard of Oz

"There is only one thing / in the world / I am afraid of."
"단 한 가지가 있어 / 　　　　　　　세상에서 / 　　　　내가 무서워하는 게."

"What is that?" asked Dorothy;
"그게 뭔데?"　　　　도로시가 물었다;

"The Munchkin farmer / who made you?"
"먼치킨 농부니 / 　　　　　　너를 만든?"

"No," answered the Scarecrow; "it's a lighted match."
"아니,"　　허수아비가 대답했다;　　　　"그건 불붙은 성냥이야"

Quiz 2

A. 단어

다음 단어의 설명을 읽고, 어떤 단어를 설명하는지 아래의 박스에서 알맞은 단어를 고르세요.

1. a long flat narrow board attached to a wall, used for putting things on
2. to make a high ringing sound
3. a violent storm in which the air moves very fast in a circular direction
4. to make a definite decision to do something
5. to open your mouth wide and take a big breath, because you are tired
6. to think that something is not honest or true
7. to make a low, rough sound, usually in anger
8. to walk or step on something
9. unusual or strange
10. the right to do what you want without being controlled by anyone

| freedom | shelf | tread | tinkle | suspect |
| queer | growl | cyclone | yawn | resolve |

B. 직독직해

아래에 제시된 문장을 직독직해로 해석해보세요.

1. Toto ran over to the trees / and began to bark / at the birds sitting there.

   →

2. There were neat fences / at the sides of the road, / painted a dainty blue color / and beyond them / were fields of grain and vegetables / in abundance.

   →

Answer **A. 단어** 1. shelf 2. tinkle 3. cyclone 4. resolve 5. yawn 6. suspect 7. growl 8. tread 9. queer 10. freedom
B. 직독직해 1. 토토는 나무로 달려가 / 짖기 시작했다 / 나무 위에 앉아있는 새를 향해. 2. 깔끔한 울타리가 있었고 / 도로 양 옆에는 / 푸른색으로 우아하게 칠해 놓은 / 그 너머로 / 곡식과 채소밭이 있었다 / 많이.

3. When she had tired / watching the dancing, / Boq led her into the house, / where he gave her a room / with a pretty bed in it.

   →

4. "I'm not feeling well," / said the Scarecrow, / with a smile, / "for it is very tedious / being perched up here / night and day / to scare away crows."

   →

5. Dorothy helped / him over the fence, / and they started along the path of yellow brick / for the Emerald City.

   →

C. 동시통역

아래에 제시된 직독직해를 보고, 영어로 말해보세요.

1. 도로시는 옷이 한 벌 밖에 없었다 / 하지만 그 옷은 우연히 깨끗하고 / 고리에 걸려 있었다 / 침대 옆에 있는.

   →

2. 도로시는 문을 닫고 / 잠그고 / 조심스럽게 열쇠를 넣었다 / 드레스 주머니에.

   →

3. 사람들은 도로시를 친절하게 맞이하고 / 그녀를 초대했다 / 저녁식사를 같이하고 함께 밤을 보내자고.

   →

4. "얼마나 먼가요 / 에메랄드 시 까지는?" 도로시가 물었다.

   →

5. 단 한 가지가 있어 / 세상에서 / 내가 무서워하는 게.

   →

Answer

3. 그녀(도로시)가 싫증이 났을 때 / 춤을 구경하는데 / 보크는 그녀를 집안으로 데려가서 / 그는 집에서 그녀에게 방을 내주었다 / 예쁜 침대가 놓여있는. 4. "난 기분이 좋지 않아" / 허수아비가 말했다 / 미소를 지으며 / "무척 지루하거든 / 여기에 있는 것은 / 밤낮으로 / 까마귀를 쫓기 위해서." 5. 도로시는 도와주었고 / 그(허수아비)가 울타리를 넘는 것을 / 그들은 노란 벽돌 길을 따라 걷기 시작했다 / 에메랄드 시를 향해.

C. 동시통역 1. Dorothy had only one other dress, / but that happened to be clean / and was hanging on a peg / beside her bed. 2. She closed the door, / locked it, / and put the key carefully / in the pocket. 3. The people greeted Dorothy kindly, / and invited her / to supper and to pass the night with them. 4. "How far is it / to the Emerald City?" the girl asked.
5. There is only one thing / in the world / I am afraid of.

Chapter 4. The Road Through the Forest
숲속을 지나는 길(줄거리)

In this short chapter / Dorothy and the Scarecrow tell /
짧은 4장에서 / 도로시와 허수아비는 말한다 /

each other their stories. When Dorothy tells /
서로에게 자신에 대한 이야기를. 도로시가 말하자 /

the Scarecrow about Kansas, / he wonders /
허수아비에게 캔자스에 대해 / 그는 궁금해 한다 /

why anyone would want go back / to such a gray place.
왜 돌아가길 원하는지 / 그렇게 우울한 곳으로.

We learn / that the Scarecrow was made just two days
독자들은 알게 된다 / 허수아비는 단지 이틀 전에 만들어졌고 /

ago / and that he has seen little / in his short life.
그는 많은 것을 경험하지 못했다는 것을 / 짧은 기간 동안.

When the farmer first set him / in the in field, /
농부가 처음에 허수아비를 설치했을 때 / 들판에 /

the Scarecrow effectively fooled the crows.
허수아비는 효과적으로 까마귀를 속였다.

Soon, however, / an old crow discovered /
하지만 곧 / 늙은 까마귀가 알아냈다 /

the Scarecrow for what he was.
허수아비의 정체를.

The old crow told the Scarecrow /
늙은 까마귀는 허수아비에게 말했다 /

that brains would make him / just as good as a man.
두뇌는 그를 만들 것이라고 / 사람과 똑같게.

By the time Dorothy and the Scarecrow finish /
도로시와 허수아비가 마쳤을 때 /

their stories, / the road paved in yellow bricks has lead /
자신들의 이야기를 / 노란벽돌이 깔린 길은 이어졌다 /

to the edge of a dark forest.
검은 숲의 끝과

They decide to go into the forest / because it is the only
그들은 숲으로 들어가기로 결정한다 / 오즈에게 가는 유일한 길이기 때문에.

way to Oz. They spend the night / in a small cabin.
그들은 밤을 보낸다 / 작은 오두막에서.

effectively 효과적으로 as good as ~와 다름없는, 마찬가지인

Chapter 5. The Rescue of the Tin Woodman
양철 나무꾼을 구출하다

When Dorothy awoke / the sun was shining / through the
도로시가 깨어났을 때 / 태양이 빛나고 있었고 / 나무 사이로 /

trees / and Toto had long been out / chasing birds around
토토는 오랫동안 밖으로 나가 있었다 / 새와 다람쥐를 쫓아다니며.

him and squirrels. She sat up / and looked around her.
도로시는 앉아서 / 주위를 둘러보았다.

Scarecrow, / still standing patiently / in his corner, /
허수아비는 / 여전히 참을성 있게 서서 / 구석에서 /

was waiting for her.
도로시를 기다리고 있었다.

"We must go and search for water," / she said to him.
"물을 찾으러 가야겠어" / 도로시가 허수아비에게 말했다.

"Why do you want water?" / he asked.
"물이 왜 필요한데?" / 허수아비가 물었다.

"To wash my face clean / after the dust of the road, /
"얼굴도 깨끗이 씻어야 하고 / 길 먼지를 뒤집어썼으니 /

and to drink, / so the dry bread will not stick /
마시려고 / 그러면 마른 빵이 달라붙지 않아 /

in my throat."
목구멍에."

"It must be inconvenient / to be made of flesh,"
"불편하겠군 / (육체가 있는 것은)인간인 것은"

said the Scarecrow thoughtfully, /
허수아비가 생각하며 말했다 /

"for you must sleep, / and eat and drink.
"너는 잠을 자야하고 / 먹고 마셔야 하니.

However, / you have brains, / and it is worth a lot of
하지만 / 넌 두뇌가 있잖아 / 그러니 귀찮아도 괜찮은 거야 /

bother / to be able to think properly."
제대로 생각할 수 있으니까."

They left the cottage / and walked through the trees /
그들은 오두막을 떠나 / 숲속을 걸었다 /

until they found / a little spring of clear water, / where
그들이 발견할 때까지 / 맑은 물이 나오는 작은 옹달샘을 /

Dorothy drank / and bathed / and ate her breakfast.
그곳에서 도로시는 물을 마시고 / 씻고 / 아침을 먹었다.

She saw there was not much bread / left in the basket, /
도로시는 빵이 얼마 없는 것을 보고 / 바구니에 남아있는 /

and the girl was thankful / the Scarecrow did not have to
그녀는 다행으로 여겼다 / 허수아비가 아무 것도 먹을 필요가 없다는 것을 /

eat anything, / for there was scarcely enough for herself
자신과 토토가 먹기에 겨우 충분하기 때문에 /

and Toto / for the day.
그날.

Key Expression

it으로 시작하고 be 동사와 형용사 다음에 to부정사가 오는 문장패턴이다. 이때 to부정사는 의미상으로 주어역할을 한다. 그래서 "to be made of flesh"는 문장의 주어가 된다.

"It must be inconvenient / to be made of flesh," said the Scarecrow thoughtfully, /
"불편하겠군 / (육체가 있는 것은)인간인 것은", 허수아비가 생각하며 말했다 /

"for you must sleep, / and eat and drink.
"너는 잠을 자야하고 / 먹고 마셔야 하니.

---

inconvenient 불편한 it is worth a lot of bother 귀찮아도 괜찮아 cottage 오두막 spring 샘, 옹달샘 bathe 씻다
scarcely 겨우, 간신히

When she had finished her meal, / and was about to go
도로시가 식사를 끝내고 / 돌아가려고 했을 때 /

back / to the road of yellow brick, / she was startled /
노란 벽돌 길로 / 그녀는 깜짝 놀랐다 /

to hear a deep groan / near by.
신음 소리를 듣고 / 근처에서.

"What was that?" she asked timidly.
"저게 뭐지?" 도로시가 겁을 내며 물었다.

"I cannot imagine," replied the Scarecrow;
"모르겠는데" 허수아비가 대답했다:

"but we can go and see."
"하지만 가보면 되지."

Just then / another groan reached their ears, /
바로 그때 / 또 다시 신음 소리가 귀에 들렸고 /

and the sound seemed to come / from behind them.
그 소리는 들려오는 듯 했다 / 뒤쪽에서.

They turned / and walked through the forest / a few
그들은 몸을 돌려 / 숲속으로 걸어갔다 / 몇 발자국 /

steps, / when Dorothy discovered something shining /
그때 도로시가 무언가가 빛나는 것을 발견했다 /

in a ray of sunshine / that fell between the trees.
햇빛 속에서 / 나무 사이로 비추는.

She ran to the place / and then stopped short, /
그녀는 그곳으로 달려가다 / 갑자기 멈췄다 /

with a little cry of surprise.
놀라 비명을 지르며.

---

be about to 막 ~하려 하다 groan 신음소리 timidly 겁을 내며 I cannot imagine 모르겠어, 짐작도 안가
stop short 갑자기 멈추다

One of the big trees had been partly chopped through,
커다란 나무 한 그루가 반쯤 베어져 있고 /

/ and standing beside it, / with an uplifted axe in his
나무 옆에 서 있었다 / 손에 도끼를 들고 /

hands, / was a man made entirely of tin.
완전히 양철로 된 남자가.

His head and arms and legs were jointed upon his body,
그의 머리와 팔과 다리는 몸통과 이어져 있었다 /

/ but he stood / perfectly motionless, / as if he could not
하지만 그는 서있었다 / 전혀 꼼짝 않고 / 마치 그가 전혀 움직일 수 없

stir at all.
는 듯이

Dorothy looked at him / in amazement, /
도로시는 그를 바라보았고 / 놀라서 /

and so did the Scarecrow, / while Toto barked sharply /
허수아비도 그랬다 / 토토는 사납게 짖어대고 /

and made a snap at the tin legs, / which hurt his teeth.
양철 다리를 물어뜯는 동안에 / 그래서 이빨을 다치고 말았다.

"Did you groan?" asked Dorothy.
"네가 신음 소리를 낸 거니?" 도로시가 물었다.

"Yes," answered the tin man, / "I did. I've been groaning
"그래" 양철 사나이가 대답했다 / "내가 그랬어. 신음하고 있었고 /

/ for more than a year, / and no one has ever heard me
1년 넘게 / 그런데 아무도 내 신음 소리를 듣고 /

before / or come to help me."
도와주러 오지 않았어"

---

chop 자르다, 팍팍 찍다 uplifted 위로 올려진 stir 움직이다 in amazement 놀라서

"What can I do for you?" she inquired softly, / for she
"무엇을 도와줄까?" 도로시가 상냥하게 물었다 /

was moved / by the sad voice / in which the man spoke.
그녀의 마음이 동했기 때문에 / 슬픈 목소리에 / 나무꾼이 말한.

"Get an oil-can / and oil my joints," he answered.
"기름통을 가져와서 / 내 이음매에 기름칠을 해줘" 그가 대답했다.

"They are rusted so badly / that I cannot move them at
"너무 녹이 슬어서 / 전혀 움직일 수가 없어;

all; if I am well oiled / I shall soon be all right again.
나에게 기름칠을 해주면 / 곧 괜찮아질 거야.

You will find an oil-can / on a shelf in my cottage."
기름통을 찾을 수 있을 거야 / 내 오두막 선반 위에서"

Dorothy at once ran back to the cottage / and found the
도로시는 즉시 오두막으로 달려갔고 / 기름통을 발견했다 /

oil-can, / and then she returned / and asked anxiously,
다시 돌아오더니 / 걱정스럽게 물었다 /

"Where are your joints?"
"이음매가 어디니?"

"Oil my neck, first," replied the Tin Woodman.
"우선 목부터 기름칠해줘" 양철 나무꾼이 대답했다.

So she oiled it, / and as it was quite badly rusted /
그녀는 그렇게 했다 / 목은 너무 심하게 녹이 슬었기 때문에 /

the Scarecrow took hold of the tin head / and moved it
허수아비가 머리를 잡고 / 부드럽게 움직였다 /

gently / from side to side / until it worked freely, /
이리저리로 / 자유롭게 움직일 때까지 /

and then the man could turn it himself.
그래서 나무꾼이 직접 목을 돌릴 수 있었다.

"Now oil the joints in my arms," he said.
"이제 팔에 기름칠을 해줘." 그가 말했다.

And Dorothy oiled them / and the Scarecrow bent them
그래서 도로시가 팔에 기름을 치고 / 허수아비가 조심스럽게 팔을 구부렸다 /

carefully / until they were quite free from rust and
녹이 떨어져 나가 새것처럼 될 때까지.

as good as new.

The Tin Woodman gave a sigh of satisfaction /
양철 나무꾼은 만족스럽게 한숨을 내쉬며 /

and lowered his axe, / which he leaned against the tree.
도끼를 내려놓고 / 그 도끼를 그는 나무에 기대어 놓았다.

"This is a great comfort," he said.
"정말로 편하구나" 그가 말했다.

"I have been holding that axe / in the air / ever since I
"나는 도끼를 계속 들고 있었어 / 허공에 / 녹이 슨 때부터 /

rusted, / and I'm glad / to be able to put it down / at last.
그래서 나는 기뻐 / 도끼를 내려놓을 수 있게 되어 / 마침내.

Now, / if you will oil the joints of my legs, /
이제, / 내 다리에 기름칠을 해주면 /

I shall be all right once more."
더 좋아질 거야."

Key Expression

as는 문장에 따라 "때, 이유, 양보, 정도, 비례" 등의 다양한 의미로 사용된다. 아래 예문의 경우 as는 "이유"를 나타내는 접속사로 사용되므로 "~때문에"라고 해석한다.

as it was quite badly rusted / the Scarecrow took hold of the tin head /
목은 너무 심하게 녹이 슬었기 때문에 / 허수아비가 머리를 잡고 /

and moved it gently / from side to side ~.
부드럽게 움직였다 / 이리저리로

joint 이음매, 접합 부분 rusted 녹이 슨 give a sigh of satisfaction 만족스럽게 한숨을 쉬다
lower 내려놓다, 내리다 lean 기대어 놓다, 기대다

So they oiled his legs / until he could move them freely;
그래서 그들은 다리에 기름을 쳤다 / 나무꾼은 자유롭게 움직일 수 있을 때까지 /

and he thanked them / again and again / for his release, /
그는 고마워했다 / 몇 번이나 / 자신을 구해준 것에 대해 /

for he seemed a very polite creature, / and very grateful.
그는 매우 공손해 보였고 / 고마워하는 듯 했다.

"I might have stood there always / if you had not come
"난 계속 서 있었을지도 몰라 / 너희들이 나타나지 않았다면."

along," he said; "so you have certainly saved my life.
그가 말했다: "그러니 너희들이 내 생명을 구한 거야.

How did you happen to be here?"
어쩌다 이곳에 오게 됐니?"

"We are on our way / to the Emerald City /
"우리는 가는 중이었어 / 에메랄드 시로 /

to see the Great Oz," she answered, /
위대한 오즈를 만나러" 도로시가 대답했다 /

"and we stopped at your cottage / to pass the night."
"우리는 네 오두막에 들렀어 / 밤을 보내려고."

"Why do you wish to see Oz?" he asked.
"왜 오즈를 만나려 하는데?" 그가 물었다.

"I want / him to send me back to Kansas, / and the
"나는 원해 / 그가 나를 캔자스로 돌려보내 주길 /

Scarecrow wants / him to put a few brains into his head,"
그리고 허수아비는 원해 / 그가 머리에 두뇌를 만들어주기를,"

she replied.
도로시가 대답했다.

The Tin Woodman appeared to think deeply /
양철 나무꾼은 깊이 생각하는 듯 했다 /

for a moment. Then he said:
잠시 동안. 그러더니 말했다:

"Do you suppose / Oz could give me a heart?"
"너희들은 생각하니 / 오즈가 내게도 심장을 줄 거라고?"

"Why, I guess so," Dorothy answered.
"글쎄, 그럴 것 같아" 도로시가 대답했다.

"It would be as easy / as to give the Scarecrow brains."
"쉬울 것 같아 / 허수아비에게 두뇌를 주는 것만큼."

"True," the Tin Woodman returned. "So, / if you will
"맞아" 양철 나무꾼이 대답했다. "그러면 / 너희들이 나에게

allow me / to join your party, / I will also go to the
허락해 주면 / 너희들과 함께 가는 것을 / 나도 에메랄드 시로 가서 /

Emerald City / and ask Oz to help me."
오즈에게 도와 달라고 부탁해볼래"

"Come along," said the Scarecrow heartily, / and
"같이 가자" 허수아비가 진심을 담아 말했고 /

Dorothy added / that she would be pleased to have his
도로시가 덧붙였다 / 기쁠 거라고 동료가 있으면.

company. So the Tin Woodman shouldered his axe /
그러자 양철 나무꾼은 도끼를 어깨에 메고 /

and they all passed through the forest / until they came
그들 모두가 함께 숲을 통해 걸어갔다 / 길에 도착할 때까지 /

to the road / that was paved with yellow brick.
노란 벽돌이 깔린.

Key Expression

아래 예문에 있는 shoulder는 동사로 사용된다. 주로 명사로 사용되는 단어에 "~ed, ~es, ~s"가 붙어 있으면 동사로 사용되었는지 확인할 필요가 있다.

So the Tin Woodman shouldered his axe / and they all passed through the forest ~.
그러자 양철 나무꾼은 도끼를 어깨에 메고 / 그들 모두가 함께 숲을 통해 걸어갔다.

release 구제, 해방 grateful 고마워하는 come along 나타나다 heartily 진심으로 shoulder 어깨에 메다

The Tin Woodman had asked Dorothy / to put the oil-can
양철 나무꾼은 도로시에게 부탁했다 / 기름통을 넣어 달라고 /

/ in her basket.
바구니 안에.

"For," he said, / "if I should get caught in the rain, /
"왜냐하면," 그가 말했다. / "내가 비를 맞아 /

and rust again, / I would need the oil-can badly."
다시 녹이 슬면 / 기름통이 몹시 필요할 거야."

It was a bit of good luck / to have their new comrade
다행스러운 일이었다 / 새로운 동료와 여행을 함께 하는 것은 /

join the party, / for / soon after they had begun their
왜냐하면 / 다시 여행을 시작한지 얼마 안 되어 /

journey again / they came to a place / where the trees and
그들은 한 장소에 도착했다 / 그곳에 나무와 나뭇가지가

branches grew so thick / over the road / that the travelers
빽빽하게 자라서 / 길 위에 / 여행자들이 지나갈 수 없다.

could not pass. But the Tin Woodman set to work / with
하지만 양철 나무꾼이 작업을 시작하고 / 도끼로

his axe / and chopped so well / that soon he cleared a
잘 쳐내서 / 그는 곧 길을 터주었다

passage / for the entire party.
일행 모두를 위해.

Dorothy was thinking so earnestly / as they walked along
도로시는 진지하게 생각하고 있어서 / 걸어가면서 /

/ that she did not notice / when the Scarecrow stumbled
그녀는 알아채지 못했다 / 허수아비가 구덩이에 빠져서 /

into a hole / and rolled over to the side of the road. Indeed
길 옆으로 굴러버린 것을 / 실제로 /

/ he was obliged to call to her / to help him up again.
허수아비는 어쩔 수 없이 그녀를 불러야 했다 / 다시 도와 달라고

---

comrade 동료 thick (나무가) 빽빽한, 울창한 clear a passage 길을 터주다 earnestly 진지하게 notice 알아채다
be obliged to 어쩔 수 없이 ~하다

"Why didn't you walk / around the hole?"
"너는 왜 걷지 않았니 / 구덩이를 돌아서?"

asked the Tin Woodman.
양철 나무꾼이 물었다.

"I don't know enough," replied the Scarecrow cheerfully.
"잘 몰라서" 허수아비가 명랑하게 대답했다.

"My head is stuffed with straw, / you know, / and that is
"내 머리는 짚으로 채워져 있어 / 너희들이 알다시피 / 그래서 /

why / I am going to Oz / to ask him / for some brains."
오즈에게 가는 거야 / 그에게 부탁하려고 / 두뇌를 달라고"

"Oh, I see," said the Tin Woodman. "But, / after all, /
"알겠어" 양철 나무꾼이 말했다. "하지만 / 결국 /

brains are not the best things / in the world."
두뇌가 가장 좋은 것은 아니야 / 세상에서."

"Have you any?" inquired the Scarecrow.
"너는 두뇌가 있니?" 허수아비가 물었다.

"No, / my head is quite empty," answered the Woodman.
"아니. / 내 머리는 비어있어." 나무꾼이 대답했다.

"But once I had brains, / and a heart also; so, / having
"하지만 한때 두뇌가 있었고 / 심장도 있었지; / 그래서 / 모두 다 가져 보

tried them both, / I should much rather have a heart."
았기에 / 나는 심장을 갖는 게 더 좋아"

Key Expression

화자가 어떤 말을 하고, "that is why"를 사용하면, "그래서, 그렇기 때문에"라는 의미로 앞에서 한 말에 대한 이유를 설명한다.

"My head is stuffed with straw, / you know, / and that is why /
"내 머리는 짚으로 채워져 있어 / 너희들이 알다시피 / 그래서 /
I am going to Oz / to ask him / for some brains."
오즈에게 가는 거야 / 그에게 부탁하려고 / 두뇌를 달라고"

cheerfully 명랑하게, 유쾌하게

"And why is that?" asked the Scarecrow.
"왜 그런 거야?" 허수아비가 말했다.

"I will tell you my story, / and then you will know."
"내 이야기를 해줄게 / 그러면 너도 이해할 거야."

So, / while they were walking / through the forest,
그래서 / 그들이 걸어가는 동안 / 숲속을 /

the Tin Woodman told / the following story:
양철 나무꾼이 말해주었다 / 다음의 이야기를:

"I was born the son of a woodman / who chopped down
"나는 나무꾼의 아들로 태어났어 / (어떤 나무꾼?) 나무를 베어서 /

trees / in the forest / and sold the wood / for a living.
숲속에서 / 나무를 파는 / 밥벌이로.

When I grew up, / I too became a woodchopper,
성장했을 때 / 나도 나무꾼이 되었지 /

and after my father died / I took care of my old mother
아버지가 돌아가신 뒤 / 늙은 어머니를 보살폈어 /

as long as she lived. Then I made up my mind
어머니가 살아있는 동안. 그러고 나서 결심했지 /

that instead of living alone / I would marry,
혼자 사는 대신 / 결혼해야겠다고 /

so that I might not become lonely.
그러면 나는 외롭지 않을 테니까.

There was one of the Munchkin girls / who was so
먼치킨 아가씨가 있었는데 / 그녀는 매우 아름다워서 /

beautiful / that I soon grew to love her / with all my
나는 곧 그녀와 사랑에 빠졌지 / 온 마음을 다해.

heart. She, on her part, / promised to marry me
그녀 쪽에서도 / 나와 결혼하기로 약속했어 /

as soon as I could earn enough money / to build a better
내가 충분히 돈을 벌게 되면 곧 / 더 좋은 집을 지을 수 있을

house for her; so I set to work harder / than ever.
만큼; 그래서 더 열심히 일하기 시작했어 / 전보다.

But the girl lived / with an old woman / who did not want
하지만 그녀는 살았고 / 늙은 할머니와 / 할머니는 딸이 결혼하는 것을

her to marry anyone, / for she was so lazy / she wished /
원하지 않았어 / 왜냐하면 할머니는 매우 게을러서 / 할머니는 바랐기에

the girl to remain with her / and do the cooking and the
아가씨가 자신의 곁에 남아있으면서 / 요리와 집안일을 해주기를.

housework. So the old woman went to the Wicked Witch
그래서 할머니는 사악한 동쪽 마녀에게 가서 /

of the East, / and promised her two sheep and a cow /
양 두 마리와 염소 한 마리를 주겠다고 약속했지 /

if she would prevent the marriage.
마녀가 결혼을 방해해주면.

Thereupon the Wicked Witch enchanted my axe, /
그래서 마녀는 내 도끼에 마술을 걸었지 /

and when I was chopping away / at my best / one day, /
내가 나무를 베고 있을 때 / 열심히 / 어느 날 /

for I was anxious to get the new house and my wife /
새 집과 아내를 얻고 싶었기 때문에 /

as soon as possible, / the axe slipped all at once /
가능한 한 빨리 / 도끼가 갑자기 미끄러지더니 /

and cut off my left leg.
내 왼쪽 다리를 베어 버렸어.

as long as ~하는 동안에 thereupon 그래서 enchant 마술을 걸다, 매혹시키다

This at first seemed a great misfortune, / for I knew /
그런 일은 처음에 엄청난 불행처럼 보였지 / 알고 있었으니까 /

a one-legged man could not do very well /
외다리인 사람은 잘 할 수 없다는 것을 /

as a wood-chopper. So I went to a tinsmith /
나무꾼으로서 그래서 양철공에게 가서 /

and had him make me a new leg / out of tin.
새 다리를 만들어 달라고 했어 / 양철로 된.

The leg worked very well, / once I was used to it.
다리는 잘 움직였어 / 일단 내가 익숙해지자.

But my action angered / the Wicked Witch of the East, /
하지만 내 행동은 노하게 했지 / 사악한 서쪽 마녀를 /

for she had promised the old woman /
마녀는 할머니에게 약속을 했으니까 /

I should not marry the pretty Munchkin girl.
내가 먼치킨 아가씨와 결혼하지 못하게 하겠다고.

When I began chopping again, / my axe slipped /
다시 도끼질을 시작했을 때 / 도끼가 미끄러져서 /

and cut off my right leg. Again I went to the tinsmith, /
내 오른쪽 다리를 베어 버렸어. 나는 다시 양철공에게 가서 /

and again / he made me a leg out of tin.
다시 / 양철 다리를 만들어 달라고 했지.

After this / the enchanted axe cut off my arms, /
이후에 / 마술 걸린 도끼는 내 두 팔을 베어 버렸지 /

one after the other; but, / nothing daunted, /
차례대로; 하지만 / 조금도 굴하지 않고 /

I had them replaced with tin ones.
난 양철로 된 팔로 대체했지.

The Wicked Witch then / made the axe slip and cut off
그러자 사악한 마녀는 / 도끼를 미끄러지게 하여 내 머리를 베어 버렸지

my head, / and at first / I thought / that was the end of me.
처음에는 / 나는 생각했어 / 이제 끝장이라고.

Key Expression

주절의 동사가 요구, 주장, 제안, 권고, 충고, 명령, 약속과 같은 의미가 있는 동사가 오면, that 절 안에 동사는 원형이거나 "should + 동사원형"으로 사용된다.

She had promised the old woman / (that) I should not marry the pretty Munchkin girl.
마녀는 할머니에게 약속을 했다 / 내가 먼치킨 아가씨와 결혼하지 못하게 하겠다고.

But the tinsmith happened to come along, /
하지만 양철공이 우연히 나타나서 /

and he made me / a new head out of tin.
그는 나에게 만들어 주었지 / 양철로 새로운 머리를.

I thought / I had beaten the Wicked Witch / then, /
나는 생각했어 / 사악한 마녀를 이겼다고 / 그때 /

and I worked harder than ever; but I little knew /
그래서 나는 더욱 열심히 일했지; 하지만 나는 몰랐어 /

how cruel my enemy could be. She thought of a new way
나의 적이 얼마나 사악한지를. 마녀는 새로운 방법을 생각해냈고 /

/ to kill my love for the beautiful Munchkin maiden, /
먼치킨 아가씨에 대한 내 사랑을 끝내기 위해 /

and made my axe slip again, / so that it cut right through
내 도끼를 다시 미끄러지게 했지 / 그래서 도끼는 내 몸을 베어 버렸고 /

my body, / splitting me into two halves.
둘로 쪼개 버렸지.

Once more / the tinsmith came to my help /
다시 한 번 / 양철공이 도우러 와서 /

and made me a body of tin, / fastening my tin arms and
양철로 몸통을 만들어 주었고 / 양철 팔 다리와 머리를 붙였지 /

legs and head / to it, / by means of joints, /
몸통에 / 이음매를 이용해서 /

so that I could move around / as well as ever.
그래서 나는 돌아다닐 수 있었어 / 전처럼

But, alas! I had now no heart / so that I lost all my love
하지만, 세상에! 이제 심장이 없어져 버린 거야 / 그래서 먼치킨 아가씨에 대한 사랑도 잃고

for the Munchkin girl, / and did not care / whether I
말았고 / 관심이 없어졌어 /

married her or not. I suppose / she is still living with the
그녀와 결혼하든 말든. 내 생각에 / 아가씨는 여전히 그 할머니와 함께 살고 /

old woman, / waiting for me to come after her.
내가 찾아오기를 기다리고 있을 거야.

wood-chopper 나무꾼 tinsmith 양철공, 양철장이 enchanted 주술(마술)에 걸린
nothing daunted 조금도 굴하지 않는, 조금도 개의치 않는 replace 대체하다, 교환하다 maiden 아가씨
split 쪼개다, 분할하다 fasten 붙이다, 고정시키다

My body shone so brightly / in the sun / that I felt very
내 몸은 이토록 밝게 빛나서 / 햇빛에 / 나는 내 몸이 무척 자랑스러

proud of it / and it did not matter now / if my axe slipped,
웠고 / 이제 괜찮아 / 도끼가 미끄러지더라도 /

/ for it could not cut me.
왜냐하면 도끼는 나를 자를 수 없으니까.

There was only one danger / --that my joints would rust;
단 한 가지 위험한 일이 있어 / 그것은 이음매가 녹슬 수 있다는 거야;

but I kept an oil-can in my cottage / and took care to oil
그러나 오두막에 기름통을 보관했고 / 내 몸에 기름칠을 했지 /

myself / whenever I needed it.
내가 / 필요할 때마다

However, / there came a day / when I forgot to do this, /
하지만 / 날이 왔지 / 내가 기름칠 하는 것을 깜빡 잊는 (날이) /

and, / being caught in a rainstorm, / before I thought
그리고 / 폭풍우를 만나게 되었을 때 / 내가 위험하다고 생각하기도 전에 /

of the danger / my joints had rusted, / and I was left to
내 이음매가 녹이 슬었고 / 그래서 난 숲속에

stand in the woods / until you came to help me.
서 있었던 거야 / 너희들이 구하러 올 때까지.

It was a terrible thing to undergo, / but during the year
그것은 끔찍한 경험이었지 / 하지만 내가 그곳에 서있는

I stood there / I had time to think / that the greatest loss /
몇 년 동안에 / 생각할 시간이 있었지 / 가장 큰 손실은 /

I had known / was the loss of my heart.
내가 알게 된 / 심장을 잃어버린 것이라고.

undergo 경험하다

While I was in love / I was the happiest man on earth;
사랑에 빠져있는 동안 / 나는 세상에서 가장 행복한 사람이었지;

but no one can love / who has not a heart, / and so I am
하지만 누구도 사랑할 수 없지 / 심장이 없는 사람을 / 그래서 결심했지 /

resolved / to ask Oz to give me one.
오즈에게 심장을 달라고 부탁하겠다고.

If he does, / I will go back to the Munchkin maiden /
그가 그렇게 해준다면, / 나는 먼치킨 아가씨에게 가서 /

and marry her."
그녀와 결혼할 거야."

Both Dorothy and the Scarecrow had been greatly
도로시와 허수아비 모두 매우 흥미를 보였다 /

interested / in the story of the Tin Woodman, / and now
양철 나무꾼의 이야기에 /

they knew / why he was so anxious to get a new heart.
그리고 이제 알게 되었다 / 그가 왜 그토록 새 심장을 가지고 싶어 했는지.

"All the same," said the Scarecrow, / "I shall ask for
"그럼에도 불구하고" 허수아비가 말했다 / "나는 두뇌를 달라고 부탁할거야 /

brains / instead of a heart; for a fool would not know /
심장 대신; 바보는 모를 테니까 /

what to do / with a heart / if he had one."
뭘 해야 할지 / 심장을 가지고 / 두뇌가 없다면."

"I shall take the heart," returned the Tin Woodman;
"나는 심장을 갖겠어" 양철 나무꾼이 대답했다;

"for brains do not make one happy, / and happiness is the
"두뇌는 사람을 행복하게 만들지 못하고 / 행복이란 가장 좋은 것이니까 /

best thing / in the world."
세상에서"

Dorothy did not say anything, / for she was puzzled to know / which of her two friends was right, / and she decided / if she could only get back / to Kansas and Aunt Em, / it did not matter so much / whether the Woodman had no brains / and the Scarecrow no heart, / or each got what he wanted.

What worried her most / was that the bread was nearly gone, / and another meal for herself and Toto / would empty the basket. To be sure / neither the Woodman nor the Scarecrow ever ate anything, / but she was not made of tin nor straw, / and could not live / unless she was fed.

all the same 그럼에도 불구하고, 아무래도 좋은 feed (feed-fed-fed) 음식을 주다

Quiz 3

A. 단어

다음 단어의 설명을 읽고, 어떤 단어를 설명하는지 아래의 박스에서 알맞은 단어를 고르세요.

1. to give food to a person or animal
2. to get rid of someone, and to put a new person in their place
3. a young woman
4. to use magic on something or someone
5. the act of giving freedom to someone
6. feeling that you want to thank someone because they have done something for you
7. to cut something into smaller pieces
8. a place in the body where two bones meet
9. a small house in the country
10. a long deep sound that you make when you are in pain

| cottage | chop | grateful | maiden | joint |
| feed | release | groan | enchant | replace |

B. 직독직해

아래에 제시된 문장을 직독직해로 해석해보세요.

1. When Dorothy tells / the Scarecrow about Kansas, / he wonders / why anyone would want go back / to such a gray place.

   →

2. When Dorothy awoke / the sun was shining / through the trees / and Toto had long been out / chasing birds around him and squirrels.

   →

Answer
A. 단어 1. feed 2. replace 3. maiden 4. enchant 5. release 6. grateful 7. chop 8. joint 9. cottage 10. groan
B. 직독직해 1. 도로시가 말할 때 / 허수아비에게 캔자스에 대해 / 그는 궁금해 한다 / 왜 돌아가길 원하는지 / 그렇게 우울한 곳으로. 2. 도로시가 깨어났을 때 / 태양이 빛나고 있었고 / 나무 사이로 / 토토는 오랫동안 밖으로 나가 있었다 / 새와 다람쥐를 쫓아다니며.

3. When she had finished her meal, / and was about to go back / to the road of yellow brick, / she was startled / to hear a deep groan / near by.
   →

4. His head and arms and legs were jointed upon his body, / but he stood / perfectly motionless, / as if he could not stir at all.
   →

5. The Tin Woodman gave a sigh of satisfaction / and lowered his axe, / which he leaned against the tree.
   →

C. 동시통역

아래에 제시된 직독직해를 보고, 영어로 말해보세요.

1. 너희들은 생각하니 / 오즈가 내게도 심장을 줄 거라고?
   →

2. 양철 나무꾼은 도로시에게 부탁했다 / 기름통을 넣어 달라고 / 바구니 안에.
   →

3. 나는 숲속에 서 있게 되었지 / 너희들이 나를 구하러 올 때까지.
   →

4. 도로시와 허수아비 모두 매우 흥미를 보였다 / 양철 나무꾼의 이야기에.
   →

5. 도로시를 가장 곤란하게 만든 것은 / 빵이 거의 다 떨어졌다는 것이었다.
   →

Answer

3. 그녀(도로시)가 식사를 끝내고 / 돌아가려고 했을 때 / 노란 벽돌 길로 / 그녀는 깜짝 놀랐다 / 신음 소리가 듣고 / 근처에서.
4. 그의 머리와 팔과 다리는 몸통과 이어져 있었다 / 하지만 그는 서있었다 / 전혀 꼼짝 않고 / 마치 그가 전혀 움직일 수 없는 듯이.
5. 양철 나무꾼은 만족스럽게 한숨을 내쉬며 / 도끼를 내려놓고 / 그 도끼를 그는 나무에 기대어 놓았다.

C. 동시통역   1. Do you suppose / Oz could give me a heart?
2. The Tin Woodman had asked Dorothy / to put the oil-can / in her basket.
3. I was left to stand in the woods / until you came to help me.
4. Both Dorothy and the Scarecrow had been greatly interested / in the story of the Tin Woodman.
5. What worried her most / was that the bread was nearly gone.

Chapter 6. The Cowardly Lion
겁쟁이 사자

All this time / Dorothy and her companions had been
줄곧 /   도로시와 친구들은 걸었다 /

walking / through the thick woods. The road was still
         울창한 숲속을.   길은 여전히 노란 벽돌로 깔려

paved with yellow brick, / but these were much covered /
있었다 /   하지만 수북이 덮여 있었고 /

by dried branches and dead leaves / from the trees, /
나뭇가지와 낙엽으로 /   나무에서 떨어진 /

and the walking was not at all good.
걷기에 전혀 적절하지 않았다.

There were few birds / in this part of the forest, /
새들도 거의 없었다 /   숲의 이 지역에는 /

for birds love the open country / where there is plenty of
새들도 탁 트인 곳을 좋아하기 때문에 /   햇빛이 많은.

sunshine. But now and then / there came a deep growl /
          하지만 때때로 /   음산한 울음소리가 들렸다 /

from some wild animal / hidden among the trees.
야생 짐승들의 /   숲속에 숨어 있는.

These sounds made the little girl's heart beat fast, /
이 소리는 도로시의 심장을 빠르게 뛰게 했다 /

for she did not know / what made them; but Toto knew, /
그녀는 몰랐기 때문에 /   어떤 동물이 그런 소리를 내는지; 하지만 토토는 알아서 /

and he walked close to Dorothy's side, /
도로시 옆에 바짝 붙은 채 걸으며 /

and did not even bark in return.
짖으려고 하지도 않았다.

"How long will it be," the child asked of the Tin
"얼마나 걸릴까"   도로시가 양철 나무꾼에게 물었다. /

Woodman, / "before we are out of the forest?"
"이 숲을 빠져 나가려면?"

"I cannot tell," was the answer, / "for I have never been to
"모르겠어"   나무꾼이 대답했다 /   "나도 에메랄드 시에 가본 적이 없으니까.

the Emerald City.

But my father went there once, / when I was a boy, /
하지만 아버지가 한 번 가본 적이 있어 /   내가 어렸을 때 /

and he said / it was a long journey / through a dangerous
아버지는 말씀했었지 / 긴 여행이라고 /   위험한 지역을 지나가는 /

country, / although nearer to the city where Oz dwells /
비록 오즈가 살고 있는 도시에 가까워지면 /

the country is beautiful. But I am not afraid / so long as
그 지역은 매우 아름답지만.   하지만 무섭지 않아 /   오랫동안

I have my oil-can, / and nothing can hurt the Scarecrow, /
내게 기름통만 있으면 /   어떤 것도 허수아비를 다치게 할 수 없어 /

while you bear upon your forehead / the mark of the
이마에 있는 동안은 /   착한 마녀의 입맞춤 표시가 /

Good Witch's kiss, / and that will protect you from harm."
그 표시가 너를 위험에서 보호해줄 거야"

"But Toto!" said the girl anxiously.
"하지만 토토는!"   도로시가 걱정스러운 듯 말했다.

"What will protect him?"
"토토는 무엇이 지켜주지?"

Key Expression

어떤 일을 시키거나 어떤 일을 하도록 허락하는 의미를 가진 동사(make, have, let) 다음에 목적격 보어로 사용되는 동사는 원형으로 사용된다.

These sounds made the little girl's heart beat fast ~ .
이 소리는 도로시의 심장을 빠르게 뛰게 했다.

companion 친구, 동반자 so long as ~하기만 하면, ~하는 동안 bear 몸에 지니다

"We must protect him ourselves / if he is in danger,"
"우리가 직접 토토를 지켜줘야지 / 그가 위험에 빠지면"

replied the Tin Woodman.
양철 나무꾼이 대답했다.

Just as he spoke / there came from the forest a terrible
바로 그가 말하는 동안에 / 숲속에서 끔찍한 울음소리가 들려왔고 /

roar, / and the next moment / a great Lion bounded
다음 순간 / 커다란 사자 한 마리가 길로 뛰어나왔다.

into the road. With one blow of his paw / he sent the
사자가 앞발로 한번 치자 / 그는 허수아비를

Scarecrow spinning over and over / to the edge of the
데굴데굴 굴러가게 했고 / 길가로 /

road, / and then he struck at the Tin Woodman /
그런 다음 사자는 양철 나무꾼을 공격했다 /

with his sharp claws.
날카로운 발톱으로.

---

bound 뛰어가다 spin over and over 데굴데굴 굴러가다 strike 공격하다, 습격하다

But, / to the Lion's surprise, / he could make no
하지만 / 놀랍게도 / 사자는 양철 몸에 흔적을 남기지 못했다 /

impression on the tin, / although the Woodman fell over
나무꾼은 길가에 쓰러져 /

in the road / and lay still.
가만히 누워있었지만.

Little Toto, / now that he had an enemy to face, /
토토는 / 적과 마주하고 있으므로 /

ran barking toward the Lion, / and the great beast had
사자를 향해 짖으며 달려갔고 / 사자는 입을 벌렸다 /

opened his mouth / to bite the dog, / when Dorothy, /
개를 물려고 / 그때 도로시가 /

fearing Toto would be killed, / and heedless of danger, /
토토가 죽을까봐 겁이 나고 / 위험을 생각하지도 않던 (도로시가) /

rushed forward / and slapped the Lion upon his nose /
앞으로 달려가 / 사자의 코를 찰싹 때렸다 /

as hard as she could, / while she cried out:
있는 힘껏 / 소리치면서:

"Don't you dare to bite Toto! You ought to be ashamed of
"감히 토토를 물 생각은 하지도 마라! 부끄러운 줄 알아 /

yourself, / a big beast like you, / to bite a poor little dog!"
너 같은 커다란 짐승이 / 작고 불쌍한 강아지를 물려하다니!"

Key Expression

형용사 역할을 하는 구와 절이 앞에 나온 명사를 수식할 수 있다. 즉 명사 다음에 오는 관계대명사, 형용사, 현재분사, 과거분사는 앞에 나온 명사를 더 자세히 설명한다. 아래 예문의 fearing (현재분사), heedless(형용사)는 Dorothy를 수식한다.

Dorothy, / fearing Toto would be killed, / and heedless of danger, /
도로시가 / 토토가 죽을까봐 겁이 나고 / 위험을 생각하지 않은 (도로시가) /
rushed forward / and slapped the Lion upon his nose ~ .
달려가 / 사자의 코를 찰싹 때렸다

---

impression 흔적, 표시 heedless 생각하지 않고, 잊고 있는 Don't you dare 감히 ~할 생각은 마라

"I didn't bite him," said the Lion, / as he rubbed his nose
"물려고 한 게 아니야" 사자가 말했다 / 앞발로 코를 문지르면서 /

with his paw / where Dorothy had hit it.
도로시가 때렸던 (코를).

"No, / but you tried to," she retorted.
"아니, / 물려고 했잖아" 도로시가 쏘아붙였다.

"You are nothing but a big coward."
"넌 덩치 큰 겁쟁이일 뿐이야."

"I know it," said the Lion, / hanging his head in shame.
"나도 알아" 사자가 말했다 / 수치심에 고개를 숙이며.

"I've always known it. But how can I help it?"
"나도 늘 알고 있었어. 하지만 어쩌겠어?"

"I don't know, / I'm sure. To think of your striking a
"나는 몰랐지 / 분명해. 짚으로 만든 허수아비를 공격한 것을 생각해보니 /

stuffed man, / like the poor Scarecrow!"
불쌍한 허수아비를!"

"Is he stuffed?" asked the Lion / in surprise, /
"그가 짚으로 만들어졌다고?" 사자가 물었다 / 놀라서 /

as he watched her pick up the Scarecrow / and set him
도로시가 허수아비를 일으켜 / 자기 발로 서게 하는 것

upon his feet, / while she patted him into shape again.
을 볼 때 / 한편 도로시는 허수아비를 두드려 모양을 다시 바로잡아 주었다.

"Of course he's stuffed," replied Dorothy, /
"물론 짚으로 만들어졌어" 도로시가 대답했다 /

who was still angry.
여전히 화가 나서.

"That's why he went over so easily," remarked the Lion.
"그래서 그가 그렇게 쉽게 넘어졌구나" 사자가 말했다.

"It astonished me / to see him whirl around so.
"깜짝 놀랐어 / 그가 그렇게 굴러가는 걸 보고.

Is the other one stuffed also?"
다른 사람(나무꾼)도 짚으로 만들어졌니?"

"No," said Dorothy, / "he's made of tin."
"아니" 도로시가 말했다 / "양철로 만들어졌어"

And she helped / the Woodman up again.
그리고 도로시는 도와주었다 / 나무꾼이 일어서는 것을.

"That's why he nearly blunted my claws," said the Lion.
"그래서 내 발톱이 약해졌구나" 사자가 말했다.

"when they scratched / against the tin / it made a cold
"발톱으로 할퀴려고 했을 때 / 양철을 / 긁히는 소리 때문에

shiver run down my back. What is that little animal /
차가운 전율로 등이 오싹했어. 저 작은 동물은 뭐니 /

you are so tender of?"
네가 그토록 소중히 여기는?"

"He is my dog, Toto," answered Dorothy.
"내 강아지, 토토야" 도로시가 대답했다.

"Is he made of tin, or stuffed?" asked the Lion.
"양철이나 짚으로 만들어졌니?" 사자가 물었다.

"Neither. He's a--a--a meat dog," said the girl.
"둘 다 아냐. 토토는 살이 있는 진짜 개야" 도로시가 말했다.

retort 말대꾸하다, 쏘아붙이다 hang one's head in shame 수치심으로 고개를 숙이다
pat ~ into shape 두드려 모양을 만들다 remark 말하다 astonish 깜짝 놀라게 하다 blunt 약하게 하다, 무디게 하다
cold shiver 차가운 전율 tender 소중히 여기는, 상냥한

"Oh! He's a curious animal / and seems remarkably small, / now that I look at him.

No one would think / of biting such a little thing, / except a coward like me," continued the Lion sadly.

"What makes you a coward?" asked Dorothy, / looking at the great beast / in wonder, / for he was as big as a small horse.

"It's a mystery," replied the Lion.

"I suppose / I was born that way.

All the other animals in the forest / naturally expect / me to be brave, / for the Lion is everywhere / thought to be the King of Beasts. I learned / that if I roared very loudly / every living thing was frightened / and got out of my way. Whenever I've met a man / I've been awfully scared; but I just roared at him, / and he has always run away / as fast as he could go. If the elephants and the tigers and the bears / had ever tried to fight me, /

I should have run myself / --I'm such a coward;
나는 달아나고 말았을 거야 / --겁쟁이니까;

but just as soon as they hear / me roar / they all try to get
하지만 그들이 듣자마자 / 내가 으르렁거리는 소리를 / 모두들 내게서

away from me, / and of course / I let them go."
달아나려고 하지 / 그러면 당연히 / 나는 그들을 놓아주지."

"But that isn't right. The King of Beasts shouldn't be a
"하지만 그건 옳지 않아. 동물의 왕이 겁쟁이여선 안 돼"

coward," said the Scarecrow.
허수아비가 말했다.

"I know it," returned the Lion, / wiping a tear from his
"나도 알아," 사자가 대답했다 / 눈물을 닦으며 /

eye / with the tip of his tail. "It is my great sorrow, /
꼬리 끝으로. "그래서 아주 슬픈 거야 /

and makes my life very unhappy. But whenever there is
그 때문에 내 삶은 매우 슬퍼. 하지만 위험이 닥칠 때마다 /

danger, / my heart begins to beat fast."
심장이 빠르게 뛰기 시작해버리거든."

"Perhaps you have heart disease," said the Tin
"어쩌면 심장병에 걸렸을지도 모르겠군" 양철 나무꾼이 말했다.
Woodman.

"It may be," said the Lion.
"그럴지도" 사자가 말했다.

> ### Key Expression
>
> "what makes"는 상대방에게 어떤 사건에 대한 이유나 원인을 물어볼 때 사용하며, "어째서, 왜"라고 해석한다.
>
> "What makes you a coward?" asked Dorothy, / looking at the great beast ~ .
> "어쩌다 겁쟁이가 되었니?" 도로시가 물었다 / 커다란 짐승을 바라보며

remarkably 매우, 대단히 It is a mystery 모르겠군 wipe 닦다 sorrow 슬픔

"If you have," continued the Tin Woodman, /
"그렇다면" 양철 나무꾼이 계속 말했다 /

"you ought to be glad, / for it proves / you have a heart.
"넌 기뻐해야 해 / 왜냐하면 증명하니까 / 네가 심장을 가졌다는.

For my part, / I have no heart; so I cannot have
내 경우엔 / 심장이 없어; 그래서 심장병도 걸릴 수 없지"

heart disease."

"Perhaps," said the Lion thoughtfully, /
"어쩌면" 사자가 골똘히 생각하며 말했다 /

"if I had no heart / I should not be a coward."
"심장이 없었다면 / 겁쟁이가 되지 않았겠지"

"Have you brains?" asked the Scarecrow.
"두뇌는 있니?" 허수아비가 말했다.

"I suppose so. I've never looked to see," replied the Lion.
"그런 것 같아. 눈으로 본 적은 없지만 " 사자가 대답했다.

"I am going to the Great Oz / to ask him to give me
"나는 위대한 오즈에게 가는 중이야 / 두뇌를 달라고 부탁하기 위해"

some," remarked the Scarecrow, / "for my head is stuffed
허수아비가 말했다 / "왜냐하면 내 머리는 짚으로 채워져

with straw."
있거든."

"And I am going to ask him / to give me a heart,"
"그리고 나는 그에게 부탁할 거야 / 나에게 심장을 달라고"

said the Woodman.
나무꾼이 말했다.

"And I am going to ask him / to send Toto and me back
"나는 그에게 부탁할 거야 / 토토와 나를 캔자스로 보내 달라고,"

to Kansas," added Dorothy.
도로시가 덧붙여 말했다.

"Do you think / Oz could give me courage?"
"생각하니 / 오즈가 내게도 용기를 줄 거라고?"

asked the Cowardly Lion.
겁쟁이 사자가 물었다.

"Just as easily / as he could give me brains,"
"쉬운 일이겠지 / 내게 두뇌를 주는 것만큼"

said the Scarecrow.
허수아비가 말했다.

"Or give me a heart," said the Tin Woodman.
"또는 내게 심장을 주는 것만큼" 양철 나무꾼이 말했다.

"Or send me back to Kansas," said Dorothy.
"또는 나를 캔자스로 돌려보내 주는 것만큼" 도로시가 말했다.

"Then, / if you don't mind, / I'll go with you,"
"그러면 / 괜찮다면 / 너희들과 함께 갈께"

said the Lion, "for my life is simply unbearable /
사자가 말했다. "내 삶은 견딜 수가 없어 /

add 덧붙여 말하다　cowardly 겁이 많은　if you don't mind 괜찮다면　unbearable 참을 수 없는

103

without a bit of courage."
용기 없이는."

"You will be very welcome," answered Dorothy, / "환영할게" 도로시가 대답했다 /

"for you will help / to keep away the other wild beasts.
"너는 도움이 될 테니까 / 다른 맹수들이 가까이 오지 못하게 하는데.

It seems to me / they must be more cowardly than you
어쩌면 / 그 동물들이 너보다 더 겁쟁이야 /

are / if they allow you to scare them so easily."
네가 그렇게 쉽게 쫓아버릴 수 있다면."

"They really are," said the Lion, / "but that doesn't make
"그건 그래" 사자가 말했다 / "하지만 그렇다고 내가 더 용감해지는

me any braver, / and as long as I know / myself to be a
건 아니야 / 내가 알고 있기에 / 내 자신이 겁쟁이라고 /

coward / I shall be unhappy."
나는 불행해."

So once more / the little company set off upon the
그래서 다시 한 번 / 작은 무리는 여행을 떠났고 /

journey, / the Lion walking with stately strides /
사자는 씩씩한 걸음으로 걸어갔다 /

at Dorothy's side. Toto did not approve / this new
도로시의 옆에서. 토토는 인정하려 하지 않았지만 / 이 새 동료를 /

comrade / at first, / for he could not forget / how nearly
처음에 / 그는 잊을 수 없었기에 / 뭉개질(잡아먹힐)

he had been crushed / between the Lion's great jaws.
뻔했던 일을 / 사자의 큰 입에.

But after a time / he became more at ease, /
하지만 얼마 후 / 토토는 더 편안해졌고 /

and presently / Toto and the Cowardly Lion had grown
곧 / 토토와 겁쟁이 사자는 좋은 친구가 되었다.

to be good friends.

During the rest of that day / there was no other adventure / to mar the peace of their journey. Once, indeed, / the Tin Woodman stepped upon a beetle / that was crawling along the road, / and killed the poor little thing.

This made the Tin Woodman very unhappy, / for he was always careful / not to hurt any living creature; and as he walked along / he wept several tears of sorrow and regret. These tears ran slowly / down his face and over the hinges of his jaw, / and there they rusted. When Dorothy presently asked him a question / the Tin Woodman could not open his mouth, / for his jaws were tightly rusted together. He became greatly frightened / at this / and made many motions to Dorothy / to relieve him, / but she could not understand.

Key Expression

"as long as"는 "~하기만 하면, ~하는 동안에, ~하기 때문에"라는 의미로 사용된다.

As long as I know / myself to be a coward / I shall be unhappy.
내가 알고 있기에 / 내 자신이 겁쟁이라고 / 나는 불행해.

keep away 가까이 오지 못하게 하다 scare 쫓아버리다 stately 씩씩한, 당당한 stride 걸음걸이 jaws 입
presently 곧, 때마침 crawl 기어가다 rust 녹슬다 relieve 구조하다, 구제하다

The Lion was also puzzled to know / what was wrong.
사자도 또한 당황하여 알지 못했다 / 무엇이 잘못 된 건지.

But the Scarecrow seized the oil-can / from Dorothy's
하지만 허수아비가 기름통을 꺼내 / 도로시의 바구니에서 /

basket / and oiled the Woodman's jaws, / so that after a
나무꾼의 턱에 기름을 칠했고 / 그러자 잠시 후에 /

few moments / he could talk / as well as before.
그는 말할 수 있게 되었다 / 전처럼 잘.

"This will serve me a lesson," said he, /
"이 일이 내게 교훈이 될 거야" 나무꾼이 말했다 /

"to look where I step. For if I should kill another bug or
"걸을 때 잘 살펴야 하는. 내가 또 다른 곤충이나 딱정벌레를 죽이게 되면 /

beetle / I should surely cry again, / and crying rusts my
다시 울게 분명하고 / 눈물이 내 턱을 녹슬게 해서 /

jaws / so that I cannot speak."
나는 말할 수 없을 테니까"

Thereafter he walked very carefully, / with his eyes on
그 후 나무꾼은 아주 조심스럽게 걸었다 / 땅바닥에 시선을 고정하고 /

the road, / and when he saw a tiny ant toiling by /
그리고 작은 개미가 느릿느릿 지나가는 것을 보면 /

he would step over it, / so as not to harm it.
그는 개미를 피해 발을 디뎠다 / 다치지 않게 하려고.

The Tin Woodman knew very well / he had no heart, /
양철 나무꾼은 잘 알고 있었다 / 자신에게 심장이 없음을 /

and therefore he took great care / never to be cruel or
그래서 이후에 매우 조심했다 / 어떤 것에도 잔인하거나

unkind to anything.
불친절하게 대하지 않으려고.

"You people with hearts," he said, / "have something to
"심장을 가진 너희들은" 나무꾼이 말했다 / "인도할 것이 있지 /

guide you, / and need never do wrong;
그래서 나쁜 짓을 저지르지 않겠지;

but I have no heart, / and so I must be very careful.
하지만 내겐 심장이 없으니 / 조심해야 해.

When Oz gives me a heart / of course I needn't mind so
오즈가 내게 심장을 주면 / 물론 나도 그렇게 신경 쓰지 않아도 되겠지"
much."

seize 잡다, 빼앗다 thereafter 그 후 toil by 느릿느릿 움직이며 지나가다

Chapter 7. The Journey to the Great Oz
위대한 오즈에게 가는 여행

They were obliged to camp out / that night / under a
그들은 야영해야 했다 / 그날 밤 / 큰 나무 밑에서 /
large tree / in the forest, / for there were no houses near.
숲속의 / 근처에 집이 없었기 때문에.
The tree made a good, thick covering / to protect them
나무는 크고 두꺼운 덮개가 되었다 / 그들을 이슬로부터 보호해
from the dew, / and the Tin Woodman chopped
주는 / 양철 나무꾼이 큰 더미의 나무를 잘랐고 /
a great pile of wood / with his axe / and Dorothy built a
  도끼로 / 도로시가 멋진 모닥불을 피웠다 /
splendid fire / that warmed her / and made her feel less
 그 모닥불은 따뜻하게 해주고, 외로움도 덜어주었다.
lonely. She and Toto ate the last of their bread, / and now
도로시와 토토는 마지막 남은 빵을 먹었고 / 이제 알 수 없
she did not know / what they would do for breakfast.
었다 / 다음날 아침으로 뭘 먹어야 할지.

"If you wish," said the Lion, "I will go into the forest
"원한다면" 사자가 말했다 / "내가 숲속에 가서 /
/ and kill a deer for you. You can roast it by the fire, /
사슴을 잡아다 줄게. 불에 구워 먹을 수 있겠지 /
since your tastes are so peculiar / that you prefer cooked
너희 사람들의 입맛은 특이해서 / 너희들은 익힌 음식을 좋아하니까 /
food, / and then you will have a very good breakfast."
 그러면 멋진 아침을 먹게 될 거야."

"Don't! Please don't," begged the Tin Woodman.
"제발 그러지 마" 양철 나무꾼이 애원했다.
"I should certainly weep / if you killed a poor deer, /
"나는 진짜 울고 말거야 / 네가 불쌍한 사슴을 죽이면 /
and then my jaws would rust again."
그러면 내 턱이 다시 녹슬겠지"

108 The Wonderful Wizard of Oz

But the Lion went away / into the forest / and found his
하지만 사자는 가버렸고 / 숲속으로 / 자신의 저녁거리를

own supper, / and no one ever knew / what it was, /
찾았다 / 아무도 몰랐다 / 그게 무엇인지 /

for he didn't mention it. And the Scarecrow found a tree
그가 말하지 않았기 때문에. 그러자 허수아비는 열매가 잔뜩 달린 나무를 찾아 /

full of nuts / and filled Dorothy's basket with them, /
도로시의 바구니를 열매로 가득 채워주었다 /

so that she would not be hungry / for a long time.
도로시가 굶주리지 않도록 / 한동안.

She thought / this was very kind and thoughtful of the
그녀는 생각했다 / 허수아비가 친절하고 생각이 깊다고 /

Scarecrow, / but she laughed heartily / at the awkward
하지만 배꼽을 잡고 웃었다 / 그 서투른 솜씨에 /

way / in which the poor creature picked up the nuts.
불쌍한 허수아비가 열매를 줍는

His padded hands were so clumsy / and the nuts were so
허수아비의 짚으로 채운 손은 무척 어설펐고 / 열매는 매우 작아서 /

small / that he dropped / almost as many as he put in the
그는 떨어뜨렸다 / 거의 바구니에 넣은 양 만큼이나.

basket. But the Scarecrow did not mind /
하지만 허수아비는 신경 쓰지 않았다 /

how long it took him / to fill the basket, / for it enabled
아무리 오랜 시간이 걸려도 / 바구니를 채우는데 / 왜냐하면 그 일이

him to keep away / from the fire, / as he feared /
떨어져 있게 해주었기에 / 모닥불에서 / 그는 두려워하여 /

Key Expression

아래 예문에는 가정법 과거와 명령법이 혼합되어 있다. 가정법 과거는 현재 사실과 반대되는 상황을 묘사하고, "and" 앞에 가정한 일이 현실로 일어나면, "and" 다음에 오는 사건이 일어날 수 있다는 의미다.

"I should certainly weep / if you killed a poor deer, /
"나는 진짜 울고 말 거야 / 네가 불쌍한 사슴을 죽이면 /
and then my jaws would rust again."
그러면 내 턱이 다시 녹슬겠지"

be obliged to 어쩔 수 없이 ~하다 chop 잘게 자르다 peculiar 특이한, 독특한 mention 언급하다, 말하다 heartily 많이, 실컷 awkward 서투른 clumsy 서투른

a spark might get into his straw / and burn him up.
불똥이 짚으로 만든 몸에 뛰어서 / 그를 태워버릴까 봐.

So he kept a good distance / away from the flames, /
그래서 그는 상당한 거리를 유지했고 / 불꽃에서 /

and only came near / to cover Dorothy with dry leaves /
가까이 왔을 뿐이었다 / 도로시에게 마른 나뭇잎을 덮어주려고 /

when she lay down to sleep. These kept her very snug and
도로시가 자려고 누웠을 때. 낙엽 이불은 도로시를 아늑하고

warm, / and she slept soundly / until morning.
따뜻하게 해 주어서 / 깊이 잠들었다 / 아침까지

---

spark 불똥, 불꽃 keep a good distance 상당한 거리를 유지하다 snug 아늑한, 편안한

When it was daylight, / the girl bathed her face /
날이 밝아왔을 때 / 도로시는 세수를 했고

in a little rippling brook, / and soon after they all started /
잔잔하게 흐르는 개울에서 / 곧 모두가 길을 떠났다 /

toward the Emerald City.
에메랄드 시를 향해.

This was to be an eventful day / for the travelers.
이 날에 많은 사건이 일어 날 운명이었다 / 일행에게.

They had hardly been walking an hour / when they saw /
그들이 한 시간도 채 걷지 않았을 때 / 그들은 보았다 /

/ before them a great ditch / that crossed the road and
눈앞에 있는 큰 수로(골짜기)를 / 길을 가로지르고 숲을 분리시키는 (골짜기가) /

divided the forest / as far as they could see / on either side.
눈에 보이는 저 멀리까지 / 양쪽으로

It was a very wide ditch, / and when they crept up to the
매우 넓은 골짜기였고 / 그들이 가장자리까지 기어가서 /

edge / and looked into it / they could see / it was also very
내려다보았을 때 / 그들은 알 수 있었고 / 골짜기가 매우

deep, / and there were many big, jagged rocks / at the
깊다는 것을 / 크고 뾰죽한 바위들이 많이 있었다 /

bottom. The sides were so steep / that none of them could
밑바닥에는. 골짜기의 양쪽은 매우 가팔라서 / 아무도 내려갈 수 없었고 /

climb down, / and for a moment / it seemed that their
그래서 잠시 동안 / 그들의 여행은 끝난 듯 했다.

journey must end.

> ### Key Expression
>
> be 동사 다음에 to 부정사가 오면, 예정, 가능, 운명, 의도, 의무와 같은 의미로 사용된다.
>
> This was to be an eventful day / for the travelers.
> 이 날에 많은 사건이 일어 날 운명이었다 / 일행에게.

rippling 잔잔하게 흐르는, 잔물결을 일으키는 brook 개울, 시내 eventful 사건이 많은, 중대한 ditch 수로, 개천
jagged 톱니 같은, 뾰죽한 steep 가파른, 험한

"What shall we do?" asked Dorothy despairingly.
"어떡해야 하지?" 도로시가 절망하여 물었다.

"I haven't the faintest idea," said the Tin Woodman, / and
"아무 생각도 안나" 양철 나무꾼이 말했고 /

the Lion shook his shaggy mane / and looked thoughtful.
사자는 털이 덥수룩한 갈기를 흔들며 / 생각에 잠긴 표정을 지었다.

But the Scarecrow said, / "We cannot fly, /
하지만 허수아비가 말했다 / "우리는 날아갈 수 없어 /

that is certain. Neither can we climb down / into this great
물론. 우리는 기어서 내려 갈수도 없어 / 이 깊은 골짜기를.

ditch. Therefore, / if we cannot jump over it, /
그러니 / 우리가 뛰어넘어갈 수 없다면 /

we must stop / where we are."
멈출 수밖에 없어 / 여기서"

"I think / I could jump over it," said the Cowardly Lion, /
"내 생각에 / 뛰어넘을 수 있어" 겁쟁이 사자가 말했다 /

after measuring the distance carefully / in his mind.
조심스럽게 거리를 재어본 후 / 마음속으로.

"Then we are all right," answered the Scarecrow, /
"그러면 좋지" 허수아비가 말했다 /

"for you can carry us all over / on your back, /
"너는 우리 모두를 옮겨줄 수 있을 테니까 / 등에 태우고 /

one at a time."
한 번에 한 명씩."

"Well, I'll try it," said the Lion. "Who will go first?"
"음, 내가 시도해볼게" 사자가 말했다. "누가 먼저 갈래?"

"I will," declared the Scarecrow, / "for, / if you found /
"내가 갈게" 허수아비가 말했다 /   "왜냐하면, / 알게 된다면 /

that you could not jump over / the gulf, / Dorothy would
네가 뛰어넘을 수 없다는 것을 /   구덩이(골짜기)를 / 도로시는 죽을 거고 /

be killed, / or the Tin Woodman badly dented /
           양철 나무꾼은 찌그러질 테니 /

on the rocks below. But if I am on your back / it will not
바위에 부딪혀.   하지만 내가 네 등에 타고 있으면 /   별 문제 없을 거야 /

matter so much, / for the fall would not hurt me at all."
              왜냐하면 떨어져도 나는 전혀 다치지 않을 테니까."

"I am terribly afraid of falling, myself,"
"난 떨어지는 게 무서워 죽겠어"

said the Cowardly Lion, /
겁쟁이 사자가 말했다 /

"but I suppose / there is nothing to do but try it.
"하지만 내 생각에 /   시도해보는 수밖에 없어.

So get on my back / and we will make the attempt."
그러니 내 등에 타고 /   한 번 해보자"

---

despairingly 절망하여 shaggy 털이 덥수룩한 mane 갈기 declare 분명히 말하다
gulf (지표면의) 갈라진 틈, 구덩이 dent 찌그러뜨리다, 움푹 들어가게 하다 attempt 시도

The Scarecrow sat upon the Lion's back, / and the big
허수아비가 사자의 등에 올라 타 앉자 / 사자는 걸어가더니 /

beast walked / to the edge of the gulf / and crouched down.
골짜기 끝으로 / 몸을 웅크리고 앉았다.

"Why don't you run and jump?" asked the Scarecrow.
"달려가다가 뛰는 게 어때?" 허수아비가 물었다.

"Because that isn't the way / we Lions do these things,"
"그건 방식이 아니거든 / 우리 사자들이 그런 일을 하는,"

he replied.
사자가 대답했다.

Then giving a great spring, / he shot through the air /
그러고 나서 높이 뛰어올라 / 공중으로 솟아올랐다가 /

and landed safely / on the other side.
안전하게 내려앉았다 / 반대편에.

They were all greatly pleased / to see / how easily he did it,
모두들 매우 기뻐했다 / 보고서 / 사자가 쉽게 해내는 것을 /

/ and after the Scarecrow had got down from his back /
그리고 허수아비가 등에서 내려오자 /

the Lion sprang across the ditch again.
사자는 다시 골짜기를 뛰어올라 건너 왔다.

Dorothy thought / she would go next; so she took Toto
도로시는 생각했다 / 자신이 다음이라; 그래서 그녀는 토토를

in her arms / and climbed on the Lion's back, /
팔에 안고 / 사자 등에 올라타고 /

holding tightly to his mane / with one hand.
사자의 갈기를 꼭 잡았다 / 한 손으로.

The next moment / it seemed as if she were flying through
다음 순간 / 마치 자신이 하늘을 나는 기분이 들었다;

the air; and then, / before she had time to think about it, /
그러고 나서 / 그 기분에 대해 생각해보기 전에 /

she was safe on the other side.
맞은편에 안전하게 도착했다.

The Lion went back a third time / and got the Tin
사자는 세 번째로 돌아와 / 양철 나무꾼을 데려왔고 /

Woodman, / and then they all sat down / for a few
그러자 모두들 바닥에 앉았다 / 잠시 동안 /

moments / to give the beast a chance to rest, /
사자에게 쉴 시간을 주려고 /

for his great leaps had made his breath short, / and he
여러 번 뛰어넘어 숨이 가빠졌기 때문에 /

panted like a big dog / that has been running too long.
사자는 커다란 개처럼 헐떡거렸다   오랫동안 뛰어다닌.

They found the forest very thick on this side, /
반대편 숲은 매우 울창했고 /

and it looked dark and gloomy. After the Lion had rested /
숲은 어둡고 음울해 보였다.   사자가 잠시 쉰 후 /

they started along the road of yellow brick, /
일행은 노란 벽돌 길을 따라 걷기 시작했다 /

silently wondering, / each in his own mind, /
말없이 궁금해 하며 / 각자 마음속으로 /

if ever they would come / to the end of the woods /
과연 자신들이 도착할지 / 숲의 끝에 /

and reach the bright sunshine again.
그리고 빛나는 햇빛을 다시 볼 수 있을지.

To add to their discomfort, / they soon heard strange
그들의 불안에 더해 / 그들은 곧 이상한 소리를 들었고 /

noises / in the depths of the forest, / and the Lion
숲속 깊은 곳에서 / 사자는 일행에게 속삭였다 /

Key Expression

"why don't you ~ ?"는 상대방에게 어떤 것을 권하거나 제안할 때 사용하며, "why not"과 같은 의미로 "~하는 게 어때, ~하지 않겠어요?"라고 해석한다.

"Why don't you run and jump?" asked the Scarecrow.
"달려가다가 뛰는 게 어때?"   허수아비가 물었다.

crouch down 웅크려 앉다, 쭈그려 앉다 give a spring 뛰어오르다 shoot through the air 공중으로 솟아오르다
land (땅에) 내려앉다 spring across 뛰어올라 건너다 leap 뜀, 도약 pant 헐떡거리다 gloomy 우울한, 음울한
discomfort 불안, 불편

whispered to them / that it was in this part of the country
(무엇이라고?) 이 지역에 /

/ that the Kalidahs lived.
칼리다들이 산다고.

"What are the Kalidahs?" asked the girl.
"칼리다가 뭔데?" 도로시가 물었다.

"They are monstrous beasts / with bodies like bears and
"무시무시한 짐승이야 / 곰과 같은 몸뚱이와

heads like tigers," replied the Lion, "and with claws so
호랑이 같은 머리가 있는" 사자가 대답했다 / "또 발톱은 매우 길고 날카로워서 /

long and sharp / that they could tear me in two / as easily
나를 둘로 찢어놓을 수도 있어 / 내가 토토를

as I could kill Toto. I'm terribly afraid of the Kalidahs."
죽이듯이 쉽게. 칼리다들이 무서워 죽겠어."

claw 발톱

"I'm not surprised / that you are," returned Dorothy.
"놀랍지 않아 / 네가 무서워하는 것은" 도로시가 대답했다.

"They must be dreadful beasts."
"정말 무서운 짐승임에 틀림없구나."

The Lion was about to reply / when suddenly they came
사자가 막 대답하려했다 / 그들이 갑자기 또 다른 골짜기에 도착했을 때 /

to another gulf / across the road. But this one was so
길 건너편에 있는. 하지만 이번 골짜기는 무척

broad and deep / that the Lion knew / at once /
넓고 깊어서 / 사자는 알아차렸다 / 즉시 /

he could not leap across it.
자신이 뛰어넘을 수 없을 거라고.

So they sat down to consider / what they should do,
그래서 그들은 생각하기 위해 앉았다 / 어떻게 해야 할지 /

and after serious thought / the Scarecrow said:
심각한 고민 끝에 / 허수아비가 말했다:

"Here is a great tree, / standing close to the ditch.
"여기 큰 나무가 있어 / 절벽 가까운 곳에 서 있는.

If the Tin Woodman can chop it down, / so that it will
양철 나무꾼이 이 나무를 벨 수 있어서 / 나무가 맞은편에

fall to the other side, / we can walk across it easily."
쓰러지면 / 우리가 쉽게 건너갈 수 있을 거야"

Key Expression

"be about to 동사원형"은 "be on the point(verge, brink) of"와 같은 의미로 사용되며, "~하려는 참이다, 막 ~을 하려하다"라고 해석한다.

The Lion was about to reply / when suddenly they came to another gulf /
사자가 막 대답하려 했다 / 그들이 갑자기 또 다른 골짜기에 도착했을 때 /
across the road.
길 건너편에 있는.

dreadful 무서운, 무시무시한 serious 진지한, 심각한

"That is a first-rate idea," said the Lion.
"훌륭한 생각이야" 사자가 말했다.

"One would almost suspect / you had brains /
"거의 생각할 거야 / 네게 두뇌가 있다고

in your head, / instead of straw."
머릿속에 / 짚이 아니라."

The Woodman set to work at once, / and so sharp was
나무꾼은 즉시 일을 시작했고 / 도끼가 무척 날카로웠기에 /

his axe / that the tree was soon chopped nearly through.
곧 나무가 거의 잘렸다.

Then the Lion put his strong front legs against the tree /
그러고 나서 사자가 강한 앞발을 나무에 대고 /

and pushed with all his might, / and slowly the big
온 힘을 다해 밀자 / 천천히 커다란 나무가

tree tipped and fell / with a crash across the ditch, /
기울더니 쓰러졌다 / 골짜기를 건너편에서 엄청난 소리를 내며 /

with its top branches on the other side.
나무 꼭대기 가지가 반대편에 걸쳐진 채.

They had just started to cross this queer bridge /
그들이 막 이 이상한 다리를 건너기 시작했다 /

when a sharp growl made them all look up, / and to their
그때 날카롭게 으르렁거리는 소리 때문에 그들 모두가 쳐다보자 / 오싹하게도 /

horror / they saw / running toward them two great beasts
그들은 보았다 / 거대한 짐승 두 마리가 그들을 향해 달려오는 것을 /

/ with bodies like bears and heads like tigers.
몸뚱이는 곰 같고 머리는 호랑이처럼 생긴.

"They are the Kalidahs!" said the Cowardly Lion, /
"저게 칼리다야" 겁쟁이 사자가 말했다 /

beginning to tremble.
부들부들 떨기 시작하며

118 The Wonderful Wizard of Oz

"Quick!" cried the Scarecrow. "Let us cross over."
"서둘러!" 허수아비가 소리쳤다. "다리를 건너자"

So Dorothy went first, / holding Toto in her arms, /
도로시가 첫 번째로 건넜고 / 토토를 팔에 안고 /

the Tin Woodman followed, / and the Scarecrow came
양철 나무꾼이 그 뒤를 따랐다 / 그리고 다음으로 허수아비가 건너갔다.

next. The Lion, / although he was certainly afraid, /
사자는 / 분명히 겁이 났지만 /

turned to face the Kalidahs, / and then he gave so loud
돌아서서 칼리다와 맞섰다 / 그리고 사자가 매우 크고 끔찍한

and terrible a roar / that Dorothy screamed / and the
으르렁 거리는 소리를 내서 / 도로시는 비명을 질렀고 /

Scarecrow fell over backward, / while even the fierce
허수아비는 뒤로 넘어졌다 / 그 동안에 맹수들조차 걸음을 멈추고 /

beasts stopped short / and looked at him / in surprise.
사자를 쳐다보았다 / 깜짝 놀라.

But, / seeing they were bigger than the Lion, /
하지만 / 칼리다는 자신이 사자보다 훨씬 큰 것을 알고 /

and remembering / that there were two of them and only
생각해서 / 그들은 둘인데 사자는 혼자뿐이라고 /

one of him, / the Kalidahs again rushed forward, /
칼리다는 다시 한 번 앞으로 돌진했다 /

and the Lion crossed over the tree / and turned to see /
그러자 사자는 나무다리를 건너 / 보려고 몸을 돌렸다 /

what they would do next. Without stopping an instant /
칼리다가 다음에 어떻게 할지. 잠시도 멈추지 않고 /

the fierce beasts also began to cross the tree.
무서운 짐승들 또한 나무다리를 건너기 시작했다.

And the Lion said to Dorothy:
그러자 사자가 도로시에게 말했다:

---

first-rate 훌륭한, 굉장한 tip 기울다 with a crash 엄청난 소리를 내며 growl 으르렁거리는 소리
roar 으르렁거리는 소리, 고함소리

"We are lost, / for they will surely tear / us to pieces /
"우린 끝났어 / 저들이 분명히 찢어놓을 거야 / 우리를 갈기갈기 /

with their sharp claws. But stand close behind me, /
날카로운 발톱으로. 하지만 내 뒤에 바싹 붙어 있어 /

and I will fight them / as long as I am alive."
내가 저들과 싸울 테니까 / 살아있는 동안"

"Wait a minute!" called the Scarecrow. He had been thinking / what was best to be done, / and now he asked the Woodman / to chop away the end of the tree / that rested on their side of the ditch. The Tin Woodman began to use his axe / at once, / and, / just as the two Kalidahs were nearly across, / the tree fell / with a crash into the gulf, / carrying the ugly, snarling brutes with it, / and both were dashed to pieces / on the sharp rocks at the bottom.

"Well," said the Cowardly Lion, / drawing a long breath of relief, / "I see we are going to live / a little while longer, and I am glad of it, / for it must be a very uncomfortable thing / not to be alive. Those creatures frightened me so badly / that my heart is beating yet."

"Ah," said the Tin Woodman sadly, /

---

snarling 으르렁거리는 be dashed to pieces 산산조각 나다 draw a long breath of relief 한숨을 길게 내쉬다

"I wish / I had a heart to beat."
"좋을 텐데 / 나도 쿵쿵 뛰는 심장이 있으면"

This adventure made / the travelers more anxious than
이 모험은 만들었다 / 여행자들을 전보다 더 바라게 /
ever / to get out of the forest, / and they walked so fast
숲을 빠져 나가려는 것을 / 그들은 매우 빨리 걸어서 /
/ that Dorothy became tired, / and had to ride on the
도로시는 지치고 / 사자 등에 올라타야 했다.
Lion's back. To their great joy / the trees became thinner
매우 기쁘게도 / 울창한 숲이 점점 옅어졌고 /
/ the farther they advanced, / and in the afternoon /
조금 더 나아감에 따라 / 오후에 /
they suddenly came upon a broad river, / flowing swiftly
그들은 갑자기 넓은 강을 만났다 / 눈앞에서 빠른 속도로
just before them.
흐르는.
On the other side of the water / they could see the road
강 건너편에 있는 / 노란 벽돌 길을 볼 수 있었다 /
of yellow brick / running through a beautiful country, /
아름다운 마을 사이로 뻗쳐나가는 (길을) /
with green meadows / dotted with bright flowers /
(그리고 마을에는) 푸른 초원이 있었다 / 밝은 색의 꽃들이 흩어져 있는 (초원이) /
and all the road bordered / with trees hanging full of
길 양쪽에 있었다 / 맛있는 과일이 주렁주렁 매달린 나무들이.
delicious fruits. They were greatly pleased /
일행은 매우 기뻐했다 /
to see this delightful country / before them.
이 아름다운 마을을 보고 / 그들 앞에 펼쳐진.

"How shall we cross the river?" asked Dorothy.
"이 강을 어떻게 건너지?" 도로시가 물었다.

"That is easily done," replied the Scarecrow.
"그건 쉽지" 허수아비가 대답했다.

122 The Wonderful Wizard of Oz

"The Tin Woodman must build us a raft, /
"양철 나무꾼이 뗏목을 만들어 주면 /

so we can float to the other side."
강 건너편으로 갈 수 있어."

So the Woodman took his axe / and began to chop down
그래서 나무꾼은 도끼를 들고 / 작은 나무들을 베기 시작했다 /

small trees / to make a raft, / and while he was busy at
뗏목을 만들기 위해 / 그리고 그가 바쁘게 일하는 동안 /

this / the Scarecrow found / on the riverbank /
허수아비는 찾았다 / 강둑에서 /

a tree full of fine fruit.
맛있는 과일이 잔뜩 달려 있는.

This pleased Dorothy, / who had eaten nothing but nuts
이것은 도로시를 기쁘게 했다 / 하루 종일 견과류 밖에 안 먹었기 때문에 /

all day, / and she made a hearty meal of the ripe fruit.
잘 익은 과일을 실컷 먹었다.

But it takes time / to make a raft, / even when one is as
하지만 시간이 걸린다 / 뗏목을 만드는 데 / 부지런하고 지칠 줄 모르는 사람이

industrious and untiring / as the Tin Woodman, /
있을 지라도 / 양철 나무꾼과 같은 /

and when night came / the work was not done.
그래서 밤이 되었을 때 / 일은 끝나지 않았다.

Key Expression

"whish" 다음에 과거 시제가 오면, 현재와 반대되는 상황을 묘사하고, 과거완료 시제가 오면, 과거와 반대되는 상황에 대해 말한다.

"I wish / I had a heart to beat."
"좋을 텐데 / 나도 쿵쿵 뛰는 심장이 있으면"

advance 앞으로 나가다, 전진하다 come upon 우연히 만나다, 발견하다 run through (도로가) 사이로 뻗쳐 있다
meadow 초원, 목초지, 목장 dotted 흩어져 있는 border ~와 접하다, 경계를 이루다 float 흘러가다, 떠가다
industrious 부지런한 untiring 지칠 줄 모르는

So they found a cozy place / under the trees / where they
그래서 일행은 아늑한 장소를 찾았고 / 　나무 밑에서 / 　그곳에서 잠을 푹

slept well / until the morning; and Dorothy dreamed /
잤다 / 　아침까지; 　그리고 도로시는 꿈을 꿨다 /

of the Emerald City, / and of the good Wizard Oz, /
에메랄드 시와 / 　위대한 마법사 오즈에 대한 /

who would soon send her back / to her own home again.
곧 도로시를 돌려보내 주는 (오즈) / 　다시 그녀의 집으로.

cozy 아늑한, 안락한

Quiz 4

A. 단어

다음 단어의 설명을 읽고, 어떤 단어를 설명하는지 아래의 박스에서 알맞은 단어를 고르세요.

1. a relaxed happy feeling that you get because something bad has not happened or a bad situation has ended

2. to go forward

3. meaning what you say or do, and not making a joke

4. making a long, loud, deep sound

5. to breathe quickly with short noisy breaths because you have been running

6. one of the sharp, curved nails at the end of each of the toes of some animals

7. rising or falling at a sharp angle

8. the long hair around the face and neck of a lion

9. to say something more that is related to what has been said already

10. the rough red substance that damages the surface of iron and steel

---

| advance | pant | rust | roar | steep |
| claw | add | serious | mane | relief |

B. 직독직해

아래에 제시된 문장을 직독직해로 해석해보세요.

1. There were few birds / in this part of the forest, / for birds love the open country / where there is plenty of sunshine.

   →

2. "Is he stuffed?" / asked the Lion / in surprise, / as he watched her pick up the Scarecrow / and set him upon his feet.

   →

Answer   A. 단어   1. relief 2. advance 3. serious 4. roar 5. pant 6. claw 7. steep 8. mane 9. add 10. rust
B. 직독직해   1. 새들도 거의 없었다 / 숲의 이 지역에는 / 새들은 탁 트인 곳을 좋아하기 때문에 / 햇빛이 많은.

3. During the rest of that day / there was no other adventure / to mar the peace of their journey.

   →

4. The Woodman set to work at once, / and so sharp was his axe / that the tree was soon chopped nearly through.

   →

5. It takes time / to make a raft, / even when one is as industrious and untiring / as the Tin Woodman.

   →

C. 동시통역

아래에 제시된 직독직해를 보고, 영어로 말해보세요.

1. "나는 모르겠어"라고 / 대답했다 / "나도 에메랄드 시에 가본 적이 없으니까."

   →

2. "어쩌다 겁쟁이가 되었니?" / 도로시가 물었다 / 커다란 짐승을 바라보며 / 놀라서.

   →

3. 위험이 닥칠 때마다 / 심장이 빠르게 뛰기 시작해.

   →

4. "원한다면" / 사자가 말했다 / "내가 숲속에 가서 / 사슴을 잡아다 줄게."

   →

5. 이 모험은 만들었다 / 여행자들을 전보다 더 바라게 / 숲을 빠져 나가려는 것을.

   →

Answer

2. "그가 짚으로 만들어졌다고?" / 사자가 물었다 / 놀라서 / 도로시가 허수아비를 일으켜 / 자기 발로 서게 하는 것을 볼 때.
3. 그 날 나머지 시간 동안에는 / 다른 모험은 없었다 / 여행의 평화를 망치는(방해하는).
4. 나무꾼은 즉시 일을 시작했고 / 도끼가 무척 날카로웠기에 / 곧 나무가 거의 잘렸다.
5. 시간이 걸린다 / 뗏목을 만드는 데 / 부지런하고 지칠 줄 모르는 사람이 있을 지라도 / 양철 나무꾼과 같은

C. 동시통역 1. "I cannot tell," / was the answer, / "for I have never been to the Emerald City."
2. "What makes you a coward?" / asked Dorothy, / looking at the great beast / in wonder.
3. Whenever there is danger, / my heart begins to beat fast.
4. "If you wish," / said the Lion, "I will go into the forest / and kill a deer for you."
5. This adventure made / the travelers more anxious than ever / to get out of the forest.

Chapter 8. The Deadly Poppy Field
죽음의 양귀비 꽃밭(줄거리)

The next morning, in the eighth chapter, / the raft is
다음날 아침, 8장에서 /   뗏목이 완성된다.

completed. But the strong current soon sweeps /
하지만 강력한 강물의 흐름은 곧 휩쓸어버린다 /

the raft far away / from the Yellow Brick Road.
뗏목을 먼 곳으로 /   노란 벽돌이 깔려있는 길에서.

In an effort to bring the raft / to the far bank,
뗏목을 움직이려고 /   멀리 떨어져 있는 강둑으로 /

the Scarecrow pushes the pole / that he is using as a
허수아비는 막대(노)를 눌러서 /   앞으로 나가게 하는 도구로 사용하고 있던 /

propulsive instrument / so deep into the river bottom /
                                   강바닥에 너무 깊이 /

that it sticks fast.
막대는 꽉 달라붙는다.

The pole and the Scarecrow soon / are left far behind by
막대(노)와 허수아비는 곧 /   뗏목에서 멀리 떨어진다 /

the raft / as a result of the strong current.
         강력한 강물의 흐름 때문에.

The Cowardly Lion jumps into the river.
겁쟁이 사자는 강물에 뛰어든다.

The Tin Woodman grabs hold of the Lion's tail.
양철나무꾼은 사자의 꼬리를 움켜잡았다.

The two get the raft to shore.
둘은 뗏목을 강가로 끌고 간다.

The travelers walk back / along the river bank /
일행들은 걸어서 돌아간다 /   강둑을 따라 /

until they can see the Scarecrow / perched on his pole /
그들이 허수아비를 볼 때까지 /   막대에 꽂혀 있는 /

in the middle of the river.
강 한가운데.

A Stork comes to the rescue / and carries the Scarecrow
황새 한 마리가 그를 구하고 와서 / 허수아비를 다시 데려 간다 /

back / to his comrades.
친구들에게.

Before the travelers can get back / to the Yellow Brick
일행들이 돌아가기 전에 / 노란 벽돌이 깔린 길로 /

Road, / they enter a field of poppies. The poppies cause
그들은 양귀비 밭으로. 양귀비는 만든다 /

/ Dorothy, Toto, and the Cowardly Lion / to fall asleep.
도로시, 토토, 겁쟁이 사자를 / 잠들게.

The Scarecrow and the Tin Woodman realize the need /
허수아비와 양철나무꾼은 필요하다는 것을 깨닫는다 /

to pull their three comrades out of the poppy field.
친구 세 명을 양귀비 밭에서.

They pick up Dorothy and Toto / and carry them out
그들은 도로시와 토토를 집어 들어 / 양귀비 밭 밖으로 옮긴다.

of the field. But the Lion is too big and heavy / to be
하지만 사자는 너무 크고 무거웠다 / 옮기기에.

carried. So he is left / sleeping among the poppies.
그래서 그를 남겨놓는다 / 양귀비꽃 사이에서 잠든 채로.

---

raft 뗏목 current 흐름, 수류 propulsive 추진하는 grab hold of 움켜잡다 perch 앉히다, 놓다
comrade 친구, 동료 poppy 양귀비

Chapter 9. The Queen of the Field Mice
들쥐 여왕 (줄거리)

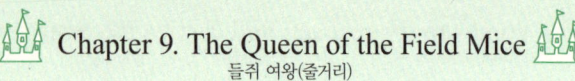

In the ninth chapter, / the Tin Woodman is beyond the
9장에서 / 양철 나무꾼은 양귀비 밭을 지나간다 /

poppy field, / but short of the Yellow Brick Road.
하지만 노란 벽돌이 깔린 길에 도달하지 못한다.

He discovers / a field mouse being pursued /
나무꾼은 발견한다 / 한 마리의 들쥐가 쫓기고 있는 것을 /

by a ravenous wildcat. To save the mouse, /
몹시 굶주린 살쾡이에 의해. 들쥐를 구하려고 /

he beheads the wildcat / with his ax.
나무꾼은 살쾡이의 목을 벤다 / 도끼로.

He then discovers / that the mouse whose life he just
그러고 나서 나무꾼은 알게 된다 / 자신이 방금 목숨을 구해준 들쥐가 /

has saved / is the Queen of the Field Mice. The Queen's
들쥐의 여왕이라는 것을. 여왕의 백성들은 알게

subjects find out / what has happened, / and one of them
되자 / 어떤 일이 일어났는지 / 한 들쥐가 묻는다 /

asks / how the mice can repay the Tin Woodman.
어떻게 양철 나무꾼에게 은혜를 갚아야 할지.

The Woodman can't think of anything.
나무꾼에게 어떤 생각도 떠오르지 않는다.

The Scarecrow suggests / that the Field Mice rescue the
허수아비는 제안한다 / 들쥐들이 겁쟁이 사자를 구해줄 것을 /

Cowardly Lion / from the poppy field.
양귀비 밭에서.

At the Scarecrow's suggestion, / the Tin Woodman cuts
허수아비의 제안에 따라 / 양철 나무꾼은 자르고 /

down / several nearby trees / and makes a truck out of
근처에 있는 몇 그루의 나무를 / 나무로 손수레를 만든다 /

them, / complete with wheels.
바퀴가 있는

Thousands of Field Mice attach strings to the truck /
수천 마리의 들쥐들은 손수레에 줄을 메고 /

and pull the truck into the poppy field.
손수레를 양귀비 밭으로 끌어당긴다.

The Scarecrow and the Tin Woodman help load /
허수아비와 나무꾼은 싣는 일을 도와준다 /

the Lion onto the truck. The mice pull the truck, Lion /
사자를 손수레에. 쥐들은 손수레에, 사자를 끌어당기고 /

and all, out of the poppy field. During this time, /
모두가 양귀비 밭 밖으로 나온다. 이때 /

Dorothy and Toto wake up and find out /
도로시와 토토는 잠에서 깨어 알게 된다 /

that they are no longer among the poppies.
자신들이 더 이상 양귀비 밭에 없다는 것을.

pursue 뒤쫓다, 추적하다 ravenous 몹시 굶주린, 게걸스럽게 먹는 wildcat 살쾡이 behead 목을 베다, 참수하다
repay 은혜를 갚다 truck 손수레, 짐수레 complete 필요한 모든 것이 갖추어진, 완전한 attach 붙이다, 첨부하다

Chapter 10. The Guardian of the Gates
문지기(줄거리)

In the tenth chapter, / the Cowardly Lion awakes and
10장에서 / 겁쟁이 사자는 잠에서 깨어나 발견한다 /

finds / that he has been pulled out of the deadly poppy
자신을 죽음의 양귀비 밭 밖으로 끌어낸 것을.

field. The travelers resume / their quest for the Yellow
일행은 다시 찾기 시작한다 / 노란 벽돌이 깔린 길을.

Brick Road. It isn't long before / they find and follow it /
머지않아 / 그들은 길을 발견하고 따라간다 /

all the way to the gates of the Emerald City.
에메랄드 시의 문까지 계속.

Along the way, / the travelers have to make an overnight
여행 중에 / 여행자들은 하룻밤 머물러야 했다 /

stop / at a farmhouse. Their host tells them / that the
농가에서. 주인은 그들에게 말한다 /

Wizard never permits / anyone to see him face to face.
오즈 마법사는 절대로 허락하지 않는다고 / 누구라도 그를 직접 만나는 것을.

The Wizard in fact / takes on whatever form he pleases.
사실 마법사는 / 자신이 원하는 모습으로 나타난다.

So no one knows / what the Wizard's natural form is.
그래서 아는 사람이 없다 / 마법사의 정상적인 모습이 어떤 것인지.

This doesn't deter / Dorothy or her companions.
이러한 것 때문에 단념하지 않는다 / 도로시와 그녀의 동료들은.

The next morning, / they resume their trip / and arrive at
다음날 아침에 / 그들은 여행을 다시 시작하여 / 에메랄드 시에

the Emerald City. There, the Guardian of the Gate /
도착한다. 그곳에서, 수문장은 /

puts spectacles with green lenses on them /
그들에게 초록색 렌즈가 있는 안경을 쓰게 한다 /

so the splendor of the city / won't blind them.
도시의 광채 때문에 /   그들의 눈이 멀지 않도록.

After that, / he leads them into the Emerald City proper.
그러고 나서 /   그는 그들을 이끌고 에메랄드 시로 간다.

resume 다시 시작하다, 계속하다 quest 탐색, 탐구 along the way (여행) 도중에, 중간에
make an overnight stop 하룻밤 머무르다 natural 정상적인, 타고난 deter 단념시키다, 저지하다
guardian 관리인, 보호자 splendor 빛남, 광채 proper (명사 뒤에서) 본래의 진정한

Chapter 11. The Wonderful City of Oz
놀라운 오즈의 도시

Even with eyes protected by the green spectacles, /
심지어 초록색 안경으로 눈을 보호했어도 /

Dorothy and her friends were at first dazzled / by the
도로시와 친구들은 처음에는 눈이 부셨다 /

brilliancy of the wonderful City.
그 놀라운 도시의 광채 때문에.

The streets were lined with beautiful houses /
거리에는 아름다운 집들이 줄지어 서 있었고 /

all built of green marble / and studded everywhere with
모두 초록색 대리석으로 지은 (집들) / 여기저기서 반짝이는 에메랄드로 장식되어 있었다.

sparkling emeralds. They walked over a pavement of the
그들은 똑같이 초록색 대리석이 깔린 도로를 걸어갔고 /

same green marble, / and where the blocks were joined
대리석 벽돌이 서로 연결된 부분에는

together / were rows of emeralds, / set closely, /
에메랄드가 줄지어 박혀 있었고 / 촘촘하게 /

and glittering / in the brightness of the sun. The window
반짝이고 있었다 / 밝은 햇빛을 받아. 창문은

panes were of green glass; even the sky above the City
초록색 유리로 만들어졌고; 도시 위에 펼쳐진 하늘도 초록색이었으며 /

had a green tint, / and the rays of the sun were green.
햇살도 초록색이었다.

There were many people / --men, women, and children--
많은 사람들이 있었다 / 남자, 여자, 어린아이들이 /

/ walking about, / and these were all dressed in green
여기저기 걸어 다니고 있는 / 이들은 모두 초록색 옷을 입고 있었고 /

clothes / and had greenish skins.
초록색 피부를 가지고 있었다.

They looked at / Dorothy and her strangely assorted
사람들은 바라보았고 / 도로시와 그녀의 낯선 여러 친구들을 /

company / with wondering eyes, / and the children all
놀란 눈으로 / 아이들은 모두 달아나고 /

ran away / and hid behind their mothers / when they saw
엄마 뒤로 숨어 버렸다 / 사자를 보았을 때;

the Lion; but no one spoke to them.
하지만 그들에게 말을 거는 사람은 없었다.

Many shops stood in the street, / and Dorothy saw / that
많은 상점들이 거리에 있었고 / 도로시는 발견했다 /

everything in them was green. Green candy and green
상점 안의 모든 물건은 초록색이라는 사실을. 초록색 사탕과

pop corn were offered for sale, / as well as green shoes,
팝콘을 팔려고 내놓았다 / 뿐만 아니라 초록색 신발과

green hats, and green clothes of all sorts.
모자와, 온갖 종류의 초록색 옷을.

At one place / a man was selling green lemonade, /
어떤 가게에서는 / 한 남자가 초록색 레모네이드를 팔고 있었고 /

and when the children bought it / Dorothy could see /
아이들이 레모네이드를 살 때 / 도로시는 볼 수 있었다 /

that they paid for it / with green pennies.
아이들이 값을 지불하는 것을 / 초록색 동전으로.

There seemed to be no horses nor animals of any kind;
말 또는 어떤 종류의 동물도 없는 것 같았다;

the men carried things around / in little green carts, /
사람들이 물건들을 운반했고 / 초록색 수레에 싣고 /

which they pushed before them.
사람들은 수레를 앞에 놓고 밀어서 움직였다.

Key Expression

아래 예문의 "even with"는 "에도 불구하고, 하지만"라는 의미로 해석한다. even에 극단적인 상황을 강조하는 의미가 있기 때문이다.

Even with eyes protected by the green spectacles, / Dorothy and her friends were
심지어 초록색 안경으로 눈을 보호했어도 / 도로시와 친구들은

at first dazzled / by the brilliancy of the wonderful City.
처음에는 눈이 부셨다 / 그 놀라운 도시의 광채 때문에.

dazzle 눈부시게 하다 brilliancy 광채 studded 장식된 pavement 포장도로 glitter 반짝이다 tint 색(조)
assorted 여러 가지, 다채로운

Everyone seemed happy and contented and prosperous.
모두 행복하고 만족스럽고 부유해 보였다.

The Guardian of the Gates led them through the streets /
문지기는 일행을 거리로 안내했다 /
until they came to a big building, / exactly in the middle
그들이 큰 건물에 도착할 때까지 / 정확히 도시의 한복판에 있던 (큰 건
of the City, / which was the Palace of Oz, the Great
물) / 그 건물이 위대한 마법사 오즈의 궁궐이었다.
Wizard. There was a soldier / before the door, /
병사가 한 명 있었다 / 성문 앞에 /
dressed in a green uniform / and wearing a long green
초록색 군복을 입고 / 긴 초록색 수염을 기르고.
beard.

"Here are strangers," said the Guardian of the Gates to
"낯선 손님들입니다" 문지기가 병사에게 말했다 /
him, / "and they demand / to see the Great Oz."
"그들은 요청합니다 / 오즈 마법사를 만나길"

"Step inside," answered the soldier,
"안으로 들어가게" 병사가 대답했다 /
"and I will carry your message / to him."
"내가 메시지를 전하지 / 마법사님께"

---

contented 만족한 prosperous 부유한 Guardian of the Gates 문지기 guardian 관리인
demand 요구하다, 요청하다

So they passed through the Palace Gates /
그래서 그들(도로시 일행)은 성문을 통과하고 /

and were led into a big room / with a green carpet /
큰 방으로 안내되었다 / 초록색 카펫이 깔려 있고 /

and lovely green furniture set / with emeralds.
아름다운 초록색 가구가 있는 / 에메랄드가 새겨진.

The soldier made / them all wipe their feet /
병사는 시켰고(했고) / 그들에게 발을 닦으라고 /

upon a green mat / before entering this room, /
초록색 깔개 위에서 / 방에 들어가기 전에 /

and when they were seated / he said politely:
그들이 자리에 앉았을 때 / 정중하게 말했다:

"Please make yourselves comfortable / while I go to the
"편안하게 계세요 / 내가 알현실로 가서

door of the Throne Room / and tell / Oz you are here."
  말하는 동안에 / 오즈님에게 너희들이 왔다고"

They had to wait a long time / before the soldier
일행은 오랫동안 기다려야 했다 / 병사가 돌아올 때까지

returned. When, at last, he came back, / Dorothy asked:
  마침내 병사가 돌아왔을 때 / 도로시가 물었다:

"Have you seen Oz?"
"오즈 마법사님을 만났나요?"

Key Expression

"before"은 "~하기까지, 하기 전에"라는 의미이므로 "before the soldier returned"는 "병사들이 돌아올 때까지"라고 해석된다.

They had to wait a long time / before the soldier returned.
일행은 오랫동안 기다려야 했다 / 병사가 돌아올 때까지

make oneself comfortable 편안하게 있다 Throne Room 알현실, 접견실

"Oh, no," returned the soldier; "I have never seen him.
"아니" 병사가 대답했다; "나는 그분을 만난 적이 없다.

But I spoke to him / as he sat behind his screen /
하지만 그분에게 말을 했고 / 휘장 뒤에 앉아 계실 때 /

and gave him your message.
너희들의 메시지를 전했단다.

He said / he will grant you an audience, / if you so
말씀하셨지 / 너희들에게 알현을 허락하겠다고 / 너희들이 그렇게

desire; but each one of you must enter / his presence
원한다면; 하지만 너희들 각자는 가야하고 / 그분이 있는 곳으로 혼자서 /

alone, / and he will admit / but one each day.
그분은 들어오는 것을 허락해 / 하루에 한 사람만.

Therefore, / as you must remain in the Palace /
그러므로 / 너희들은 성안에 머물러야 하기에 /

for several days, / I will have you shown to rooms /
며칠 동안 / 방을 안내해줄게 /

where you may rest in comfort / after your journey."
너희들이 편히 쉴 수 있는 (방을) / 긴 여행을 해서"

"Thank you," replied the girl; "That is very kind of Oz."
"감사합니다" 도로시가 대답했다; "오즈님은 정말 친절하시군요"

The soldier now blew upon a green whistle, / and at
병사는 초록색 호루라기를 불었고 /

once a young girl, / dressed in a pretty green silk gown,
그러자 갑자기 어린 소녀가 / 초록색 비단 옷을 입은 /

/ entered the room. She had lovely green hair and green
방으로 들어왔다. 소녀는 아름다운 초록색 머리와 눈이 있었고 /

eyes, / and she bowed low before Dorothy / as she said, /
도로시 앞에서 고개 숙여 절을 했다 / 말하면서 /

"Follow me / and I will show you your room."
"저를 따라오세요 / 방으로 안내해 드릴게요"라고

So Dorothy said good-bye / to all her friends except
그래서 도로시는 작별인사를 하고 / 토토를 제외한 친구들에게 /

Toto, / and taking the dog in her arms / followed the
토토를 품에 안고 / 초록색 소녀를 따라갔다 /
green girl / through seven passages / and up three flights
일곱 개의 복도를 지나고 / 세 개의 계단을 오르며 /
of stairs / until they came to a room / at the front of
어느 방에 도착할 때까지 / 궁궐 앞쪽에 있는.
the Palace. It was the sweetest little room in the world,
세상에서 가장 아름다운 작은 방이었다 /
/ with a soft comfortable bed / that had sheets of green
부드럽고 편안한 침대가 있었고 / 그 침대에는 초록색 비단으로 만든 요와
silk and a green velvet counterpane.
초록색 벨벳 이불이 깔려 있었다.
There was a tiny fountain / in the middle of the room, /
작은 분수도 있었고 / 방 한가운데 /
that shot a spray of green perfume into the air, / to fall
그 분수는 초록색 향수를 공중으로 뿜었고 / 떨어졌다 /
back / into a beautifully carved green marble basin.
아름다운 조각이 새겨진 초록색 대리석 받침대로.
Beautiful green flowers stood / in the windows,
아름다운 녹색 꽃들이 놓여 있었고 / 창가에 /
/ and there was a shelf / with a row of little green books.
책꽂이가 하나 있었다 / 작은 초록색 책이 가지런히 꽂혀 있는.
When Dorothy had time to open these books / she found
도로시가 이 책들을 펼쳐 보고 / 그녀는 발견했다
/ them full of queer green pictures / that made her laugh,
/ 책에는 이상한 초록색 그림으로 가득 차 있는 것을 / 그림을 보고 도로시는 웃었고 /
/ they were so funny.
그림은 무척 재미있었다.

---

grant an audience 알현을 허락하다 admit (입장, 입학)을 허락하다 counterpane 이불 perfume 향수

basin 세면대, 세면대 모양의 받침대 queer 이상한

In a wardrobe / were many green dresses, / made of
옷장 안에 / 초록색 드레스가 가득 있었고 /

silk and satin and velvet; and all of them fitted Dorothy
비단과 새틴과 벨벳으로 만들어진; 모두 도로시에게 딱 맞았다.

exactly.

"Make yourself perfectly at home," said the green girl, /
"편히 쉬세요" 초록색 소녀가 말했다 /

"and if you wish for anything / ring the bell.
"원하는 게 있으면 / 벨을 울리세요.

Oz will send for you / tomorrow morning."
오즈님이 당신에게 오라고 전갈을 보내실 거예요 / 내일 아침에"

She left Dorothy alone / and went back to the others.
소녀는 도로시를 혼자 남겨놓고 떠났고 / 다른 일행에게 돌아갔다.

These she also led to rooms, / and each one of them
소녀는 또한 일행을 방으로 안내했고 / 각각은 묵게 되었다 /

found himself lodged / in a very pleasant part of the
궁궐의 유쾌한 방에.

Palace. Of course / this politeness was wasted on the
물론 / 이런 친절은 허수아비에게는 헛된 일이었다;

Scarecrow; for when he found himself alone in his
왜냐하면 허수아비는 방안에 혼자 있게 되었을 때 /

room / he stood stupidly / in one spot, / just within the
그는 멍청하게 서있었다 / 한 곳에 / 문 바로 안쪽에 /

doorway, / to wait till morning.
아침이 될 때까지 기다리며.

It would not rest him / to lie down, / and he could not
허수아비에게는 휴식이 아니었다 / 누워있는 것이 / 그는 눈을 감을 수도 없었다;

close his eyes; so he remained all night staring / at a little
그래서 허수아비는 밤새도록 계속 쳐다봤다 / 작은 거미를 /

spider / which was weaving its web / in a corner of the
거미줄을 치고 있던 / 방안 구석에서.

room, / just as if it were not one of the most wonderful
그 방이 좋은 방이 아니라는 듯이 /

rooms / in the world. The Tin Woodman lay down on his
bed / from force of habit, / for he remembered /
when he was made of flesh; but not being able to sleep, /
he passed the night / moving his joints up and down /
to make sure they kept in good working order.
The Lion would have preferred / a bed of dried leaves
in the forest, / and did not like being shut up in a room;
but he had too much sense / to let this worry him, / so he
sprang upon the bed / and rolled himself up like a cat /
and purred himself asleep / in a minute.

The next morning, / after breakfast, / the green maiden
came to fetch Dorothy, / and she dressed her / in one
of the prettiest gowns, / made of green brocaded satin.
Dorothy put on a green silk apron / and tied a green
ribbon around Toto's neck, / and they started /
for the Throne Room of the Great Oz.

---

wardrobe 옷장 send for ~에게 오라고 전갈을 보내다 lodge 묵다, 숙박하다 politeness 친절
remain ~ing 계속 ~하다 remain staring 계속 쳐다보다 from force of habit 습관대로
sense 판단력, 사리, 분별 pur oneself asleep 가르랑거리며 잠들다 maiden 하녀 fetch 데리러 오다

First they came to a great hall / in which were many
그들이 먼저 넓은 방에 들어갔다 / 그곳에는 많은 신사 숙녀들이 있었다 /

ladies and gentlemen of the court, / all dressed in rich
비싼 옷을 차려 입고.

costumes. These people had nothing to do / but talk to
이 사람들은 할 일이 전혀 없었다 / 서로 이야기를 나누는

each other, / but they always came to wait / outside the
것 외에는 / 하지만 항상 와서 기다렸다 / 알현실 밖에서 /

Throne Room / every morning, / although they were
매일 아침 / 비록 그들은 허락받지 못했지만 /

never permitted / to see Oz. As Dorothy entered / they
오즈를 만나는 것을. 도로시가 들어가자 / 사람들은

looked at her curiously, / and one of them whispered:
호기심에서 그녀를 쳐다보았고 / 그 중 한 사람이 속삭이며 물었다:

"Are you really going to look upon / the face of Oz the
"너는 정말로 볼 거니 / 무서운 오즈님의 얼굴을?"
Terrible?"

"Of course," answered the girl, / "if he will see me."
"물론이죠" 도로시가 대답했다 / "저를 만나주시기만 하면요"

"Oh, he will see you," said the soldier / who had taken
"오즈님은 너를 만나실 거야" 병사가 말했다 / 도로시의 메시지를

her message to the Wizard, / "although he does not like /
마법사에게 전달했던 / "비록 그분은 좋아하지 않으시지만 /

to have people ask to see him.
사람들이 만나기를 청하는 것을.

Indeed, at first / he was angry and said / I should send
사실 처음에는 / 화를 내며 말씀하셨지 / 너희들을 돌려보내라고 /

you back / where you came from. Then he asked me /
너희들이 온 곳으로. 그 다음에 나에게 물으셨지 /

what you looked like, / and when I mentioned your silver
네가 어떻게 생겼는지 / 그래서 내가 네 은색 구두에 대해 말씀 드렸을 때 /

shoes / he was very much interested.
그분은 매우 흥미를 보이셨어.

142 The Wonderful Wizard of Oz

At last / I told him / about the mark upon your forehead,
마침내 / 나는 말씀 드렸지 / 네 이마에 있는 자국에 대해 /

/ and he decided / he would admit / you to his presence."
그러니까 그분은 결심하셨지 / 허락하신다고 / 그분이 있는 곳으로 네가 오는 것(너와 만나는 것)을"

Just then a bell rang, / and the green girl said to Dorothy,
바로 그 때 종이 울렸고 / 초록색 소녀가 도로시에게 말했다 /

/ "That is the signal. You must go into the Throne Room
"저게 신호예요. / 접견실에 들어가셔야 해요 /

/ alone."
혼자"

She opened a little door / and Dorothy walked boldly
소녀가 작은 문을 열자 / 도로시는 대담하게 걸어 들어갔고 /

through / and found herself in a wonderful place.
멋진 곳에 있게 되었다.

It was a big, round room / with a high arched roof, / and
그곳은 크고 둥근 방이었고 / 높고 둥근 천장이 있는 /

the walls and ceiling and floor were covered / with large
벽과 천장과 바닥에는 깔려 있었다 /

emeralds set closely together. In the center of the roof /
커다란 에메랄드가 촘촘히 박힌. 천장 한복판에는 /

Key Expression

"in which"는 관계부사 where와 같은 의미로 사용되고, "in which" 다음에 주어와 동사가 도치되어 있다. 주어인 "many ladies and gentlemen"을 전치사구와 형용사구로 수식하기 때문이다.

First they came to a great hall / in which were many ladies and gentlemen of the court, /
그들이 먼저 넓은 방에 들어갔다 / 그곳에는 많은 신사 숙녀들이 있었다 /
all dressed in rich costumes.
비싼 옷을 차려 입고.

costume 의상, 옷 curiously 진기하게, 호기심에서 throne 옥좌

was a great light, / as bright as the sun, / which made the
커다란 등이 있었고 / 태양만큼 밝게 빛나는 / 에메랄드를 반짝거리게

emeralds sparkle / in a wonderful manner.
했다 / 멋진 모습으로.

But what interested Dorothy most / was the big throne of
그러나 도로시에게 가장 흥미로운 것은 / 커다란 초록색 대리석 옥좌였다 /

green marble / that stood in the middle of the room.
방 한가운데에 놓여 있는.

It was shaped like a chair / and sparkled with gems, /
의자 모양이었고 / 보석이 반짝거렸다 /

as did everything else. In the center of the chair /
다른 모든 것처럼. 의자 가운데에 /

was an enormous Head, / without a body to support it /
거대한 머리가 놓여 있었다 / 머리를 떠받치는 몸도 없었고 /

or any arms or legs whatever. There was no hair upon
팔 다리도 없는 (머리가) 머리에 털이 없었다 /

this head, / but it had eyes and a nose and mouth, / and
하지만 눈과 코와 입은 있었고 /

was much bigger / than the head of the biggest giant.
훨씬 컸다 / 세상에서 가장 큰 거인의 머리보다

gem 보석

As Dorothy gazed upon this / in wonder and fear, /
도로시가 이 머리를 바라보고 있을 때 / 놀라움과 두려움에 /

the eyes turned slowly / and looked at her /
눈이 서서히 돌더니 / 그녀를 바라보았다 /

sharply and steadily. Then the mouth moved, /
날카롭고 침착하게. 그리고 나서 입이 움직였고 /

and Dorothy heard a voice say:
도로시가 말하는 목소리를 들었다:

"I am Oz, / the Great and Terrible.
"나는 오즈다 / 위대하고 무시무시한 마법사.

Who are you, / and why do you seek me?"
너는 누구이며 / 그리고 왜 나를 찾아 왔는가?

It was not such an awful voice / as she had expected /
무서운 목소리는 아니었다 / 도로시가 기대한 만큼 /

to come from the big Head; so she took courage and
커다란 머리에서 나올 것이라고; 그래서 용기를 내어 대답했다:

answered:

"I am Dorothy, / the Small and Meek.
"저는 도로시예요 / 작고 얌전한 아이예요.

I have come / to you for help."
저는 왔어요 / 당신에게 도움을 청하러"

The eyes looked at her thoughtfully / for a full minute.
눈은 생각에 잠긴 듯 그녀를 바라보았다 / 한참동안.

Then said the voice:
그러고 나서 말했다:

"Where did you get the silver shoes?"
"그 은 구두는 어디서 얻었는가?"

gaze 지켜보다, 바라보다 meek 순한, 얌전한

"I got them / from the Wicked Witch of the East, /
"얻었어요 / 동쪽 사악한 마녀에게서 /

when my house fell on her / and killed her," / she replied.
제 집이 마녀 위에 떨어져서 / 마녀를 죽였을 때" 그녀가 대답했다.

"Where did you get / the mark upon your forehead?"
"어디서 얻은 것이냐 / 이마에 있는 자국은?"

continued the voice. "That is / where the Good Witch of
목소리가 말을 이었다. "그것은 / 북쪽의 착한 마녀가 제게 입맞춤 해준 것이에요 /

the North kissed me / when she bade me good-bye /
작별인사를 하고 /

and sent me to you," said the girl.
당신에게 저를 보낼 때," 그녀가 말했다.

Again the eyes looked at / her sharply, / and they saw /
눈이 또 다시 바라보고 / 그녀를 날카롭게 / 알았다 /

she was telling the truth.
그녀가 진실을 말하고 있음을.

Then Oz asked / "What do you wish me to do?"
그러자 오즈가 물었다 / "내가 어떻게 하길 원하니?"

"Send me back to Kansas, / where my Aunt Em and
"저를 캔자스로 돌려보내 주세요 / 그곳에 엠 숙모와 헨리 삼촌이 있어요"

Uncle Henry are," she answered earnestly.
그녀는 진심으로 대답했다.

"I don't like your country, / although it is so beautiful.
"저는 이 나라가 싫어요 / 매우 아름다운 곳이지만.

And I am sure / Aunt Em will be dreadfully worried /
그리고 분명히 / 엠 숙모는 무척 걱정하실 거예요 /

over my being away so long."
제가 오랫동안 사라져 버린 것에 대해"

The eyes winked three times, / and then they turned up
눈은 윙크를 세 번 하고 / 그리고 나서 천장을 올려다보았다가 /

to the ceiling / and down to the floor / and rolled around
바닥을 내려다보고 / 이상한 모습으로 돌아서 /

so queerly / that they seemed to see every part of the
방안의 이 곳 저 곳을 둘러보는 듯이 보였다.

room. And at last / they looked at Dorothy again.
그리고 마침내 / 도로시를 다시 바라보았다.

"Why should I do this for you?" asked Oz.
"내가 왜 그래야 하지?" 오즈가 물었다.

"Because you are strong / and I am weak; because you
"오즈님은 강하고 / 저는 약하니까요; 오즈님은

are a Great Wizard / and I am only a little girl."
위대한 마법사이고 / 저는 어린아이일 뿐이니까요"

"But you were strong / enough to kill the Wicked Witch
"하지만 너도 강하잖니 / 동쪽의 사악한 마녀를 죽일 만큼"

of the East," said Oz.
오즈가 말했다.

"That just happened," returned Dorothy simply;
"그건 우연히 일어난 일이에요" 도로시가 간단하게 대답했다;

"I could not help it."
"어쩔 수가 없었어요"

"Well," said the Head, / "I will give you my answer.
"음" 머리가 말했다 / "네게 대답을 하겠다.

You have no right to expect / me to send you back to
너는 기대할 권리가 없다 / 내게 너를 캔자스로 돌려보내 달라고 할

Kansas / unless you do something / for me in return.
(권리가) / 네가 무언가 해주지 않으면 / 내게 보답으로.

> ### Key Expression
>
> "my being away so long"은 동명사구이며, "my"가 의미상 주어다. 동명사의 의미상 주어는 소유격이나 목적격을 사용할 수 있다.
>
> And I am sure / Aunt Em will be dreadfully worried / over my being away so long.
> 그리고 분명히 / 엠 숙모는 무척 걱정하실 거예요 / 제가 오랫동안 사라져 버린 것에 대해

bid (bid-bade-bidden) 인사를 하다, 작별을 고하다 earnestly 진심으로 dreadfully 몹시, 대단히

In this country / everyone must pay / for everything he
이 나라에서는 / 누구나 대가를 치러야 하지 / 무언가를 얻으려면.

gets. If you wish / me to use my magic power / to send
네가 원한다면 / 내가 마법의 힘을 사용하길 /

you home again / you must do something / for me first.
너를 다시 집으로 돌려보내주려고 / 너는 무언가 해야 해 / 먼저 나를 위해.

Help me / and I will help you."
나를 도와주면 / 나도 너를 도와주겠다"

"What must I do?" asked the girl.
"제가 무엇을 해야 하나요?" 도로시가 물었다.

"Kill the Wicked Witch of the West," answered Oz.
"서쪽의 사악한 마녀를 죽여라" 오즈가 대답했다.

"But I cannot!" exclaimed Dorothy, / greatly surprised.
"하지만 못해요!" 도로시가 큰소리로 말했다 / 깜짝 놀라서

"You killed the Witch of the East / and you wear the
"너는 동쪽 마녀를 죽였고 / 은 구두를 신고 있어 /

silver shoes, / which bear a powerful charm.
강력한 마법을 지닌.

There is now but one Wicked Witch / left in all this land,
이제 사악한 마녀는 하나뿐이다 / 이 나라에 남아있는 /

/ and when you can tell me / she is dead / I will send you
네가 말해주면 / 그 마녀가 죽었다고 / 너를 캔자스로 돌려보내

back to Kansas / --but not before."
주겠다 / 하지만 그 전에는 안 돼"

The little girl began to weep, / she was so much
도로시는 울기 시작했다 / 그녀는 무척 실망했다;

disappointed; and the eyes winked again /
그러자 눈이 다시 윙크를 하고 /

148 The Wonderful Wizard of Oz

and looked upon her anxiously / as if the Great Oz felt /
도로시를 걱정스러운 눈빛으로 바라보았다 / 마치 오즈는 생각하는 듯 했다 /

that she could help him / if she would.
그녀가 자신을 도와줄 수 있다고 / 마음만 먹으면.

"I never killed anything, / willingly," she sobbed.
"저는 아무 것도 죽여본 적이 없어요 / 원해서" 그녀는 흐느꼈다.

"Even if I wanted to, / how could I kill the Wicked
"제가 그러고 싶다 해도 / 어떻게 사악한 마녀를 죽일 수 있겠어요? /

Witch? / if you, / who are Great and Terrible, / cannot
마녀? 오즈님도 / 위대하고 무시무시한 마법사인 /

kill her yourself, / how do you expect / me to do it?"
직접 죽일 수 없다면 / 어떻게 기대하세요 / 제가 할 수 있다고?"

"I do not know," said the Head; "but that is my answer,
"나도 모른다" 머리가 말했다; "하지만 그게 내 대답이다 /

/ and until the Wicked Witch dies / you will not see
사악한 마녀가 죽을 때까지 / 네 삼촌과 숙모를 다시 볼 수

your uncle and aunt again. Remember / that the Witch
없을 것이다. 기억해라 / 그 마녀는 사악하고

is Wicked / --tremendously Wicked-- / and ought to be
엄청나게 사악하지 / 죽여야 한다는 것을.

killed. Now go, / and do not ask to see me again /
이제 가라 / 내게 다시 찾아오지 말거라 /

until you have done your task."
네가 임무를 완수할 때까지는."

Key Expression

to 부정사의 의미상 주어가 문장의 주어와 다른 경우 부정사 바로 앞에 목적어로 의미상 주어를 표현할 수 있다.

If you wish / me to use my magic power / to send you home again /
네가 원한다면 / 내가 마법의 힘을 사용하길 / 너를 다시 집으로 돌려보내주려고 /
you must do something / for me first.
너는 무언가 해야 해 / 먼저 나를 위해.

exclaim 외치다, 큰소리로 말했다 anxiously 걱정스러운 듯, 염려하듯이 willingly 자진해서, 원해서

Sorrowfully / Dorothy left the Throne Room / and went
슬퍼하며 /　　　　도로시는 알현실을 떠나고 /　　　　　　　　돌아갔다 /

back / where the Lion and the Scarecrow and the Tin
　　　사자와 허수아비와 양철 나무꾼이 기다리는 곳으로 /

Woodman were waiting / to hear what Oz had said to
　　　　　　　　　　　오즈가 그녀에게 한 말을 들으려고.

her. "There is no hope for me," she said sadly, /
　　"이제 희망이 없어"　　　　　　　도로시가 슬프게 말했다 /

"for Oz will not send me home / until I have killed /
"오즈는 나를 집으로 보내 주지 않을 것이기에 /　내가 죽일 때까지 /

the Wicked Witch of the West; and that I can never do."
사악한 서쪽 마녀를;　　　　　　　　　그런데 난 그럴 수 없어"

Her friends were sorry, / but could do nothing to help
친구들은 가엾어 했다 /　　　하지만 도와줄 방법이 없었다;

her; so Dorothy went to her own room / and lay down on
　　　그래서 도로시는 자신의 방으로 돌아가 /　　　침대에 누워 /

the bed / and cried herself to sleep.
　　　　　　울다가 잠이 들었다.

sorrowfully 슬퍼하며　cry oneself to sleep 울다가 잠들다

150　The Wonderful Wizard of Oz

The next morning / the soldier with the green whiskers /
다음날 아침 / 초록색 수염이 있는 병사가 /

came to the Scarecrow / and said:
허수아비에게 와서 / 말했다:

"Come with me, / for Oz has sent for you."
"나를 따라와 / 오즈님이 너를 데려오라고 보내셨다"

So the Scarecrow followed him / and was admitted into
그래서 허수아비는 병사를 따라갔고 / 알현실로 들어갔다 /

the great Throne Room, / where he saw, /
그곳에서 그는 보았다 /

sitting in the emerald throne, / a most lovely Lady.
에메랄드 옥좌에 앉아있는 / 매우 아름다운 부인을.

She was dressed in green silk gauze / and wore upon her
그녀는 초록색 비단 옷을 입고 / 흘러내린 초록색 머리 위에

flowing green locks a crown of jewels.
보석 왕관을 쓰고 있었다.

Growing from her shoulders were wings, /
어깨에 날개가 돋아 있었다 /

gorgeous in color and so light / that they fluttered /
색깔이 화려하고 가벼워서 / 펄럭거렸다 /

if the slightest breath of air reached them.
가벼운 바람이 닿기만 해도.

Key Expression

"admit"에는 "누군가를 어떤 장소로 입장시키다, 들어가게 하다"라는 의미가 있으며, "saw"의 목적어는 "a mostly lovely lady"이다.

So the Scarecrow followed him / and was admitted into the great Throne Room, /
그래서 허수아비는 병사를 따라갔고 / 알현실로 들어갔다 /
where he saw, / sitting in the emerald throne, / a most lovely Lady.
그곳에서 그는 보았다 / 에메랄드 옥좌에 앉아있는 / 매우 아름다운 부인을.

locks 머리털, 머리타래 gorgeous 화려한 flutter 펄럭이다

When the Scarecrow had bowed, / as prettily / as his
허수아비가 절을 했을 때 / 얌전하게 /

straw stuffing would let him, / before this beautiful
짚으로 된 몸으로 허락하는 한 / 이 아름다운 여성 앞에서 /

creature, / she looked upon him sweetly, / and said:
부인은 상냥하게 그를 바라보며 / 말했다:

"I am Oz, / the Great and Terrible.
"나는 오즈다 / 위대하고 무시무시한 마법사.

Who are you, / and why do you seek me?"
너는 누구냐 / 그리고 왜 나를 찾아 왔느냐?"

Now the Scarecrow, / who had expected / to see the great
이때 허수아비는 / 기대하고 있었던 / 거대한 머리를 보게

Head / Dorothy had told him of, / was much astonished;
될 거라고 / 도로시가 말했던 / 깜짝 놀랐다;

but he answered her bravely.
하지만 용기를 내어 대답했다.

"I am only a Scarecrow, / stuffed with straw.
"저는 그저 허수아비입니다 / 짚으로 채워진.

Therefore I have no brains, / and I come to you praying
그래서 저는 두뇌가 없어서 / 부탁을 드리러 왔습니다 /

/ that you will put brains in my head / instead of straw, /
제 머리 속에 두뇌를 넣어 달라고 / 짚 대신에 /

so that I may become / as much a man as any other /
그러면 저는 될 수 있겠지요 / 다른 사람처럼 /

in your dominions."
당신 영토(나라)의"

"Why should I do this for you?" asked the Lady.
"내가 왜 그래야 하지?" 부인이 물었다.

"Because you are wise and powerful, / and no one else
"오즈님은 현명하고 강한 분이며 / 아무도 절 도와줄 수

can help me," answered the Scarecrow.
없으니까요" 허수아비가 대답했다.

"I never grant favors / without some return," said Oz;
"나는 부탁을 들어주지 않는다 / 어떤 대가 없이" 오즈가 말했다;

"but this much I will promise. If you will kill for me /
"하지만 이것은 약속하겠다. 네가 나를 위해 죽이면 /

the Wicked Witch of the West, / I will bestow upon you a
사악한 서쪽 마녀를 / 나는 네게 훌륭한 두뇌를 주겠다 /

great many brains, / and such good brains / that you will
아주 좋은 두뇌를 /

be the wisest man / in all the Land of Oz."
가장 현명한 사람이 될 수 있을 만한 / 오즈 전체에서."

"I thought / you asked Dorothy to kill the Witch," /
"저는 생각했는데요. / 도로시에게 마녀를 죽이라고 하셨다고" /

said the Scarecrow, / in surprise.
허수아비가 말했다 / 놀라서

"So I did. I don't care / who kills her.
"그랬지. 상관하지 않는다 / 누가 죽이든.

But until she is dead / I will not grant your wish.
하지만 마녀가 죽기 전까지 / 네 부탁을 들어주지 않겠다.

Now go, / and do not seek me again / until you have
이제 가라 / 다시는 나를 찾아오지 마라 / 두뇌를 얻을 때까지 /

earned the brains / you so greatly desire."
네가 그토록 간절히 바라는"

prettily 얌전하게, 공손하게 sweetly 상냥하게 astonish 깜짝 놀라게 하다 dominion 영토, 영지
grant a favor 부탁을 들어주다. 호의를 베풀다 bestow 주다

The Scarecrow went sorrowfully back / to his friends
허수아비는 슬픈 표정으로 돌아가 / 친구들에게 /

/ and told them / what Oz had said; and Dorothy was
말했다 / 오즈가 한 말을; 그러자 도로시는 놀랐다 /

surprised / to find / that the Great Wizard was not a
알고서 / 위대한 마법사 오즈가 머리가 아니라 /

Head, / as she had seen him, / but a lovely Lady.
자신이 본 것처럼 / 아름다운 부인이라는 사실에.

"All the same," said the Scarecrow, /
"마찬가지야" 허수아비가 말했다 /

"she needs a heart / as much as the Tin Woodman."
"그 부인은 심장이 필요해 / 양철 나무꾼이 바라는 만큼이나"

On the next morning / the soldier with the green
다음날 아침 / 초록색 수염의 병사가 /

whiskers / came to the Tin Woodman / and said:
양철 나무꾼에게 와서 / 말했다:

"Oz has sent for you. Follow me."
"오즈님이 보내셨다. 나를 따라와라"라고

So the Tin Woodman followed him / and came to the
그래서 양철 나무꾼은 그를 따라가 / 알현실로 들어갔다.

great Throne Room.

He did not know / whether he would find Oz /
그는 몰랐다 / 자신이 오즈를 볼지 /

a lovely Lady / or a Head, / but he hoped /
아름다운 부인의 모습으로 / 아니면 머리의 모습으로 / 하지만 바랐다 /

it would be the lovely Lady. "For," he said to himself, /
아름다운 부인의 모습이길. "왜냐하면" 중얼거렸다 /

"if it is the head, / I am sure / I shall not be given a heart,
"오즈가 머리의 모습이라면 / 분명히 / 심장을 받지 못할 거야 /

/ since a head has no heart of its own /
머리에는 심장이 없고 /

154 The Wonderful Wizard of Oz

and therefore cannot feel for me. But if it is the lovely
그러면 나를 동정하지 않을 테니까.   하지만 오즈가 아름다운 부인의

Lady / I shall beg hard for a heart, / for all ladies are
모습이라면 / 심장을 달라고 청해 볼 거야 /   모든 부인들은

themselves said to be kindly hearted."
친절한 마음씨를 가지고 있다고 하니까"

But when the Woodman entered the great Throne Room
하지만 나무꾼이 알현실로 들어갔을 때 /

/ he saw neither the Head nor the Lady,
그는 머리도 부인도 보지 못했다 /

for Oz had taken the shape of a most terrible Beast.
오즈는 무시무시한 짐승의 모습을 하고 있었기에.

It was nearly as big as an elephant, / and the green throne
그것은 코끼리만큼이나 큰 짐승이었고 /   옥좌는 단단하지 못한 듯 보였다 /

seemed hardly strong / enough to hold its weight.
   그 무게를 견딜 수 있을 만큼.

The Beast had a head / like that of a rhinoceros, /
그 짐승은 머리가 있었다 / 코뿔소 같은 /

only there were five eyes in its face.
얼굴에 다섯 개의 눈이 있었다.

There were five long arms / growing out of its body, /
다섯 개의 긴 팔이 있었고 /   몸통에서 자라고 있는 /

and it also had five long, slim legs.
다섯 개의 길고 가는 다리가 있었다.

Key Expression

"not A but B"는 "A가 아니라 B"라는 의미로 A와 B에는 대등한 어구가 사용되어야 한다.
즉 예문의 경우처럼 A에 해당되는 말이 명사가 쓰이면 B에 해당되는 말도 명사가 쓰여야한다.

Dorothy was surprised / to find / that the Great Wizard was not a Head, /
도로시는 놀랐다 /   알고서 /   위대한 마법사 오즈가 머리가 아니라 /
as she had seen him, / but a lovely Lady.
자신이 본 것처럼 /   아름다운 부인이라는 사실에.

Thick, woolly hair covered every part of it, / and a more
덥수룩하게 많은 털이 온몸을 덮고 있어서 /

dreadful-looking monster could not be imagined.
더 무서워 보이는 동물을 상상할 수 없을 정도였다.

It was fortunate / the Tin Woodman had no heart /
다행이었다 / 양철 나무꾼에게 심장이 없는 것이 /

at that moment, / for it would have beat loud and fast /
그 순간 / 가슴이 쿵쿵 뛰었을 테니까 /

from terror. But being only tin, / the Woodman was not
공포로. 하지만 양철로만 되어있기에 / 나무꾼은 전혀 무서워하지 않았다 /

at all afraid, / although he was much disappointed.
비록 그는 무척 실망하긴 했지만.

"I am Oz, / the Great and Terrible," spoke the Beast, /
"나는 오즈다 / 위대하고 무시무시한 마법사" 짐승이 말했다 /

in a voice that was one great roar.
으르렁거리는 목소리로.

"Who are you, / and why do you seek me?"
"너는 누구이며 / 왜 나를 찾아왔느냐?"

"I am a Woodman, / and made of tin.
"저는 나무꾼이고 / 양철로 만들어졌습니다.

Therefore I have no heart, / and cannot love.
그래서 저는 심장이 없어 / 사랑을 할 수 없습니다.

I pray / you to give me a heart / that I may be as other
간청합니다 / 제게 심장을 주길 / 다른 사람들처럼 될 수 있도록"

men are."

---

thick 털이 많은 wooly 덥수룩한 dreadful 무서워 보이는 roar 으르렁거리는 소리 pray 간청하다

"Why should I do this?" demanded the Beast.
내가 왜 그래야 하지?" 짐승이 물었다.

"Because I ask it, / and you alone can grant my request,"
"제가 부탁하고 / 오즈님만이 제 부탁을 들어주실 수 있으니까요"

answered the Woodman.
나무꾼이 대답했다.

Oz gave a low growl at this, / but said, / gruffly:
오즈는 작은 소리로 으르렁거렸다 / 하지만 말했다 / 퉁명스럽게:

"If you indeed desire a heart, / you must earn it."
"제가 정말로 심장을 원한다면 / 그럴만한 자격이 되어서 얻어야 한다."

"How?" asked the Woodman.
"어떻게요?" 나무꾼이 물었다.

"Help Dorothy / to kill the Wicked Witch of the West,"
"도로시를 도와줘라 / 사악한 서쪽 마녀를 죽이는 일을"

replied the Beast. "When the Witch is dead, / come to
짐승이 대답했다. "마녀가 죽으면 / 내게 오거라 /

me, / and I will then give you / the biggest and kindest
그러면 내게 주겠다 / 가장 크고 친절하고 사랑하는 마음이 있는

and most loving heart / in all the Land of Oz."
심장을 / 오즈 전체에서."

So the Tin Woodman was forced to return /
그래서 양철 나무꾼은 어쩔 수 없이 돌아가서 /

sorrowfully to his friends / and tell them of the terrible
슬픈 표정으로 친구들에게 / 무시무시한 짐승에 대해 말했다 /

Beast / he had seen.
자신이 보았던.

demand 묻다 grant one's request 부탁을 들어주다 give a low growl 작은 소리로 으르렁거리다
gruffly 퉁명스럽게 earn 그럴만한 자격이 되어서 얻다 be forced to 어쩔 수 없이 ~하다

They all wondered greatly / at the many forms / the Great
모두들 무척 궁금해 했다   다양한 모습에 /

Wizard could take upon himself, / and the Lion said:
위대한 마법사가 취할 수 있는 /   그러자 사자가 말했다:

"If he is a Beast / when I go to see him, / I shall roar my
"오즈가 짐승이라면 /   내가 보러 갔을 때 /   나는 큰 소리로 으르렁거

loudest, / and so frighten him / that he will grant /
릴 거야 /   그러면 오즈를 놀라게 하여 /   그는 들어주겠지 /

all I ask. And if he is the lovely Lady, / I shall pretend to
내가 부탁한 모든 것을. 그리고 그가 아름다운 부인이라면 /   덤벼드는 척할 거야 /

spring upon her, / and so compel her to do my bidding.
            그러면 어쩔 수 없이 내 요청을 들어주지.

And if he is the great Head, / he will be at my mercy;
또 커다란 머리라면 /   내 뜻대로 될 거야;

for I will roll this head all about the room / until he
내가 그 머리를 온 방안에 굴릴 거야 /   그가 약속할 때까지 /

promises / to give us what we desire. So be of good cheer,
우리가 바라는 대로 하겠다고.   그러니까 기운 내 /

/ my friends, / for all will yet be well."
친구들아 /   모두 잘 될 거야"

The next morning / the soldier with the green whiskers /
다음날 아침 /   초록색 수염의 병사가 /

led the Lion / to the great Throne Room / and bade him /
사자를 데리고 가서 /   알현실로 /   사자에게 말했다 /

enter the presence of Oz.
오즈가 있는 곳에 들어가라고.

The Lion at once passed through the door, /
사자는 즉시 문을 통과하고 /

and glancing around saw, / to his surprise, /
주위를 둘러보고 발견했다 /   놀랍게도 /

that before the throne / was a Ball of Fire, /
옥좌 앞에 /   불덩어리가 있는 것을 /

so fierce and glowing / he could scarcely bear to gaze
맹렬하게 타오르고 있는 / 그는 겨우 쳐다보았다.

upon it. His first thought was / that Oz had by accident
그는 처음에는 생각했다 / 우연히 오즈의 몸에 불이 붙어서 /

caught on fire / and was burning up;
타고 있다고;

but when he tried to go nearer, /
하지만 가까이 다가가려 했을 때 /

the heat was so intense / that it singed his whiskers, /
열기가 너무 강렬해서 / 사자의 수염을 태웠다 /

and he crept back tremblingly / to a spot nearer the door.
사자는 부들부들 떨면서 뒤쪽으로 갔다 / 문에 가까운 곳으로.

Then a low, quiet voice came / from the Ball of Fire, /
그때 낮고 조용한 목소리가 들려오고 / 불덩어리로부터 /

and these were the words it spoke:
이렇게 말했다:

"I am Oz, / the Great and Terrible.
"나는 오즈다 / 위대하고 무시무시한 마법사.

Who are you, / and why do you seek me?"
너는 누구이며 / 왜 나를 찾아왔는가?"

spring upon ~에게 달려(덤벼)들다 compel ~시키다, 어쩔 수 없이 ~하게 하다 bidding 요청, 명령
be at one's mercy ~의 마음대로 되다, 처분대로 하다 be of good cheer 기운 내라, 정신 차려라
glance around 주의를 둘러보다, 두리번거리다 could scarcely bear to 거의(간신히) ~하다 by accident 우연히
intense 강렬한 singe 가볍게 태우다, 그슬리다 spot 장소, 지점

And the Lion answered, / "I am a Cowardly Lion, /
그러자 사자가 대답했다 / "저는 겁쟁이 사자입니다 /

afraid of everything. I came to you to beg /
모든 것을 무서워하는. 저는 부탁하러 왔습니다 /

that you give me courage, / so that in reality /
제게 용기를 달라고 / 그래서 실제로 /

I may become the King of Beasts, / as men call me."
짐승의 왕이 될 수 있도록 / 사람들이 저를 부르듯이"

"Why should I give you courage?" demanded Oz.
"내가 왜 네게 용기를 주어야 하지?" 오즈가 물었다.

"Because of all Wizards you are the greatest, / and alone
"모든 마법사 중에 오즈님은 가장 위대하고 / 오즈님만이

have power / to grant my request," answered the Lion.
힘이 있으니까요 / 제 부탁을 들어줄 만한" 사자가 대답했다.

The Ball of Fire burned fiercely / for a time, / and the
불덩어리가 맹렬히 타올랐고 / 잠시 동안 /

voice said, / "Bring me proof / that the Wicked Witch is
목소리로 말했다 / "내게 증거를 가져와라 / 사악한 마녀가 죽었다는 /

dead, / and that moment I will give you courage. But as
그러면 네게 용기를 주겠다.

long as the Witch lives, / you must remain a coward."
하지만 마녀가 살아있는 한 / 너는 겁쟁이로 남아 있어야 해"

The Lion was angry at this speech, / but could say
사자는 이 말을 듣고 화가 났다 / 하지만 한 마디도

nothing in reply, / and while he stood silently gazing at /
대답할 수 없었고 / 그가 가만히 서서 쳐다보는 동안 /

the Ball of Fire / it became so furiously hot /
불덩어리를 / 불이 몹시 뜨거워져서 /

that he turned tail / and rushed from the room.
사자는 휙 돌아서서 / 방으로 달려 나왔다.

He was glad / to find his friends waiting for him, / and
사자는 기뻐서 / 친구들이 자기를 기다리고 있는 것을 보고 /

told them of his terrible interview / with the Wizard.
무시무시한 대화에 대해 이야기했다 / 마법사와.

"What shall we do now?" asked Dorothy sadly.
"이제 어떻게 해야 하지?" 도로시가 슬픈 표정으로 물었다.

"There is only one thing / we can do," returned the Lion,
"하나뿐이야 / 우리가 할 수 있는 일은" 사자가 대답했다 /

/ "and that is to go to the land of the Winkies, /
"그것은 윙키들이 사는 나라에 가서 /

seek out the Wicked Witch, / and destroy her."
사악한 마녀를 찾아 / 그녀를 죽이는 것이야."

"But suppose we cannot?" said the girl.
"하지만 할 수 없으면?" 도로시가 말했다.

"Then I shall never have courage," declared the Lion.
"그러면 나는 용기를 갖지 못하겠지" 사자가 말했다.

"And I shall never have brains," added the Scarecrow.
"그러면 나는 두뇌를 갖지 못하겠지" 허수아비도 덧붙여 말했다.

"And I shall never have a heart," spoke the Tin
"그러면 나는 심장을 갖지 못하겠지" 양철 나무꾼도 말했다.
Woodman.

"And I shall never see / Aunt Em and Uncle Henry,"
"그러면 나는 볼 수 없겠지 / 엠 숙모와 헨리 삼촌을"

grant one's request ~의 부탁을 들어주다 gaze at 응시하다, 쳐다보다 interview 회담, 대담
suppose 가령 ~라면, 만일 ~라면 declare 확실하게 말하다, 주장하다 add 덧붙여 말하다

said Dorothy, / beginning to cry.
도로시가 말했다 / 울기 시작하면서

"Be careful!" cried the green girl.
"조심해!" 초록색 소녀가 소리쳤다.

"The tears will fall on your green silk gown / and spot it."
"눈물이 네 초록색 비단 옷에 떨어지면 / 얼룩이 생기니까"

So Dorothy dried her eyes / and said, /
그래서 도로시는 눈물을 닦고 / 말했다 /

"I suppose we must try it; but I am sure / I do not want to
"시도해봐야겠구나; 하지만 분명히 / 나는 누구도 죽이고 싶지

kill anybody, / even to see Aunt Em again."
않아 / 엠 숙모를 다시 본다해도."

"I will go with you; but I'm too much of a coward /
"나는 너랑 갈 거야; 하지만 나는 너무 겁이 많아서 /

to kill the Witch," said the Lion.
마녀를 죽일 수는 없어" 사자가 말했다.

"I will go too," declared the Scarecrow; "but I shall not be
"나도 갈께" 허수아비가 말했다; "하지만 난 별로 도움이

of much help / to you, / I am such a fool."
안 될 거야 / 너희들에게 / 나는 바보니까"

"I haven't the heart / to harm even a Witch,"
"나는 용기가 없어 / 마녀를 해치고 싶은"

remarked the Tin Woodman;
양철 나무꾼이 말했다;

"but if you go / I certainly shall go with you."
"하지만 너희들이 간다면 / 물론 나도 함께 갈 거야"

spot 얼룩지게 하다 of a coward 겁이 많은, 비겁한 haven't the heart 용기가 없다

Therefore it was decided / to start upon their journey /
그래서 결정되었다 / 여행을 떠나기로 /

the next morning, / and the Woodman sharpened his axe
다음날 아침 / 나무꾼은 도끼의 날을 갈았고 /

/ on a green grindstone / and had all his joints properly
초록색 숫돌에 / 모든 이음매에 충분히 기름을 쳐두었다.

oiled. The Scarecrow stuffed himself / with fresh straw
허수아비는 자신의 몸을 채웠고 / 새 짚으로 /

/ and Dorothy put new paint on his eyes / that he might
도로시는 새로 허수아비의 눈을 그려주었다 / 더 잘 볼 수 있도록.

see better.

The green girl, / who was very kind to them, /
초록색 소녀는 / 그들에게 매우 친절했던, /

filled Dorothy's basket / with good things to eat, /
도로시의 바구니를 채워주고 / 먹을 것을 잔뜩 /

and fastened a little bell / around Toto's neck /
작은 방울을 매어 주었다 / 토토의 목에 /

with a green ribbon.
초록색 리본으로.

They went to bed quite early / and slept soundly / until
그들은 아주 일찍 잠자리에 들었고 / 깊은 잠을 잤다 /

daylight, / when they were awakened / by the crowing of
동이 틀 때까지 / 그 무렵 그들은 잠에서 깨었다 / 초록색 수탉이 우는 소리로 /

a green cock / that lived in the back yard of the Palace, /
궁궐 안 뒤뜰에 살고 있는 /

and the cackling of a hen / that had laid a green egg.
암탉이 우는 소리가 들렸다 / 초록색 알을 낳은.

---

grindstone 숫돌 fasten 묶다, 매다 crow 수탉이 울다 back yard 뒤뜰 cackle (암탉이) 꼬꼬댁 울다

Quiz 5

A. 단어

다음 단어의 설명을 읽고, 어떤 단어를 설명하는지 아래의 박스에서 알맞은 단어를 고르세요.

1. a flat, floating structure made of pieces of wood tied together
2. very hungry
3. to shine brightly with flashing points of light
4. an open round container shaped like a bowl, used for holding water
5. to pay to live in a room in someone's house
6. clothes that are typical of a particular place or period of time in the past
7. to look at someone or something for a long time
8. quiet, gentle, and easily persuaded by other people to do what they want
9. to surprise someone very much
10. to ask a question in a very firm or angry way

raft	basin	astonish	lodge	meek
ravenous	gaze	demand	glitter	costume

B. 직독직해

아래에 제시된 문장을 직독직해로 해석해보세요.

1. The strong current soon sweeps / the raft far away / from the Yellow Brick Road.

   →

2. The Scarecrow suggests / that the Field Mice rescue the Cowardly Lion / from the poppy field.

   →

Answer   A. 단어 1. raft 2. ravenous 3. glitter 4. basin 5. lodge 6. costume 7. gaze 8. meek 9. astonish 10. demand
B. 직독직해 1. 강력한 강물의 흐름은 곧 휩쓸어버린다 / 뗏목을 먼 곳으로 / 노란 벽돌이 깔려있는 길에서.
2. 허수아비는 제안한다 / 들쥐들이 겁쟁이 사자를 구해줄 것을 / 양귀비 밭에서.

3. They passed through the Palace Gates / and were led into a big room / with a green carpet / and lovely green furniture set / with emeralds.

   →

4. If you wish / me to use my magic power / to send you home again / you must do something / for me first.

   →

5. The Lion was angry at this speech, / but could say nothing in reply.

   →

C. 동시통역

아래에 제시된 직독직해를 보고, 영어로 말해보세요.

1. 사자는 너무 크고 무거워 / 옮기기에 힘들었다.

   →

2. 오즈 마법사는 절대로 허락하지 않아 / 누구라도 그를 직접 만나는 것을.

   →

3. 마침내 / 나는 그분에게 말씀 드렸지 / 네 이마에 있는 자국에 대해 / 그러니까 그분은 결심하셨지 / 허락하신다고 / 그분이 있는 곳으로 네가 오는 것(너와 만나는 것)을

   →

4. "나는 너랑 갈 거야; 하지만 나는 너무 겁이 많아서 / 마녀를 죽일 수는 없어"

   →

5. 그들은 아주 일찍 잠자리에 들었고 / 깊은 잠을 잤다 / 동이 틀 때까지.

   →

Answer

3. 그들(도로시 일행)은 성문을 통과하고 / 큰 방으로 안내되었다 / 초록색 카펫이 깔려 있고 / 아름다운 초록색 가구가 있는 / 에메랄드가 새겨진. 4. 네가 원한다면 / 내가 마법의 힘을 사용하길 / 너를 다시 집으로 돌려보내주려고 / 너는 무언가 해야 해 / 먼저 나를 위해.
5. 사자는 이 말을 듣고 화가 났다 / 하지만 한 마디도 대답할 수 없었다.
C. 동시통역 1. The Lion is too big and heavy / to be carried.
2. The Wizard never permits / anyone to see him face to face. 3. At last / I told him / about the mark upon your forehead, / and he decided / he would admit / you to his presence.
4. "I will go with you; but I'm too much of a coward / to kill the Witch."
5. They went to bed quite early / and slept soundly / until daylight.

Chapter 12. The Search for the Wicked Witch
악한 마녀를 찾아서

The soldier with the green whiskers / led them /
초록색 수염의 병사는 /   일행을 안내했다 /
through the streets of the Emerald City / until they
에메랄드 시의 거리를 지나서 /   그들이 방에 도착할 때까지 /
reached the room / where the Guardian of the Gates lived.
그곳(그 방)에 문지기가 살고 있었다.
This officer unlocked their spectacles / to put them back
문지기는 쓰고 있던 안경을 벗었다 /   커다란 상자에 넣으려고 /
in his great box, / and then he politely opened the gate /
그리고 나서 그는 정중하게 성문을 열었다 /
for our friends.
도로시 일행을 위해.

"Which road leads / to the Wicked Witch of the West?"
"어느 길로 가야하나요 /   서쪽의 사악한 마녀에게 가려면?"
asked Dorothy.
도로시가 물었다.

"There is no road," answered the Guardian of the Gates.
"길은 없단다"   문지기가 대답했다.
"No one ever wishes to go / that way."
"아무도 가려 하지 않으니까 /   그 쪽으로"

"How, then, / are we to find her?" inquired the girl.
"그러면 어떻게 /   마녀를 찾을 수 있죠?"   도로시가 물었다.

"That will be easy," replied the man, / "for when she
"그건 쉬울 거야"   문지기가 대답했다 /   "왜냐하면 마녀가 알면 /
knows / you are in the country of the Winkies /
너희들이 윙키 나라에 있는 것을 /

she will find you, / and make you all her slaves."
마녀가 너희들을 찾을 것이고 / 너희들을 노예로 삼으려 할 거야"

"Perhaps not," said the Scarecrow, /
"그렇지는 않을 거예요" 허수아비가 말했다 /

"for we mean to destroy her."
"우리는 마녀를 죽일 작정이니까"

"Oh, that is different," said the Guardian of the Gates.
"그렇다면 얘기가 다르겠군" 문지기가 말했다.

"No one has ever destroyed / her before, / so I naturally
"아무도 죽이지 못했으니까 / 마녀를 전에 / 그래서 당연하다고

thought / she would make slaves of you, / as she has of
생각했지 / 마녀가 너희들을 노예로 삼는 것이 / 다른 사람들에게

the rest. But take care; for she is wicked and fierce, /
한 것처럼. 하지만 조심해; 왜냐하면 그 마녀는 사악하고 사나워 /

and may not allow / you to destroy her. Keep to the West,
놔두지 않을 거야 / 너희들이 자신을 죽이도록. 서쪽으로 계속 가 /

/ where the sun sets, / and you cannot fail to find her."
해가 지는 쪽으로 / 그러면 마녀를 찾게 될 거야"

They thanked him / and bade him good-bye, / and turned
일행은 그에게 고맙다고 말하고 / 작별인사를 하고 / 서쪽으로 방향을

toward the West, / walking over fields of soft grass /
돌리고 / 부드러운 풀밭을 걸어갔다 /

Key Expression

naturally는 문장전체를 수식하는 문장부사로 thought를 수식하는 것이 아니라, "she would make slaves of you"를 수식한다. 그래서 "마녀가 너희들을 노예로 삼는 것이 당연하다고 생각했다"라고 해석한다.

So I naturally thought / she would make slaves of you ~.
그래서 당연하다고 생각했지 / 마녀가 너희들을 노예로 삼는 것이.

mean to ~할 작정이다, 할 셈이다 fierce 몹시 사나운

dotted here and there / with daisies and buttercups.
여기저기 산재해 있는 (피어있는) / 데이지와 미나리아재비 꽃이.

Dorothy still wore the pretty silk dress / she had put on
도로시는 여전히 예쁜 비단 드레스를 입고 있었다 / 궁궐에서 입던 /

in the palace, / but now, / to her surprise, / she found /
하지만 이제 / 놀랍게도 / 그녀는 발견했다 /

it was no longer green, / but pure white.
옷의 색은 더 이상 초록색이 아니라 / 새하얀 색이라는 것을.

The ribbon around Toto's neck / had also lost its green
토토 목에 감긴 리본도 / 초록색 빛이 없어졌고 /

color / and was as white as Dorothy's dress.
도로시의 옷처럼 흰 색이었다.

The Emerald City was soon left far behind.
에메랄드 시는 금세 멀어졌다.

As they advanced / the ground became rougher and
그들이 앞으로 나아감에 따라 / 땅은 점점 더 황량하고 언덕이 많아졌다 /

hillier, / for there were no farms nor houses / in this
농장이나 집도 없었기에 /

country of the West, / and the ground was untilled.
서쪽 나라에는 / 땅은 경작되지 않았다.

dotted 산재해 있는, 흩어져 있는 buttercup 미나리아재비 advance 앞으로 나아가다
untilled 경작되지 않은, 미경작의

In the afternoon / the sun shone hot in their faces, /
오후에 / 태양이 그들의 얼굴에 뜨겁게 내리쬐었다 /

for there were no trees / to offer them shade; so that
나무가 한 그루도 없었기에 / 그늘을 드리워주는; 그래서

before night / Dorothy and Toto and the Lion were tired,
밤이 되기도 전에 / 도로시와 토토와 사자는 지쳤고 /

/ and lay down upon the grass / and fell asleep, /
풀밭에 누워서 / 잠이 들었다 /

with the Woodman and the Scarecrow keeping watch.
그리고 양철 나무꾼과 허수아비가 보초를 섰다.

Now the Wicked Witch of the West had but one eye, /
그때 서쪽의 사악한 마녀는 눈이 하나 밖에 없었다 /

yet that was as powerful as a telescope, / and could see
하지만 그 눈은 망원경처럼 강력했고 / 어디든지 볼 수 있었다.

everywhere. So, / as she sat in the door of her castle, /
그래서 / 마녀는 성문 앞에 앉아 있을 때 /

she happened to look around / and saw Dorothy lying
마녀가 주변을 돌아보다가 / 도로시가 잠든 모습을 보았다 /

asleep, / with her friends all about her.
친구들이 그녀 주위에 있는 가운데.

They were a long distance off, / but the Wicked Witch
일행은 멀리 떨어져 있었다 / 하지만 사악한 마녀는 화가 났다 /

was angry / to find them in her country; so she blew
그들이 자기 땅에 있는 것을 보고; 그래서 마녀는

upon a silver whistle / that hung around her neck.
은색 호루라기를 불었다 / 목에 매달고 있던.

Key Expression

"with the woodman and the Scarecrow keeping watch"는 "with+목적어+보어"의 패턴으로 동시상황 또는 부대상황을 나타내는 분사구라고 부른다. 이런 패턴을 보면, 간단하게 "그리고 ~하다"라고 해석하면 자연스럽다.

Dorothy and Toto and the Lion were tired, / and lay down upon the grass /
도로시와 토토와 사자는 지쳤고 / 풀밭에 누워서 /
and fell asleep, / with the Woodman and the Scarecrow keeping watch.
잠이 들었다 / (그리고) 양철 나무꾼과 허수아비가 보초를 서고 있었다.

keep watch 보초를 서다, 망을 보다 a long distance off 멀리 떨어진

At once / there came running to her from all directions /
갑자기 / 사방에서 달려 나왔다 /

a pack of great wolves.
커다란 늑대 떼가.

They had / long legs and fierce eyes and sharp teeth.
늑대들에게는 있었다 / 긴 다리, 사나운 눈, 날카로운 이빨이

"Go to those people," said the Witch, /
"저들에게 가서" 마녀가 말했다 /

"and tear them to pieces."
"갈기갈기 찢어버려라."

"Are you not going to make / them your slaves?"
"만들지 않을 거예요 / 저들을 노예로?"

asked the leader of the wolves.
늑대 무리의 우두머리가 물었다.

"No," she answered, "one is of tin, / and one of straw;
"아니" 마녀가 대답했다 "한 놈은 양철로 / 한 놈은 짚으로 만들어 졌고;

one is a girl and another a Lion. None of them is fit to
여자애랑 사자라서. 아무도 일을 할 수 없으니 /

work, / so you may tear them into small pieces."
그러니 너희들은 갈기갈기 찢어버려도 돼"

"Very well," said the wolf, / and he dashed away at full
"알겠습니다" 늑대는 말하고 / 전속력으로 달려갔다 /

speed, / followed by the others.
나머지 늑대 떼를 거느리고.

It was lucky / the Scarecrow and the Woodman were
다행이었다 / 허수아비와 양철 나무꾼이 깨어 있었고 /

wide awake / and heard the wolves coming.
늑대들이 다가오는 소리를 들었기에.

"This is my fight," said the Woodman, /
"이건 내 싸움이군," 나무꾼이 말했다 /

"so get behind me / and I will meet them / as they come."
"그러니 내 뒤에 숨어 / 내가 상대할게 / 늑대들이 오면"

He seized his axe, / which he had made very sharp, / and
나무꾼은 도끼를 잡았다 / 날카롭게 갈아 놓은 /

as the leader of the wolves came on / the Tin Woodman
우두머리 늑대가 다가오자 / 나무꾼은 팔을 휘둘러서 /

swung his arm / and chopped the wolf's head from its
늑대 머리를 몸통에서 잘라버렸다 /

body, / so that it immediately died.
그래서 늑대는 곧 죽어 버렸다.

As soon as he could raise his axe / another wolf came up,
나무꾼이 도끼를 들자마자 / 다른 늑대가 달려들었고 /

/ and he also fell / under the sharp edge of the
그 늑대도 쓰러져버렸다 / 양철 나무꾼의 무기인 날카로운 도끼날 앞에서.

Tin Woodman's weapon. There were forty wolves, /
늑대 40마리가 있었고 /

and forty times a wolf was killed, / so that at last /
한 마리씩 40번을 죽였다 / 그리하여 마침내 /

they all lay dead in a heap / before the Woodman.
늑대들 모두가 죽어서 무더기로 쌓여 있었다 / 나무꾼의 앞에.

pack 한 떼, 일행 dash away 쏜살같이 달려가다 chop 자르다 in a heap 무더기로

Then he put down his axe / and sat beside the Scarecrow,
그러고 나서 나무꾼이 도끼를 내려놓고 / 허수아비 옆에 앉았다 /

/ who said, / "It was a good fight, friend."
허수아비가 말했다 / "잘 싸웠네, 친구"

They waited / until Dorothy awoke / the next morning.
둘은 기다렸다 / 도로시가 깨어날 때까지 / 다음날 아침.

The little girl was quite frightened / when she saw /
도로시는 깜짝 놀랐다 / 그녀가 보았을 때 /

the great pile of shaggy wolves, / but the Tin Woodman
털이 덥수룩한 늑대들의 거대한 더미를 / 하지만 양철 나무꾼이 설명해주었다.

told her all. She thanked him / for saving them /
그녀는 고맙다고 말하고 / 목숨을 구해준 것에 대해 /

and sat down to breakfast, / after which they started
앉아서 아침을 먹었다 / 그 후에 일행은 다시 여행을 떠났다.

again upon their journey.

Now this same morning / the Wicked Witch came to the
같은 날 아침에 / 사악한 마녀는 성문에 나와서 /

door of her castle / and looked out / with her one eye /
살펴보았다 / 애꾸눈으로 /

that could see far off.
멀리까지 볼 수 있는.

She saw / all her wolves lying dead, / and the strangers
마녀는 보았다 / 늑대들이 모두 죽은 채로 누워있었고 / 낯선 이들이 여전히 자신의 땅을

still traveling through her country. This made her angrier
여행하고 있는 것을. 이것은 마녀를 전보다 더 화나게

than before, / and she blew her silver whistle twice.
만들었고 / 마녀는 은색 호루라기를 두 번 불었다.

Straightway a great flock of wild crows / came flying
곧 수많은 야생 까마귀 떼가 / 마녀에게 날아왔다 /

toward her, / enough to darken the sky.
하늘을 캄캄하게 뒤덮을 정도로

And the Wicked Witch said to the King Crow, /
그러자 사악한 마녀는 까마귀의 왕에게 말했다 /

"Fly at once to the strangers; peck out their eyes /
"즉시 낯선 이들에게 날아가서; 저들의 눈을 쪼아 먹고 /

and tear them to pieces."
갈기갈기 찢어버리라고"

The wild crows flew in one great flock /
야생 까마귀들은 거대한 무리를 지어 날아갔다 /

toward Dorothy and her companions.
도로시와 동료들에게

When the little girl saw them coming / she was afraid.
도로시는 까마귀 떼가 몰려오는 것을 보았을 때 / 그녀는 겁이 났다.

But the Scarecrow said, / "This is my battle, /
하지만 허수아비가 말했다 / "이건 내 싸움이군 /

so lie down beside me / and you will not be harmed."
그러니 내 뒤에 엎드려 있어 / 그러면 너희들은 다치지 않을 거야"

So they all lay upon the ground / except the Scarecrow, /
그러자 그들 모두가 땅에 엎드렸고 / 허수아비만 제외하고 /

and he stood up / and stretched out his arms.
허수아비는 서서 / 두 팔을 활짝 뻗었다.

And when the crows saw him / they were frightened, /
까마귀들이 허수아비를 보았을 때 / 그들은 깜짝 놀랐다 /

Key Expression

아래 예문의 lying과 traveling은 목적격 보어로 현재분사가 사용되기 때문에, 목적어와 목적격 보어의 관계는 능동관계. 그래서 마녀는 "늑대들이 죽은 채로 누워있고, 낯선 이들이 여행하고 있는 것을 보았다"라고 해석한다.

She saw / all her wolves lying dead, / and the strangers still traveling through her country.
그녀는 보았다 / 늑대들이 모두 죽은 채로 누워있었고 / 낯선 이들이 여전히 자신의 땅을 여행하고 있는 것을.

shaggy 털이 덥수룩한 straightway 곧, 즉시 flock 떼, 무리 peck out 쪼아 내다, 쪼아 먹다

as these birds always are by scarecrows, / and did not
까마귀들은 늘 허수아비를 보면 놀라기 때문에 /

dare to come any nearer. But the King Crow said:
감히 더 가까이 가지 못했다.   그러나 까마귀 왕이 말했다:

"It is only a stuffed man. I will peck his eyes out."
"짚으로 만든 허수아비일 뿐이야.   내가 저놈의 눈을 쪼아 버릴 거야"

The King Crow flew at the Scarecrow, / who caught it
까마귀 왕은 허수아비에게 날아갔고 /   허수아비는 까마귀의

by the head / and twisted its neck / until it died.
머리를 잡아 /   목을 비틀어 버렸다 /   까마귀가 죽을 때까지.

And then another crow flew at him, / and the Scarecrow
그러자 다른 까마귀가 날아왔고 /   허수아비는

twisted its neck also. There were forty crows, /
그 놈의 목도 비틀어버렸다.   40마리의 까마귀가 있었고 /

and forty times the Scarecrow twisted a neck, /
허수아비가 40번 까마귀 목을 비틀었다 /

until at last / all were lying dead beside him.
마침내 /   모든 까마귀가 죽을 때까지.

Then he called to his companions to rise, / and again /
허수아비는 동료에게 일어서라고 말했고 /   다시 /

they went upon their journey.
여행을 떠났다.

When the Wicked Witch looked out again / and saw /
사악한 마녀는 다시 둘러보고 /   보았을 때 /

all her crows lying in a heap, / she got into a terrible
까마귀들이 모두 죽어 더미로 쌓여 있는 것을 /   마녀는 미친 듯이 화를 내고 /

rage, / and blew three times upon her silver whistle.
은색 호루라기를 세 번 불었다.

get into a rage 화를 내다 rage 격정, 흥분상태

Forthwith / there was heard a great buzzing / in the air, /
곧 /   요란하게 윙윙거리는 소리가 들렸고 /   하늘에서 /

and a swarm of black bees came flying toward her.
검은 벌떼가 마녀에게 날아왔다.

"Go to the strangers / and sting them to death!"
"낯선 자들에게 가서 /   그들을 쏘아 죽여 버려라!"

commanded the Witch, / and the bees turned and flew
마녀가 명령했다 /   그러자 벌은 방향을 돌려 재빨리 날아갔다

rapidly / until they came / to where Dorothy and her
그들이 갈 때까지 /   도로시와 동료들이 걷고 있는 곳으로.

friends were walking. But the Woodman had seen them
하지만 나무꾼이 벌떼가 오는 것을 보았고 /

coming, / and the Scarecrow had decided / what to do.
허수아비는 결정했다 /   어떻게 해야 할지.

"Take out my straw / and scatter it / over the little girl
"내 몸 속의 짚을 꺼내 /   뿌려줘 /   도로시와 개와 사자 위에"

and the dog and the Lion," he said to the Woodman, /
허수아비가 나무꾼에게 말했다 /

"and the bees cannot sting them."
"그러면 벌이 그들을 쏘지 못할 거야"

This the Woodman did, / and as Dorothy lay close beside
나무꾼이 시키는 대로 했고 /   도로시가 사자 옆에 누워 /

the Lion / and held Toto in her arms, / the straw covered
토토를 품에 안았을 때 /   짚으로 그들을 완전히

them entirely.
덮어주었다.

The bees came and found / no one but the Woodman to
벌떼가 다가와서 발견했다   쏠 대상이 나무꾼 밖에 없는 것을 /

forthwith 곧, 즉시 buzzing 윙윙거리는 소리 swarm 떼, 무리 sting (벌이) 찌르다, 쏘다 scatter 뿌리다

sting, / so they flew at him / and broke off all their stings
그래서 벌떼가 나무꾼에게 날아가 / 모든 침이 부러졌다 /

/ against the tin, / without hurting the Woodman at all.
양철에 부딪쳐 / 나무꾼에게 전혀 상처 입히지 못하고.

And as bees cannot live / when their stings are broken /
그리고 벌들은 살지 못하기에 / 자신들의 침이 부러지면 /

that was the end of the black bees, /
벌은 최후를 맞았고 /

and they lay scattered thick about the Woodman, /
나무꾼 주위에 가득 쌓였다 /

like little heaps of fine coal.
작은 석탄 더미처럼.

Then Dorothy and the Lion got up, / and the girl
그러자 도로시와 사자가 일어났고 / 도로시는 나무꾼을 도와주었다 /

helped the Tin Woodman / put the straw back into the
짚을 허수아비의 몸에 다시 넣는 것을 /

Scarecrow again, / until he was as good as ever.
허수아비가 전의 모습이 될 때까지.

So they started upon their journey / once more.
그리고 그들은 여행을 떠났다 / 다시 한 번.

The Wicked Witch was so angry / when she saw her
사악한 마녀는 몹시 화가 나서 / 자신의 검은 벌을 보았을 때 /

black bees / in little heaps like fine coal / that she
석탄처럼 쌓여 있는 것을 /

stamped her foot / and tore her hair / and gnashed her
마녀는 발을 동동 구르고 / 머리를 쥐어뜯고 / 이를 북북 갈았다.

teeth. And then she called a dozen of her slaves, /
그리고 나서 열두 명의 노예를 불렀다 /

who were the Winkies, / and gave them sharp spears, /
윙키족인 / 그들에게 날카로운 창을 주고 /

telling them / to go to the strangers / and destroy them.
명령했다 / 낯선 자들에게 가서 / 그들을 죽이라고.

The Winkies were not a brave people, / but they had to
윙키들은 용감한 사람들이 아니었다 /   하지만 해야만 했다 /

do / as they were told. So they marched away / until they
명령대로.   그래서 그들은 (성을 떠나) 행진했다 /   도로시에게 다가

came near to Dorothy. Then the Lion gave a great roar /
갈 때까지.   그러자 사자가 큰 소리로 으르렁거리며 /

and sprang towards them, / and the poor Winkies were
그들에게 덤벼들었고 /   불쌍한 윙키들은 몹시 놀라서 /

so frightened / that they ran back / as fast as they could.
        달아나 버렸다 /   최대한 빨리.

When they returned to the castle / the Wicked Witch
그들이 성으로 돌아왔을 때 /   사악한 마녀는 그들을 심하게 때리고 /

beat them well / with a strap, / and sent them back to
        채찍으로 /   일터로 돌려보냈다 /

their work, / after which she sat down to think /
        그 후 마녀는 앉아 생각에 잠겼다 /

what she should do next. She could not understand /
다음에 어떻게 해야 할지.   마녀는 이해할 수 없었다 /

how all her plans to destroy these strangers / had failed;
어떻게 낯선 놈들을 죽이려는 자신의 모든 계획이 /   실패했는지;

but she was a powerful Witch, / as well as a wicked one,
하지만 마녀는 힘이 셌고 /   또한 사악한 마녀였다 /

/ and she soon made up her mind / how to act.
    그래서 마녀는 곧 결심했다 /   어떻게 할지.

Key Expression

아래 예문의 전치사 at은 목표나 대상을 의미하므로 "~을 향하여"라는 의미가 있고, 전치사 against는 접촉을 의미하여 "~에 부딪쳐, 접촉하여"라는 의미로 사용된다.

They flew at him / and broke off all their stings / against the tin ~.
벌떼가 나무꾼에게 날아가 / 모든 침이 부러졌다 /   양철에 부딪쳐

---

stamp 발을 구르다 gnash (분노로) 이를 갈다 spear 창 give a great roar 큰소리로 으르렁거리다
spring towards ~에게 덤벼들다 strap 채찍, 가죽

There was, / in her cupboard, / a Golden Cap, /
있었다 / 선반에 / 황금 모자가 /

with a circle of diamonds and rubies running round it.
다이아몬드와 루비가 모자 주위에 둥근 원으로 박혀있는.

This Golden Cap had a charm. Whoever owned it /
이 황금 모자에는 마력이 있었다. 모자를 소유한 사람은 누구든지 /

could call three times upon the Winged Monkeys, /
날개 달린 원숭이들을 세 번 불러낼 수 있고 /

who would obey any order / they were given.
원숭이들은 어떤 명령이라도 따른다 / 자신들이 받은.

But no person could command these strange
하지만 누구도 이 기묘한 생물들에게 명령할 수는 없다 /

creatures / more than three times. Twice already /
세 번 이상. 이미 두 번 /

the Wicked Witch had used / the charm of the Cap.
사악한 마녀는 사용했다 / 모자의 마력을.

Once was / when she had made the Winkies her slaves, /
한 번은 / 윙키들을 노예로 삼아 /

and set herself to rule over their country.
윙키 나라를 직접 다스리려 했을 때였다.

The Winged Monkeys had helped / her do this.
날개 달린 원숭이들은 도왔다 / 마녀가 그런 일을 하도록.

The second time was / when she had fought against the
두 번째는 / 위대한 오즈 마법사에 맞서 싸워서 /

Great Oz himself, / and driven him / out of the land of
그를 쫓아냈을 때였다 / 서쪽 나라에서.

the West.

The Winged Monkeys had also helped her / in doing
날개 달린 원숭이들은 역시 도와주었다 / 이런 일을 할 때.

this. Only once more / could she use this Golden Cap, /
이제 단 한 번만 / 마녀는 황금 모자를 사용할 수 있었다 /

for which reason she did not like to do so / until all her
그래서 마녀는 모자를 사용하고 싶지 않았다 / 다른 모든 마력을

other powers were exhausted. But now that her fierce
써버릴 때까지. 하지만 자신의 사나운 늑대들과 /

wolves / and her wild crows / and her stinging bees were
까마귀 떼와 / 벌들이 모두 죽어 버렸고 /

gone, / and her slaves had been scared away /
그리고 노예들은 겁을 먹고 도망쳤기 때문에 /

by the Cowardly Lion, / she saw / there was only one
겁쟁이 사자에 의해 / 마녀는 알았다 / 한 가지 방법 밖에 없다는 것을 /

way left / to destroy Dorothy and her friends.
도로시와 동료를 죽일 수 있는.

So the Wicked Witch took the Golden Cap /
그래서 사악한 마녀는 황금 모자를 꺼냈고 /

from her cupboard / and placed it upon her head.
선반에서 / 모자를 머리에 썼다.

Then she stood upon her left foot / and said slowly:
그리고 나서 왼발로 서서 / 천천히 주문을 외웠다:

"Ep-pe, pep-pe, kak-ke!"
"에페, 페페, 카케!"

Next she stood upon her right foot / and said:
그런 다음 오른발로 서서 / 외쳤다:

"Hil-lo, hol-lo, hel-lo!"
"힐로, 홀로, 헬로!"

Key Expression

whoever는 "~한 사람은 누구든지"라는 의미로 "anyone who"와 같은 의미로 쓰인다.

Whoever owned it / could call three times upon the Winged Monkeys, /
모자를 소유한 사람은 누구든지 / 날개 달린 원숭이들을 세 번 불러낼 수 있고 /
who would obey any order ~ .
원숭이들은 어떤 명령이라도 따른다.

charm 마력, 주문 set oneself to ~하려고 애쓰다, 열심히 ~하다 exhaust 다 써버리다
scare away 겁을 주어 쫓아버리다

After this she stood upon both feet /
그러고 나서 두발로 서서 /

and cried in a loud voice:
큰 소리로 외쳤다:

"Ziz-zy, zuz-zy, zik!"
"지지, 주지, 지크!"

Now the charm began to work. The sky was darkened, /
그러자 마력이 나타나기 시작됐다.   하늘이 어두워지고 /

and a low rumbling sound was heard / in the air.
낮게 우르릉거리는 소리가 들렸다 /   하늘에서.

There was a rushing of many wings, / a great chattering
수많은 날개가 갑자기 움직이는 소리와 /   큰 소리로 떠들며

and laughing, / and the sun came out of the dark sky /
웃는 소리가 들렸고 /   어두운 하늘에서 태양이 나타나 /

to show / the Wicked Witch surrounded by a crowd of
보여주었다 /   원숭이 떼에 둘러싸인 사악한 마녀를 /

monkeys, / each with a pair of immense and powerful
        그리고 한 쌍씩 크고 튼튼한 날개가 달려 있었다 /

wings / on his shoulders.
       원숭이들의 어깨에는.

One, / much bigger than the others, / seemed to be their
한 마리가 / 다른 원숭이보다 훨씬 큰 /   우두머리처럼 보였다.

leader. He flew close to the Witch / and said, /
우두머리 원숭이가 마녀에게 다가와 /   말했다 /

"You have called us / for the third and last time.
"당신은 우리를 불렀습니다 /   세 번째이자 마지막으로.

What do you command?"
무슨 명령을 내리시겠습니까?"

---

rumbling 우르릉거리는 소리 surround 에워싸다, 둘러싸다 immense 거대한, 큰

"Go to the strangers / who are within my land / and destroy them all / except the Lion," said the Wicked Witch. "Bring that beast to me, / for I have a mind to harness him / like a horse, / and make him work."

"Your commands shall be obeyed," said the leader. Then, / with a great deal of chattering and noise, / the Winged Monkeys flew away / to the place where Dorothy and her friends were walking.

Some of the Monkeys seized the Tin Woodman / and carried him through the air / until they were over a country / thickly covered with sharp rocks. Here they dropped the poor Woodman, / who fell a great distance to the rocks, / where he lay so battered and dented / that he could neither move nor groan.

---

harness 마구를 달다 chatter 원숭이가 캑캑 울다 seize 잡다 battered 상처를 입고 dented 움푹 찌그러진
groan 신음소리를 내다

Others of the Monkeys caught the Scarecrow, /
다른 원숭이들은 허수아비를 잡았고 /

and with their long fingers / pulled all of the straw /
긴 손가락으로 / 짚을 모조리 꺼냈다 /

out of his clothes and head. They made his hat and boots
허수아비의 몸과 머리에서. 그들은 허수아비의 모자와 장화와

and clothes into a small bundle / and threw it /
옷으로 작은 꾸러미로 만들었고 / 그것을 던져 버렸다 /

into the top branches of a tall tree.
키 큰 나무 꼭대기에.

The remaining Monkeys threw pieces of stout rope /
나머지 원숭이들은 튼튼한 밧줄을 던졌고 /

around the Lion / and wound many coils / about his body
사자에게 / 여러 번 감았다 / 사자의 몸과

and head and legs, / until he was unable to bite or scratch
머리와 다리를 / 사자가 물거나, 할퀴거나, 버둥거리지 못할 때까지 /

or struggle / in any way. Then they lifted him up and
어떤 방법으로도. 그 다음에 원숭이들은 사자를 들고

flew away with him / to the Witch's castle, /
날아갔다 / 마녀의 성으로 /

where he was placed / in a small yard / with a high iron
그곳에 사자를 놓았다 / 작은 정원에 / 높은 쇠 울타리가 쳐져 있는 /

fence around it, / so that he could not escape.
그래서 사자는 탈출할 수 없었다.

But Dorothy / they did not harm at all.
하지만 도로시에게 / 원숭이들이 전혀 해를 입히지 못했다.

She stood, / with Toto in her arms, / watching the sad
그녀는 서있었다 / 토토를 품 안에 안고 / 친구들의 슬픈 운명을 쳐다보고 /

fate of her comrades / and thinking it would soon be
곧 자신의 차례일 거라고 생각하면서.

her turn. The leader of the Winged Monkeys flew up to
우두머리 원숭이가 그녀에게 날아왔다 /

her, / his long, hairy arms stretched out / and his ugly
길고 털투성이의 팔을 내밀고 / 흉측한 얼굴로

face grinning terribly; but he saw the mark of the Good
무섭게 웃으면서; 하지만 그는 착한 마녀의 입맞춤 자국을 보고 /

Witch's kiss / upon her forehead / and stopped short, /
도로시 이마에 있는 / 갑자기 멈춰 서서 /

motioning the others / not to touch her.
다른 원숭이들에게 몸짓으로 알렸다 / 그녀를 건드리지 말라고

"We dare not harm this little girl," he said to them, /
"우리는 감히 이 아이를 해칠 수 없어" 원숭이가 부하들에게 말했다 /

"for she is protected by the Power of Good, /
"이 아이는 착한 힘에 보호받고 있고 /

and that is greater than the Power of Evil.
그 힘은 악한 힘보다 강하니까.

All we can do / is to carry her to the castle of the Wicked
우리가 할 수 있는 일은 / 이 아이를 사악한 마녀의 성으로 데려가 /

Witch / and leave her there."
그곳에 아이를 두는 것뿐이다."

Key Expression

예문의 관계대명사 who와 관계부사 where를 계속적 용법으로 사용한다. who를 "그래서 그 (나무꾼는)"이라고 해석하고 where를 "그래서 그곳에"라고 해석한다.

Here they dropped the poor Woodman, / who fell a great distance to the rocks, /
그들은 여기에 불쌍한 나무꾼을 던져버렸다 / 그래서 나무꾼은 먼 곳에 바위로 떨어졌고 /
where he lay so battered and dented / that he could neither move nor groan.
그래서 그곳에 상처를 입고 찌그러져 있어 / 움직이거나 신음 소리도 내지 못했다.

stout 튼튼한, 단단한 wind (wind-wound-wound) 감다 struggle 버둥거리다, 허우적거리다 grin 빙긋 웃다
motion 몸짓으로 알리다

So, / carefully and gently, / they lifted Dorothy in their
그래서 / 조심스럽고 부드럽게 / 원숭이들은 도로시를 품에 안고 /

arms / and carried her swiftly through the air / until they
도로시를 들고 빠르게 하늘을 날았다 /

came to the castle, / where they set her down / upon the
성에 도착할 때까지 / 그곳에 그녀를 내려놓았다 /

front doorstep. Then the leader said to the Witch:
현관 계단 위에. 그리고 우두머리 원숭이는 마녀에게 말했다:

"We have obeyed you / as far as we were able.
"우리는 당신의 명령에 따랐습니다 / 할 수 있는 한.

The Tin Woodman and the Scarecrow are destroyed, /
양철 나무꾼과 허수아비는 죽었고 /

and the Lion is tied up / in your yard. The little girl we
사자는 묶어두었습니다 / 정원에. 이 아이를 우리가

dare not harm, / nor the dog she carries in her arms.
감히 해칠 수 없고 / 그녀의 품에 안겨 있는 개도 마찬가지입니다.

Your power over our band is now ended, /
우리 무리에 대한 당신의 지배는 이제 끝났고 /

and you will never see us again."
당신은 이제 우리를 다시 볼 수 없을 것입니다"

Then all the Winged Monkeys, / with much laughing and
그리고 나서 모든 날개 달린 원숭이들은 / 요란한 소리로 웃고

chattering and noise, / flew into the air / and were soon
캑캑 울고 떠들면서 / 하늘로 날아가 / 곧 사라졌다.

out of sight.

The Wicked Witch was both surprised and worried /
사악한 마녀는 놀라면서 걱정이 되었다 /

when she saw / the mark on Dorothy's forehead, / for she
그녀가 보았을 때 / 도로시 이마 위의 입맞춤 자국을 /

knew well / that neither the Winged Monkeys nor she,
잘 알고 있었기 때문에 / 날게 달린 원숭이도 자신도 /

herself, / dare hurt the girl / in any way.
감히 해칠 수 없다는 것을 / 어떤 방법으로든.

She looked down at Dorothy's feet, / and seeing the
마녀는 도로시의 발을 내려다보았고 / 은색 구두를 보자 /

Silver Shoes, / began to tremble with fear, / for she knew
공포로 떨기 시작했다 / 마녀는 알고 있었기 때문에 /

/ what a powerful charm belonged to them.
구두에 얼마나 강력한 마력이 있는지.

At first / the Witch was tempted to run away / from
처음에 / 마녀는 달아나고 싶었다 /

Dorothy; but she happened to look into the child's eyes /
도로시에게서; 우연히 마녀가 도로시의 눈을 보고 /

and saw / how simple the soul behind them was, / and /
알게 되었다 / 눈 뒤에 있는 도로시의 영혼이 얼마나 순진한 지 / 그리고 생각했다 /

that the little girl did not know / of the wonderful power /
이 아이가 모를 거라고 / 놀라운 마력을 /

the Silver Shoes gave her.
은 구두가 아이에게 줄 수 있는.

So the Wicked Witch laughed to herself, / and thought, /
그래서 사악한 마녀는 속으로 웃으면서 / 생각했다 /

"I can still make her my slave, / for she does not know /
"아직도 내 노예로 만들 수 있겠군 / 이 아이는 모를 테니까 /

how to use her power."
자신의 힘을 사용하는 방법을"

Then she said to Dorothy, / harshly and severely:
그래서 마녀는 도로시에게 말했다 / 단호하고 엄하게:

Key Expression

"seeing the Silver Shoes"는 때를 나타내는 분사구문이며 she가 의미상 주어이므로, "그녀가 은색 구두를 보았을 때"라고 해석한다.

She looked down at Dorothy's feet, / and seeing the Silver Shoes, /
그녀는 도로시의 발을 내려다보았고 / 그녀(마녀)가 은색 구두를 보았을 때 /
began to tremble with fear ~.
공포로 떨기 시작했다

yard 정원, 마당 chatter 캑캑 울다 charm 마력, 마법의 힘 be tempted to ~하고 싶어지다, 하려는 유혹을 받다

"Come with me; and see that you mind / everything I tell
"따라 오너라; 그리고 명심해라 / 내가 너에게 하는 모든 말을 /

you, / for if you do not / I will make an end of you, /
그렇게 하지 않으면 / 내가 너를 죽일 거야 /

as I did of the Tin Woodman and the Scarecrow."
양철 나무꾼과 허수아비에게 한 것처럼"

Dorothy followed her / through many of the beautiful
도로시는 마녀를 따라갔다 / 수많은 아름다운 방을 통과하여 /

rooms / in her castle / until they came to the kitchen, /
성 안에 있는 / 그들이 부엌에 도착할 때까지 /

where the Witch bade her / clean the pots and kettles /
그곳에서 마녀가 명령했다 / 솥과 주전자를 깨끗하게 닦고 /

and sweep the floor / and keep the fire fed with wood.
마루를 쓸고 / 난로 불에 장작을 지피라고.

Dorothy went to work meekly, / with her mind made up /
도로시는 순순히 일을 하기 시작했다 / 결심하면서 /

to work as hard as she could; for she was glad /
가능한 열심히 일하겠다고; 다행으로 여겼기 때문에 /

the Wicked Witch had decided / not to kill her.
사악한 마녀가 결심한 것을 / 자신을 죽이지 않겠다고.

---

bid(bid-bade-bidden) 말하다, 명령하다 meekly 순순히, 온순하게

With Dorothy hard at work, / the Witch thought /
도로시가 열심히 일하는 동안 / 마녀는 생각했다 /

she would go into the courtyard / and harness the
자신은 정원에 들어가서 / 겁쟁이 사자에게 굴레를 씌워야겠다고 /

Cowardly Lion / like a horse; it would amuse her, /
말처럼; 자신을 즐겁게 할 것 같았다 /

she was sure, / to make him draw her chariot /
분명 / 사자에게 마차를 끌게 하는 것은 /

whenever she wished to go to drive.
마차를 타고 싶을 때마다.

But as she opened the gate / the Lion gave a loud roar /
하지만 마녀가 문을 열었을 때 / 사자가 큰 소리로 으르렁거리며 /

and bounded at her so fiercely / that the Witch was
사납게 덤벼들었다 / 마녀는 겁이 나서 /

afraid, / and ran out / and shut the gate again.
뛰어 나와 / 문을 다시 닫아 버렸다.

"If I cannot harness you," said the Witch to the Lion, /
"너에게 굴레를 씌울 수 없다면" 마녀가 사자에게 말했다 /

speaking through the bars of the gate, "I can starve you.
문의 창살 사이로 / "너를 굶겨 죽일 수 있어.

You shall have nothing to eat / until you do as I wish."
너는 아무 것도 먹지 못할 거야 / 네가 내 말대로 할 때까지."

So after that / she took no food to the imprisoned Lion;
그 후에 / 마녀는 갇혀 있는 사자에게 먹이를 주지 않았다;

Key Expression

to 부정사는 사용되는 문장에 따라 명사, 형용사, 부사처럼 쓰인다. 아래 예문의 "to eat"은 바로 앞에 있는 nothing을 수식하여 형용사처럼 쓰인다.

You shall have nothing to eat / until you do as I wish.
너는 아무 것도 먹지 못할 거야 / 네가 내 말대로 할 때까지.

---

chariot 마차, 전차 bound ~에게 덤벼들다, 뛰어오르다 starve 굶겨 죽이다, 굶주리게 하다 imprisoned 갇혀 있는

but every day / she came to the gate / at noon / and
하지만 매일 / 마녀는 문으로 와서 / 정오에 /

asked, / "Are you ready to be harnessed / like a horse?"
물었다 / "굴레를 쓸 준비가 되었느냐 / 말처럼?"

And the Lion would answer, /
그러나 사자는 대답했다 /

"No. If you come in this yard, / I will bite you."
"아니. 네가 이 뜰 안으로 들어오면 / 물어 버리겠다."

The reason the Lion did not have to do / as the Witch
사자가 하지 않아도 된 이유는 / 마녀가 원하는 대로 /

wished / was that every night, / while the woman was
매일 밤 / 마녀가 잠들어 있는 동안 /

asleep, / Dorothy carried him food / from the cupboard.
도로시가 음식을 가져다주었기 때문이었다 / 찬장에서.

After he had eaten / he would lie down on his bed of
사자는 음식을 먹은 후 / 짚으로 만든 침대에 눕고 /

straw, / and Dorothy would lie beside him / and put her
도로시는 사자 옆에 누우면 / 도로시의 머리를 기대

head / on his soft, shaggy mane, / while they talked of
고 / 사자의 부드럽고, 털이 덥수룩한 갈기에 / 자신들의 문제를 이야기하는 동안에 /

their troubles / and tried to plan some way to escape.
탈출할 방법을 찾으려고 했다.

But they could find no way / to get out of the castle, /
하지만 그들은 방법을 찾을 수 없었다 / 성에서 빠져나갈 수 있는 /

for it was constantly guarded / by the yellow Winkies, /
성을 계속 지키고 있었기 때문에 / 노란 윙키들이 /

who were the slaves of the Wicked Witch /
그들은 사악한 마녀의 노예였고 /

and too afraid of her / not to do as she told them.
마녀를 너무 두려워하여 / 시키는 대로 하지 않을 수 없었다.

The girl had to work hard / during the day, /
도로시는 열심히 일해야 했다 / 하루 종일 /

and often the Witch threatened to beat her / with the
그리고 마녀는 자주 도로시를 때리겠다고 위협했다 /

same old umbrella / she always carried in her hand.
자신의 낡은 우산으로 /   항상 손에 들고 다니는

But, / in truth, / she did not dare to strike Dorothy, /
하지만 / 사실 /   마녀는 감히 도로시를 때리지 못했다 /

because of the mark upon her forehead.
도로시 이마의 입맞춤 자국 때문에.

The child did not know this, / and was full of fear for
도로시는 이 사실을 몰랐고 /   자신과 토토에 대한 걱정으로 가득차 있었다.

herself and Toto. Once the Witch struck Toto a blow /
한 번 마녀가 토토를 때리자 /

with her umbrella / and the brave little dog flew at her /
자신의 우산으로 /   용감한 토토는 마녀에게 달려들어서 /

and bit her leg in return.
다리를 물어버렸다.

The Witch did not bleed / where she was bitten, /
마녀는 피를 흘리지 않았다 /   물린 부분에서 /

for she was so wicked / that the blood in her had dried up
마녀는 매우 사악해서 /   몸속의 피가 모두 말라버렸기 때문이었다 /

/ many years before.
수 년 전에

---

shaggy 털이 덥수룩한 mane (사자의) 갈기

Dorothy's life became very sad / as she grew to
도로시의 삶은 매우 슬퍼졌다 / 그녀는 알게 되었기 때문에 /

understand / that it would be harder than ever /
전보다 더 어려워졌다는 것을 /

to get back to Kansas and Aunt Em again.
캔자스에 있는 엠 숙모에게 돌아가는 일이.

Sometimes she would cry bitterly / for hours, /
가끔 그녀는 괴로워 울기도 했다 / 몇 시간 동안 /

with Toto sitting at her feet / and looking into her face, /
(이 때) 토토는 도로시 발치에 앉아서 / 그녀의 얼굴을 바라보며 /

whining dismally / to show / how sorry he was for his
우울하게 낑낑거렸다 / 보여주려 하듯이 / 자신이 어린 주인을 얼마나 가엾게 여기는지.

little mistress. Toto did not really care / whether he was
사실 토토는 별로 신경 쓰지 않았다 / 자신이 캔자스에 있든

in Kansas or the Land of Oz / so long as Dorothy was
오즈의 나라에서 살든 / 오랫동안 도로시가 자기 옆에 있기만 하면;

with him; but he knew the little girl was unhappy, /
하지만 그는 도로시가 불행하다는 것을 알았고 /

and that made him unhappy too.
그 사실 때문에 토토도 불행해졌다.

Now the Wicked Witch had a great longing / to have for
이제 사악한 마녀에게는 강한 열망이 있었다 /

her own the Silver Shoes / which the girl always wore.
도로시의 은 구두를 자신의 것으로 만들려는 / 도로시가 항상 신고 있는.

Her bees and her crows and her wolves / were lying in
마녀의 벌과 까마귀와 늑대들도 / 무더기로 쌓여서 /

heaps / and drying up, / and she had used up all the
말라가고 있었고 / 황금 모자의 마력도 모두 써버렸다;

power of the Golden Cap; but if she could only get hold
하지만 마녀가 도로시의 은 구두를 빼앗을 수만

of the Silver Shoes, / they would give her more power /
있다면 / 은 구두가 마녀에게 더 큰 힘을 줄 것이다 /

than all the other things she had lost.
자신이 잃어버린 모든 힘보다도.

She watched Dorothy carefully, / to see / if she ever took
마녀는 도로시를 주의 깊게 살폈다 / 알아보려고 / 도로시가 구두를 벗는지 /

off her shoes, / thinking she might steal them.
자신이 구두를 훔칠 수 있을 것이라고 생각했기에.

But the child was so proud of her pretty shoes /
하지만 도로시는 자신의 구두에 자부심을 느끼고 있어서 /

that she never took them off / except at night /
그녀는 결코 벗으려 하지 않았다 / 밤에 잘 때와 /

and when she took her bath. The Witch was too much
목욕할 때를 제외하고는. 마녀는 어둠을 무척 무서워하여 /

afraid of the dark / to dare go in Dorothy's room at night
밤에는 도로시의 방에 감히 가려 하지 않았고 /

/ to take the shoes, / and her dread of water was greater
구두를 벗기러 / 물에 대한 두려움은 훨씬 컸다 /

/ than her fear of the dark, / so she never came near /
어둠에 대한 두려움보다 / 그래서 마녀는 가까이 가지 못했다 /

when Dorothy was bathing. Indeed, / the old Witch never
도로시가 목욕하고 있을 때에는. 사실 / 마녀는 물을 만져본 적도

touched water, / nor ever let water touch her / in any way.
없었고 / 물이 몸에 닿도록 하지도 않았다 / 어떤 경우라도.

But the wicked creature was very cunning, /
하지만 마녀는 매우 교활했기에 /

and she finally thought of a trick / that would give her
마녀는 마침내 나쁜 꾀를 생각해냈다 / 자신이 원하는 것을 손에 넣을 수 있는

what she wanted. She placed a bar of iron /
(꾀를). 마녀는 철봉을 놓았고 /

> ### Key Expression
>
> 아래 예문의 grow 동사는 "시간이 지나면서 차츰 ~하게 되다"라는 의미로 사용된다. grow는 get이나 go동사 보다 격식을 갖춘 표현이다.
>
> Dorothy's life became very sad / as she grew to understand /
> 도로시의 삶은 매우 슬퍼졌다 / 그녀는 알게 되었기 때문에 (무엇을) /
> that it would be harder than ever / to get back to Kansas and Aunt Em again.
> 전보다 더 어려워졌다는 것을 / 캔자스에 있는 엠 숙모에게 돌아가는 일이.

bitterly 괴로워하며, 고통에 가득 차 whine 낑낑거리다 dismally 우울하게, 울적하게 longing 열망, 갈망
dread 두려움, 공포 cunning 교활한, 약삭빠른

in the middle of the kitchen floor, / and then / by her
부엌 바닥 한 가운데에 / 그 다음 / 마법을 사용하여 /

magic arts / made the iron invisible to human eyes.
그 철봉이 사람 눈에 보이지 않도록 했다.

So that when Dorothy walked across the floor /
그래서 도로시는 마루를 건너갈 때 /

she stumbled over the bar, / not being able to see it, /
그녀는 철봉에 발이 걸려 넘어졌다 / 철봉을 볼 수 없었기에 /

and fell at full length.
벌렁 나가 자빠졌다.

She was not much hurt, / but in her fall / one of the Silver
그다지 다치지는 않았다 / 하지만 넘어질 때 / 은 구두 한 짝이 벗겨졌고;

Shoes came off; and before she could reach it, /
그리고 그녀가 미처 줍기 전에 /

the Witch had snatched it away / and put it on her own
마녀가 구두를 낚아채서 / 자신의 앙상한 발에 구두를 신었다.

skinny foot.

The wicked woman was greatly pleased /
마녀는 무척 기뻤다 /

with the success of her trick, / for as long as she had one
자신이 꾀가 성공해서 / 자신이 은 구두 한 짝을 가지고 있는 한 /

of the shoes / she owned half the power of their charm, /
그녀는 마력의 절반을 가지게 되었고 /

and Dorothy could not use it against her, /
도로시가 자신에게 마법을 사용할 수 없었기 때문에 /

even had she known / how to do so.
도로시가 알게 될지라도 / 마법을 사용하는 방법을 .

---

invisible 눈에 보이지 않는 stumble (발이 걸려) 넘어지다 fall at full length 벌렁 나가빠지다
snatch 잡아채다, 낚아채다

The little girl, / seeing she had lost one of her pretty
도로시는 / 자신의 예쁜 구두 한 짝을 빼앗긴 것을 알자 /

shoes, / grew angry, / and said to the Witch, /
화가 나서 / 마녀에게 말했다 /

Give me back my shoe!"
"내 구두를 돌려주세요!"

"I will not," retorted the Witch, /
"싫어" 마녀가 쏘아붙였다 /

"for it is now my shoe, and not yours."
"이제 이 구두는 내 것이지, 네 것이 아니니까"

"You are a wicked creature!" cried Dorothy.
"사악한 마녀 같으니!" 도로시가 외쳤다.

"You have no right / to take my shoe from me."
"당신에겐 권리가 없어요 / 내 구두를 빼앗을."

"I shall keep it, / just the same," said the Witch, /
"나는 가지고 있을 거야 / 그래도" 마녀가 말했다 /

laughing at her, "and someday / I shall get the other one
도로시를 비웃으며 / "그리고 언젠가는 / 나머지 한 짝도 빼앗고 말 거야."

from you, too."

This made Dorothy so very angry / that she picked up
이 말은 도로시를 매우 화나게 했다 / 그래서 그녀는 물통을 집어 들어 /

the bucket of water / that stood near / and dashed it over
옆에 놓여 있던 / 마녀에게 던져 버렸고 /

the Witch, / wetting her / from head to foot.
마녀를 흠뻑 젖게 했다 / 머리끝부터 발끝까지.

retort 쏘아붙이다, 대꾸하다　just the same 그래도, 그럼에도 불구하고　dash 내던지다

Instantly the wicked woman gave a loud cry of fear, /
즉시 마녀는 겁에 질려 큰 소리로 고함을 질렀고 /

and then, / as Dorothy looked at her / in wonder, /
그 다음 / 도로시가 쳐다보는 동안 / 놀라서 /

the Witch began to shrink and fall away.
마녀는 점점 오그라들면서 작아지기 시작했다.

"See what you have done!" she screamed.
"네가 한 짓을 봐" 마녀가 소리쳤다.

"In a minute I shall melt away."
"잠시 후 난 녹아 없어지고 말 거야"

"I'm very sorry, / indeed," said Dorothy, / who was truly
"죄송해요 / 정말로" 도로시가 말했다 / 너무나 놀라서 /

frightened / to see the Witch actually melting away /
마녀가 녹아 없어지는 모습을 보고 /

like brown sugar / before her very eyes.
마치 흑설탕처럼 / 자신의 눈앞에서.

"Didn't you know / water would be the end of me?"
"몰랐어 / 물이 닿으면 나는 끝장난다는 것을?"

asked the Witch, / in a wailing, despairing voice.
마녀가 물었다 / 울부짖으며, 절망적인 목소리로.

"Of course not," answered Dorothy. "How should I?"
"물론 몰랐어요" 도로시가 대답했다. "어떻게 알겠어요?"

"Well, in a few minutes / I shall be all melted, /
"어쨌든, 잠시 후 / 나는 완전히 녹아 버릴 것이고 /

and you will have the castle to yourself.
너는 이 성을 갖게 될 거야.

I have been wicked in my day, / but I never thought /
나는 평생 못되게 살았지 / 하지만 생각해 본적이 없었지 /

a little girl like you would ever be able to melt me /
너 같은 어린애가 나를 녹여 버리고 /

194 The Wonderful Wizard of Oz

and end my wicked deeds. Look out --here I go!"
내 악행을 멈추게 할 수 있다고 / 조심해--이제 난 간다!"

With these words / the Witch fell down / in a brown,
이 말을 남기고 / 마녀는 쓰러졌고 / 녹아버려서 형체가 없는 갈

melted, shapeless mass / and began to spread /
색 덩어리가 되어 / 퍼지기 시작했다 /

over the clean boards of the kitchen floor.
깨끗한 부엌 바닥 위에.

Seeing / that she had really melted away to nothing, /
보고나서 / 마녀가 모양이 없는 것으로 완전히 녹은 것을 /

Dorothy drew another bucket of water / and threw it over
도로시는 물통에 다시 물을 담아서 / 찌꺼기에 쏟아 부었다.

the mess. She then swept it all / out the door.
그 다음 그녀는 찌꺼기를 모두 쓸어냈다 / 문 밖으로.

After picking out the silver shoe, / which was all that
은 구두 한 짝을 집어 들고 / 마녀의 몸에서 남은 유일한

was left of the old woman, / she cleaned and dried it /
물건이었던 / 그것을 깨끗하게 닦고 말렸다 /

with a cloth, / and put it on her foot again.
걸레로 / 그리고 다시 자신의 발에 신었다.

Then, being at last free / to do as she chose, /
그리고 자유의 몸이 되었기에 / 마침내 원하는 대로 할 수 있는 /

she ran out to the courtyard / to tell the Lion /
그녀는 정원으로 달려갔다 / 사자에게 말하려고 /

that the Wicked Witch of the West had come to an end, /
사악한 서쪽의 마녀가 최후를 맞이했으니 /

and that they were no longer prisoners / in a strange
자신들은 더 이상 죄수가 아니라고 / 낯선 땅에서.

land.

---

instantly 즉시 give a loud cry of fear 겁에 질려 큰 소리로 고함을 지르다 shrink 오그라들다, 줄다
melt away 녹아 없어지다 wail 울부짖다 despairing 절망적인 wicked 악한, 사악한 deed 행동(위)
mess 오물, 쓰레기 come to an end 최후를 맞이하다

Quiz 6

A. 단어

다음 단어의 설명을 읽고, 어떤 단어를 설명하는지 아래의 박스에서 알맞은 단어를 고르세요.

1. to make a quick answer that sometimes expresses anger or annoyance
2. to make a long high sound when a dog is in pain or unhappy
3. to suffer or to die because there is not enough food
4. strong and thick
5. to use all that you have of something
6. a large group of insects moving together
7. covered with long, messy hair
8. a very strong feeling of anger
9. to hit the floor or ground hard with a foot
10. to smile widely

starve	stamp	grin	rage	retort
swarm	stout	exhaust	shaggy	whine

B. 직독직해

아래에 제시된 문장을 직독직해로 해석해보세요.

1. The soldier with the green whiskers / led them / through the streets of the Emerald City / until they reached the room / where the Guardian of the Gates lived.

   →

2. As the leader of the wolves came on / the Tin Woodman swung his arm / and chopped the wolf's head / from its body.

   →

Answer A. 단어 1. retort 2. whine 3. starve 4. stout 5. exhaust 6. swarm 7. shaggy 8. rage 9. stamp 10. grin
B. 직독직해   1. 초록색 수염의 병사는 / 그들을 안내했다 / 에메랄드 시의 거리를 지나서 / 그들이 방에 도착할 때까지 / 그곳(그 방)에 문지기가 살고 있었다.
2. 우두머리 늑대가 다가오자 / 나무꾼은 팔을 휘둘러서 / 늑대 머리를 잘라버렸다 / 몸통에서.

The Wonderful Wizard of Oz

3. The bees came and found / no one but the Woodman to sting.
   →

4. The Wicked Witch was both surprised and worried / when she saw / the mark on Dorothy's forehead.
   →

5. Often the Witch threatened to beat her / with the same old umbrella / she always carried in her hand.
   →

C. 동시통역

아래에 제시된 직독직해를 보고, 영어로 말해보세요.

1. 그들은 그에게 고맙다고 말하고 / 작별인사를 하고 / 서쪽으로 방향을 돌리고 / 부드러운 풀밭을 걸어갔다.
   →

2. 그들은 기다렸다 / 도로시가 깨어날 때까지 / 다음날 아침.
   →

3. "낯선 자들에게 가서 / 그들을 쏘아 죽여 버려라!" / 마녀가 명령했다.
   →

4. "사악한 마녀 같으니!" / 도로시가 외쳤다. / "당신에겐 권리가 없어요 / 내 구두를 빼앗을."
   →

5. 어쨌든, 잠시 후 / 나는 완전히 녹아 버릴 것이고 / 너는 이 성을 갖게 될 거야.
   →

Answer

3. 벌떼가 다가와서 발견했다 / 쏠 대상이 나무꾼 외에는 아무도 없는 것을.
4. 사악한 마녀는 놀라면서 걱정이 되었다 / 그녀가 보았을 때 / 도로시 이마 위의 입맞춤 자국을.
5. 마녀는 자주 도로시를 때리겠다고 위협했다 / 자신의 낡은 우산으로 / 항상 손에 들고 다니는.

C. 동시통역 1. They thanked him / and bade him good-bye, / and turned toward the West, / walking over fields of soft grass.
2. They waited / until Dorothy awoke / the next morning.
3. "Go to the strangers / and sting them to death!" / commanded the Witch.
4. "You are a wicked creature!" / cried Dorothy. "You have no right / to take my shoe from me."
5. Well, in a few minutes / I shall be all melted, / and you will have the castle to yourself.

Chapter 13. The Rescue
구조(줄거리)

In the thirteenth chapter, / Dorothy sets the Lion free
13장에서 / 도로시는 갇혀 있던 사자를 구한다.

from his prison.

She calls the Winkies together / to tell them / that they
그녀는 윙키들을 불러 모은다 / 말하려고 / 그들은

now are free / from the Witch's tyranny. She asks them /
이제 자유로워졌다고 / 마녀의 학대에서. 그녀는 그들에게 부탁한다 /

to rescue the Scarecrow and the Tin Woodman.
허수아비와 나무꾼을 구조해달라고.

The Winkies restuff the Scarecrow / and solder together
윙키들은 허수아비를 (지푸라기로) 다시 채우고 / 양철 나무꾼을 납으로 때우고

and repair the Tin Woodman.
수선한다.

A few days later, / the travelers decide to return to
며칠 후에 / 여행자들은 에메랄드 시로 돌아가기로 결정한다 /

the Emerald City / to tell the Wizard / that they've
에메랄드 시로 / 오즈 마법사에게 말하려고 / 자신들의 임무를

accomplished their mission. On this occasion,
완성했다고. 이때,

Dorothy notices the Golden Cap. She doesn't know /
도로시가 황금모자를 발견한다. 그녀는 모르고 있다 /

what it's supposed to be used for. But she decides to take
그것을 어떻게 사용해야 하는지. 하지만 그녀는 모자를 가지고 가기로

it with her. The travelers all bid farewell / to the Winkies
결심한다. 여행자들은 작별인사를 하고 / 윙키들에게 /

/ and start off for the Emerald City.
에메랄드 시를 향해 떠난다.

---

prison 감금된 상태, 구속된 곳 tyranny 폭정, 학대 solder 납으로 때우다 accomplish 완수하다, 성취하다
occasion 경우, 때

Chapter 14. The Winged Monkeys
날개 달린 원숭이(줄거리)

In the fourteenth chapter, / the travelers soon become lost / because of the lack of a road / between the Witch's castle and the Emerald City. Dorothy summons the Queen of the Field Mice. The Queen tells the travelers / that they have traveled / in the wrong direction. She then notices the Golden Cap and suggests / that Dorothy use it / to summon the Winged Monkeys. The Queen tells Dorothy of the charm / that's on the inside of the Cap and that summons the Winged Monkeys.

Dorothy uses the charm. The Winged Monkeys appear / and carry the travelers through the air / to the Emerald City. On the way there, / the King explains / why his Winged Monkeys must obey / the commands of the possessor of the Golden Cap. He also explains / why the Cap can be used / by any given person only three times.

summon 부르다, 호출하다 charm 마법, 마력 possessor 소유자, 주인

Chapter 15. The Discovery of Oz, the Terrible
무서운 오즈의 정체가 들통 나다

The four travelers walked up / to the great gate of
네 명의 여행자들은 걸어갔고 /   에메랄드 시의 성문으로 /
Emerald City / and rang the bell.
           종을 울렸다.
After ringing several times, / it was opened / by the same
여러 번 종을 울린 후 /   성문이 열렸다 /   같은 문지기에 의해 /
Guardian of the Gates / they had met before.
                    그들이 예전에 만났던.

"What! Are you back again?" he asked, / in surprise.
"아니!   너희들이 돌아온 거야?"   문지기가 물었다 / 놀라서

"Do you not see us?" answered the Scarecrow.
"보고 있잖아요?"   허수아비가 대답했다.

"But I thought / you had gone to visit / the Wicked Witch
"하지만 난 알고 있었는데 / 너희들이 찾아간 것으로 /   서쪽의 사악한 마녀를"
of the West."

"We did visit her," said the Scarecrow.
"우리는 마녀를 만났지"   허수아비가 말했다.

"And she let you go again?" asked the man, / in wonder.
"그런데 너희들을 돌려보냈다고?"   문지기가 물었다 /   놀라서.

"She could not help it, / for she is melted," explained the
"마녀도 어쩔 수 없었지 /   마녀는 녹아버렸기에"   허수아비가 설명했다.

Scarecrow.

"Melted! Well, that is good news, indeed," said the man.
"녹다니! 그것 참 기쁜 소식이구나, 정말로" 문지기가 말했다.

"Who melted her?"
"누가 녹인 거니?"

"It was Dorothy," said the Lion gravely.
"도로시가" 사자가 엄숙하게 말했다.

"Good gracious!" exclaimed the man, /
"잘했구나!" 문지기는 큰소리로 말하고 /

and he bowed very low indeed / before her.
고개 숙여 절을 했다 / 도로시에게.

Then he led them / into his little room / and locked the
그 다음 그는 일행을 안내하고 / 작은 방으로 / 안경을 씌워주었다

spectacles / from the great box / on all their eyes, /
커다란 상자에서 안경을 꺼내 / 그들 모두의 눈에 /

just as he had done before. Afterward they passed on
예전에 했던 것처럼. 그 후에 일행은 성문을 통과하였다 /

through the gate / into the Emerald City.
에메랄드 시로 들어가는.

Key Expression

"be 동사+동사의 과거분사+by 명사 or 대명사"는 수동태의 기본 패턴이다. 즉 어떤 사건이 일어났는데 그 사건이 일어나게 한 사람은 "by"로 표시한다.

After ringing several times, / it was opened / by the same Guardian of the Gates /
여러 번 종을 울린 후 / 성문이 열렸다 / 같은 문지기에 의해 /
they had met before.
그들이 예전에 만났던.

gravely 엄숙하게, 근엄하게 exclaim 외치다, 큰소리로 말하다

When the people heard / from the Guardian of the Gates
사람들은 소식을 듣자 / 문지기로부터 /

/ that Dorothy had melted the Wicked Witch of the West,
도로시가 사악한 서쪽 마녀를 녹여버렸다는 소식을 /

/ they all gathered around the travelers / and followed
모든 사람들이 그들 주위에 모여들었고 / 그들을 따라갔다 /

them / in a great crowd / to the Palace of Oz.
무리를 지어 / 오즈의 궁궐까지.

The soldier with the green whiskers / was still on guard
초록색 수염을 기른 병사는 / 여전히 문 앞에서 망을 보고

before the door, / but he let them in at once, /
있었다 / 하지만 그는 그들을 즉시 들여보냈고 /

and they were again met / by the beautiful green girl, /
그들은 다시 만나게 되었고 / 아름다운 초록색 소녀를 /

who showed / each of them to their old rooms / at once, /
그 소녀는 안내해주었다 / 일행 각자에게 예전에 묵었던 방을 / 즉시 /

so they might rest / until the Great Oz was ready to
그래서 그들은 쉴 수 있었다 / 위대한 오즈가 만날 준비가 될 때까지.

receive them.

The soldier had the news carried straight to Oz /
병사는 바로 오즈에게 소식을 전했다 /

that Dorothy and the other travelers had come back
도로시와 친구들이 다시 돌아왔다는 소식을 /

again, / after destroying the Wicked Witch;
사악한 마녀를 죽인 후;

but Oz made no reply.
하지만 오즈는 대답하지 않았다.

They thought / the Great Wizard would send for them /
그들은 생각했다 / 위대한 마법사가 자신들을 부를 것이라고 /

at once, / but he did not. They had no word from him /
즉시 / 그는 그러지 않았다. 일행은 아무 말도 듣지 못했다 /

the next day, / nor the next, / nor the next.
이튿날에도 / 그 다음에도 / 그 다음에도.

The waiting was tiresome and wearing, / and at last /
기다리는 일은 지루하고 피곤해졌고 / 마침내 /

they grew vexed / that Oz should treat them /
그들은 짜증이 났다 / 오즈가 자신들을 대하는 것에 /

in so poor a fashion, / after sending them /
매우 형편없이 / 자신들을 보내고 나서 /

to undergo hardships and slavery.
어려움과 노예 노릇을 당하도록.

So the Scarecrow at last / asked the green girl /
그래서 허수아비는 마침내 / 초록색 소녀에게 부탁했다 /

to take another message to Oz, /
오즈에게 또 다른 메시지를 전해달라고 /

saying / if he did not let them in to see him / at once /
말하면서 / 오즈가 자신들을 만나지 않는다면 / 당장 /

they would call the Winged Monkeys to help them, /
날개 달린 원숭이를 불러서 도움을 청하고 /

and find out / whether he kept his promises or not.
알아낼 것이라고 / 오즈가 약속을 지킬 것인지 아닌지.

When the Wizard was given this message /
마법사는 이 메세지를 들었을 때 /

he was so frightened / that he sent word for them /
그는 무척 놀라서 / 그는 그들에게 답변을 전했다 /

to come to the Throne Room / at four minutes after nine
알현실로 오라고 / 9시 4분에 /

o'clock / the next morning. He had once met the Winged
이튿날 아침. 오즈는 한 번 날개 달린 원숭이를 만난 적이

Monkeys / in the Land of the West, / and he did not wish
있었다 / 서쪽 나라에서 / 그래서 그는 바라지 않았다 /

/ to meet them again.
날개 달린 원숭이를 다시 만나길.

---

tiresome 지치는, 지루한 wearing 피곤하게 하는 vex 짜증나게 하다, 애타게 하다
in so poor a fashion 매우 형편없는 태도로, 매우 형편없이 undergo 겪다, 당하다 hardship 어려움, 고난

The four travelers passed a sleepless night, / each
네 명의 여행자들은 잠을 못 이루는 밤을 보냈다 / 각자

thinking of the gift Oz had promised / to bestow on him.
오즈가 약속한 선물을 생각했기에 / 자신에게 주기로 한.

Dorothy fell asleep only once, / and then she dreamed /
도로시는 딱 한 번 잠이 들었고 / 그 다음에 꿈을 꾸었다 /

she was in Kansas, / where Aunt Em was telling her /
자신이 캔자스로 돌아간 / 그곳에서 엠 숙모는 도로시에게 말했다 /

how glad she was / to have her little girl at home again.
자신은 아주 기쁘다고 / 도로시가 다시 집에 돌아와서.

Promptly at nine o'clock / the next morning / the green-
아홉 시 정각에 / 이튿날 아침 / 초록색

whiskered soldier came to them, / and four minutes later
수염의 병사가 그들에게 왔고 / 4분 후

/ they all went into the Throne Room of the Great Oz.
모두 함께 오즈의 알현실로 들어갔다.

Of course / each one of them expected /
물론 / 각자는 기대했다 /

to see the Wizard / in the shape he had taken before, /
마법사를 보게 되리라고 / 이전에 마법사가 보여줬던 모습으로 /

and all were greatly surprised / when they looked about /
그래서 모두 깜짝 놀랐다 / 주위를 둘러보고 /

and saw no one / at all in the room.
아무도 보이지 않아서 / 방 안 어디에도.

They kept close to the door / and closer to one another, /
그들은 문을 닫고 / 서로 가까이 붙어있었다 /

for the stillness of the empty room was more dreadful /
비어 있는 방안의 고요함은 더욱 무서웠기 때문에 /

than any of the forms / they had seen Oz take.
어떤 형태보다도 / 자신들이 오즈가 변한 것을 보았던.

Presently they heard a solemn Voice, / that seemed to
곧 그들은 엄숙한 목소리를 들었다 / 들려오는 것 같았던 /

204 The Wonderful Wizard of Oz

come / from somewhere near the top of the great dome, /
돔 천장 가까운 어딘가에서 /

and it said:
그 목소리는 이렇게 말했다:

"I am Oz, / the Great and Terrible.
"나는 오즈다 / 위대하고 무서운 마법사.

Why do you seek me?"
왜 나를 찾아왔느냐?"

They looked again / in every part of the room, / and then,
그들은 다시 살펴보았다 / 방안 구석구석을 / 그 다음 /

/ seeing no one, / Dorothy asked, / "Where are you?"
아무도 볼 수 없었기 때문에 / 도로시가 물었다 / "어디 계세요?"

Key Expression

아래 예문의 부정사 구(to have her little girl at home again)는 glad를 수식하며, 엠 숙모가 왜 기뻐하는지 그 이유를 설명하므로 부사적 용법으로 쓰인 것이다.

Aunt Em was telling her / how glad she was / to have her little girl at home again.
엠 숙모는 도로시에게 말했다 / 자신은 아주 기쁘다고 / 도로시가 다시 집에 돌아와서.

---

bestow 주다, 수여하다 promptly 정확히 제시간에, 지체 없이 stillness 고요, 정적 presently 곧 solemn 엄숙한

"I am everywhere," answered the Voice, /
"나는 어디에나 있다" 목소리가 대답했다 /

"but to the eyes of common mortals / I am invisible.
"하지만 보통 사람들의 눈에는 / 나는 보이지 않는다.

I will now seat myself upon my throne, / that you may
이제 내 옥좌에 앉겠다 / 너희들이 나와 대화를

converse with me." Indeed, / the Voice seemed just then
나눌 수 있도록" 진짜로 / 그때 목소리는 들려오는 듯 했다 /

to come / straight from the throne itself; so they walked
바로 옥좌에서; 그래서 그들은 옥좌로

toward it / and stood in a row / while Dorothy said:
다가가서 / 한 줄로 섰다 / 도로시가 말하는 동안:

"We have come to claim our promise, / O Oz."
"우리의 약속에 대한 권리를 주장하러 왔어요 / 마, 마법사님"

"What promise?" asked Oz.
"무슨 약속 말이냐?" 오즈가 물었다.

"You promised / to send me back to Kansas /
"약속하셨잖아요 / 저를 캔자스로 돌려보내 준다고 /

when the Wicked Witch was destroyed," said the girl.
사악한 마녀를 죽이면" 도로시가 말했다.

"And you promised to give me brains,"
"그리고 제게 두뇌를 주겠다고 약속했고요"

said the Scarecrow.
허수아비가 말했다.

"And you promised to give me a heart,"
"그리고 제게 심장을 주기로 약속했고요"

said the Tin Woodman.
나무꾼이 말했다.

"And you promised to give me courage,"
"그리고 제게 용기를 주겠다고 약속했고요"

said the Cowardly Lion.
겁쟁이 사자가 말했다.

"Is the Wicked Witch really destroyed?" asked the Voice,
"사악한 마녀가 정말 죽었느냐?" 목소리가 물었고 /

/ and Dorothy thought / it trembled a little.
도로시는 생각했다 / 그 목소리가 약간 떨리는 것 같다고.

"Yes," she answered, / "I melted her / with a bucket of
"네," 도로시가 대답했다 / "제가 녹여버렸어요 / 한 양동이의 물로"

water."

"Dear me," said the Voice, / "How sudden! Well, come to
"저런" 목소리가 말했다 / "정말 놀랍구나! 그럼, 내일 오렴 /

me tomorrow, / for I must have time to think it over."
나는 생각할 시간이 필요하기에"

"You've had plenty of time already,"
"이미 생각할 시간은 충분했잖아요"

said the Tin Woodman angrily.
양철 나무꾼이 화를 내며 말했다.

"We shan't wait a day longer," said the Scarecrow.
"하루도 더 기다릴 수 없어요" 허수아비가 말했다.

"You must keep your promises to us!" exclaimed
"약속을 지키셔야 해요!" 도로시가 소리쳤다.

mortal 인간 invisible 눈에 보이지 않는 converse 대화하다 throne 옥좌 in a row 한 줄로
claim 권리를 주장하다 shan't(shall not) ~하지 않을 것이다(의지)

Dorothy.

The Lion thought / it might as well frighten the Wizard,
사자는 생각했다 / 마법사에게 겁을 주는 것이 좋겠다고 /

/ so he gave a large, loud roar, / which was so fierce and
그래서 그는 큰 소리로 으르렁거렸다 / 그 소리가 매우 사납고 무서워서 /

dreadful / that Toto jumped away from him in alarm /
토토가 놀라서 물러서다가 /

and tipped over the screen / that stood in a corner.
휘장을 뒤엎었다 / 한쪽 구석에 세워져 있던.

As it fell with a crash / they looked that way, / and the
휘장이 쿵 소리를 내며 넘어질 때 / 그들은 그쪽을 돌아보았고 /

next moment / all of them were filled with wonder.
다음 순간 / 모두가 깜짝 놀랐다.

For they saw, / standing in just the spot / the screen
그들은 보았기 때문에 / 바로 그 장소에 / 휘장이 가리고 있던 /

had hidden, / a little old man, / with a bald head and a
키 작은 노인을 / 대머리와

wrinkled face, / who seemed to be as much surprised / as
주름살 투성이의 얼굴이 있는 / 그 노인은 똑같이 놀란 듯 보였다 /

they were. The Tin Woodman, / raising his axe, / rushed
그들만큼이나. 양철 나무꾼은 / 도끼를 치켜들고 /

toward the little man / and cried out, "Who are you?"
그 노인에게 달려가면서 / 소리쳤다 / "너는 누구냐?"

"I am Oz, / the Great and Terrible," said the little man, /
"나는 오즈다 / 위대하고 무서운 마법사" 노인이 말했다 /

in a trembling voice.
떨리는 목소리로

"But don't strike me / --please don't-- /
"하지만 때리지 마 / 제발 /

and I'll do anything / you want me to."
어떤 것이든 다 할게 / 너희들이 원하는"

might as well ~하는 편이 좋다 in alarm 놀라서 tip over 뒤엎다 wrinkled 주름살투성이의

Our friends looked at him / in surprise and dismay.
도로시와 친구들은 그를 바라보았다 /   놀라고 낙담하여

"I thought / Oz was a great Head," said Dorothy.
"나는 알고 있었는데 / 오즈가 커다란 머리인줄"   도로시가 말했다.

"And I thought / Oz was a lovely Lady,"
"나는 알고 있었는데 /   오즈가 아름다운 부인인줄"

said the Scarecrow.
허수아비가 말했다.

"And I thought / Oz was a terrible Beast,"
"나는 알고 있었는데 /   오즈가 무서운 짐승인줄"

said the Tin Woodman.
양철 나무꾼이 말했다.

"And I thought / Oz was a Ball of Fire,"
"나는 알고 있었는데 /   오즈가 불덩이인줄"

exclaimed the Lion.
사자가 외쳤다.

"No, you are all wrong," said the little man meekly.
"너희 모두 틀렸다"   노인이 온순한 목소리로 말했다.

"I have been making believe."
"그런 척 했을 뿐이야"

"Making believe!" cried Dorothy.
"그런 척 했다고!"   도로시가 소리쳤다.

"Are you not a Great Wizard?"
"당신은 위대한 마법사가 아닌가요?"

dismay 낙담, 당황 meekly 온순하게 make believe ~인 척하다

"Hush, my dear," he said.
"쉿, 애야" 오즈가 말했다.

"Don't speak so loud, / or you will be overheard / --and
"그렇게 크게 말하지 마 / 그러면 너의 목소리가 밖에서 들릴 것이고 /

I should be ruined. I'm supposed to be a Great Wizard."
나는 끝장이야. 나는 위대한 마법사가 되어야 하거든"

"And aren't you?" she asked.
"그럼 아닌가요?" 도로시가 말했다.

"Not a bit of it, my dear; I'm just a common man."
"전혀 아니야, 아가씨; 나는 보통 사람일 뿐이야"

"You're more than that," said the Scarecrow, /
"그 이상이야" 허수아비가 말했다 /

in a grieved tone; "you're a humbug."
슬픈 목소리로; "당신은 사기꾼이야"

"Exactly so!" declared the little man, / rubbing his hands
"맞아!" 오즈가 말했다 / 두 손을 비비며 /

together / as if it pleased him. "I am a humbug."
애원하는 듯이 "나는 사기꾼이네"

"But this is terrible," said the Tin Woodman.
"끔찍하군" 양철 나무꾼이 말했다.

"How shall I ever get my heart?"
"내 심장은 어떻게 얻어야 하지?"

"Or I my courage?" asked the Lion.
"내 용기는?" 사자가 말했다.

"Or I my brains?" wailed the Scarecrow, / wiping the tears from his eyes / with his coat sleeve.

"My dear friends," said Oz, / "I pray you / not to speak of these little things. Think of me, / and the terrible trouble / I'm in / at being found out."

"Doesn't anyone else know / you're a humbug?" asked Dorothy.

"No one knows it / but you four / --and myself," replied Oz. "I have fooled everyone so long / that I thought I should never be found out. It was a great mistake / my ever letting you into the Throne Room. Usually / I will not see even my subjects, / and so they believe / I am something terrible."

"But, I don't understand," said Dorothy, / in bewilderment. "How was it that / you appeared to me / as a great Head?"

hush 쉿, 조용히 해 overhear 몰래 엿듣다, 도청하다 grieved 슬픈 humbug 사기꾼
declare 분명히 말하다, 주장하다 wail 소리 내어 울다 pray 간절히 바라다, 간청하다 subject 신하, 국민
in bewilderment 어리둥절하여, 당황하여

"That was one of my tricks," answered Oz.
"그건 내 속임수였어" 오즈가 대답했다.

"Step this way, please, / and I will tell you all about it."
"이리와라 / 내가 너희들에게 모든 것을 이야기할게."

He led the way to a small chamber / in the rear of the
오즈는 작은 방으로 이끌었고 / 알현실 뒤에 있는 /

Throne Room, / and they all followed him.
그들 모두가 그를 따라갔다.

He pointed to one corner, / in which lay the great Head, /
오즈는 한쪽 구석을 가리켰다 / 그곳에는 커다란 머리가 있었다 /

made out of many thicknesses of paper, /
여러 겹의 종이로 만들고 /

and with a carefully painted face.
조심스럽게 얼굴을 그려 넣은.

"This I hung / from the ceiling / by a wire," said Oz.
"이것을 나는 걸어놓았지 / 천장에 / 철사로" 오즈가 말했다.

"I stood behind the screen / and pulled a thread, /
"나는 휘장 뒤에 서서 / 실을 잡아당겼어 /

to make the eyes move / and the mouth open."
눈을 움직이고 / 입을 벌리게 하려고."

"But how about the voice?" she inquired.
"하지만 목소리는요?" 도로시가 물었다.

"Oh, I am a ventriloquist," said the little man.
"나는 복화술사야" 오즈가 말했다.

"I can throw the sound of my voice / wherever I wish, /
"목소리를 낼 수 있어 / 원하는 곳 어디에서든지 /

so that you thought / it was coming out of the Head.
그래서 너희들은 생각한 거야 / 목소리가 머리에서 나오는 것이라고.

Here are the other things / I used to deceive you."
여기 다른 것도 있어 / 너희들을 속이기 위해 사용했던"

He showed the Scarecrow / the dress and the mask he had worn / when he seemed to be the lovely Lady.

And the Tin Woodman saw / that his terrible Beast / was nothing but a lot of skins, / sewn together, / with slats to keep their sides out.

As for the Ball of Fire, / the false Wizard had hung / that also from the ceiling. It was really a ball of cotton, / but when oil was poured upon it / the ball burned fiercely.

"Really," said the Scarecrow, / "you ought to be ashamed of yourself / for being such a humbug."

"I am --I certainly am," answered the little man sorrowfully; "but it was the only thing / I could do. Sit down, please, / there are plenty of chairs; and I will tell you my story."

---

chamber 방 in the rear of ~의 뒤에 ventriloquist 복화술사 deceive 속이다

sew (sew-sewed-sewn) 꿰매다, 깁다 slat 널빤지 as for ~에 대해 말하면 fiercely 맹렬하게, 격심하게

sorrowfully 비탄에 잠겨, 애처롭게

So they sat down and listened / while he told the
그래서 그들은 앉아서 들었다 / 오즈가 다음의 이야기를 하는 동안.
following tale.

"I was born in Omaha--"
"나는 오마하에서 태어났지"

"Why, that isn't very far from Kansas!" cried Dorothy.
"아니, 거긴 캔자스에서 멀지 않은 곳이잖아요!" 도로시가 소리쳤다.

"No, but it's farther from here," he said, / shaking his
"그래, 하지만 여기서는 훨씬 멀지" 오즈가 말했다, / 슬픈 듯이 고개를 저으며.
head at her sadly.

"When I grew up / I became a ventriloquist, /
"나는 성장하여 / 복화술사가 되었지 /
and at that I was very well trained / by a great master.
그리고 훈련을 잘 받았어 / 훌륭한 스승으로부터.
I can imitate any kind of a bird or beast."
나는 어떤 새나 짐승의 소리도 흉내 낼 수 있어."
Here he mewed so like a kitten / that Toto pricked up his
이때 오즈는 새끼 고양이처럼 소리를 내서 / 토토가 귀를 쫑긋 세우고 /
ears / and looked everywhere / to see where she was.
사방을 둘러보았다 / 고양이가 어디 있는지 보려고.
"After a time," continued Oz, /
"얼마 후" 오즈가 말을 이었다 /
"I tired of that, / and became a balloonist."
"나는 그것(복화술)에 싫증이 나서 / 열기구 타는 사람이 되었지"

imitate 흉내 내다 kitten 새끼 고양이 prick up one's ears 귀를 쫑긋 세우다 balloonist 열기구 타는 사람

"What is that?" asked Dorothy.
"그게 뭔데요?" 도로시가 물었다.

"A man who goes up in a balloon / on circus day, /
"풍선을 타고 올라가는 사람이야 / 서커스가 열리는 날 /

so as to draw a crowd of people together /
사람들을 끌어 모아 /

and get them to pay / to see the circus," he explained.
그들이 돈을 내게 하는 / 서커스를 보기 위해" 오즈가 설명했다.

"Oh," she said, / "I know."
"아" 도로시가 말했다 / "알겠어요"

"Well, one day / I went up in a balloon / and the ropes
"그런데, 어느 날 / 기구를 타고 올라갔는데 / 밧줄이 꼬여 버렸지 /

got twisted, / so that I couldn't come down again.
그래서 나는 다시 내려갈 수가 없었어.

It went way up above the clouds, / so far that a current of
기구는 구름 위로 올라가 버렸고 / 그때까지 바람이 불어와서 /

air struck it / and carried it many, many miles away.
기구를 수마일 밖으로 데려가 버렸지.

For a day and a night / I traveled through the air, / and on
꼬박 하루 낮과 밤 동안 / 하늘을 여행했고 /

the morning of the second day / I awoke and found / the
둘째 날 아침에 / 잠에서 깨어보니 알게 됐다 /

balloon floating / over a strange and beautiful country.
기구가 떠다니고 있는 것을 / 낯설고 아름다운 나라 위에서.

Key Expression

"awoke and found"는 "잠에서 깨어보니 ~을 알게 되었다"라는 의미로 "awoke to find"와 같은 의미로 사용된다.

I awoke and found / the balloon floating / over a strange and beautiful country.
나는 잠에서 깨어보니 알게 됐다 / 기구가 떠다니고 있는 것을 / 낯설고 아름다운 나라 위에서.

twisted 꼬인 so far 이 시점까지, 이때까지

It came down gradually, / and I was not hurt a bit.
기구는 서서히 내려왔고 / 그래서 나는 조금도 다치지 않았어.

But I found / myself in the midst of a strange people, /
하지만 알았지 / 내가 낯선 사람들 사이에 있다는 것을 /

who, / seeing me come from the clouds, / thought /
그 사람들은 / 내가 하늘에서 내려오는 것을 보았기 때문에 / 생각했지 /

I was a great Wizard. Of course / I let them think so, /
내가 위대한 마법사라고. 물론 / 나는 그들이 그렇게 생각하게 했지 /

because they were afraid of me, and promised /
그들이 나를 두려워했고 약속했으니까 /

to do anything / I wished them to.
무엇이든 하겠다고 / 내가 원하는 일이면.

Just to amuse myself, / and keep the good people busy, /
내 자신이 즐기고 / 착한 사람들을 바쁘게 만들기 위해 /

I ordered them to build this City, and my Palace;
그들에게 이 도시와 궁궐을 짓게 했지;

and they did it all / willingly and well.
그들은 그 모든 일을 해주었지 / 기꺼이 잘.

Then I thought, / as the country was so green and
그러자 나는 생각했지 / 이 나라가 푸르고 아름다우니까 /

beautiful, / I would call it the Emerald City; and to make
나는 에메랄드 시라고 부르겠다고; 그래서 그 이름에

the name fit better / I put green spectacles on all the
더 어울리도록 / 모든 사람들에게 초록색 안경을 쓰게 했지 /

people, / so that everything they saw / was green."
그래서 그들이 보는 모든 것이 / 초록색이 되도록"

"But isn't everything here green?" asked Dorothy.
"하지만 이곳의 모든 게 초록색이지 않나요?" 도로시가 물었다.

"No more than in any other city," replied Oz;
"다른 도시랑 마찬가지야" 오즈가 대답했다;

"but when you wear green spectacles, / why of course
"하지만 네가 초록색 안경을 쓰면 / 당연히

216 The Wonderful Wizard of Oz

everything you see / looks green to you.
너희들이 보는 모든 것이 / 너희들에게 초록색으로 보이지.

The Emerald City was built / a great many years ago, /
에메랄드 시는 세워졌다 / 아주 오래 전에 /

for I was a young man / when the balloon brought me
그 이유는 나는 젊은이였고 / 기구가 나를 이곳으로 데려왔을 때 /

here, / and I am a very old man now.
이제 늙은이가 되었으니까.

But my people have worn green glasses on their eyes /
하지만 내 백성들은 눈에 초록색 안경을 썼지 /

so long / that most of them think / it really is an Emerald
오랫동안 / 그래서 대부분의 사람들이 생각하지 / 이곳이 정말 에메랄드 시이고 /

City, / and it certainly is a beautiful place, / abounding in
분명히 아름다운 곳이라고 / 보석과 귀금속이

jewels and precious metals, and every good thing /
풍부하고, 모든 좋은 것들이 있는 (아름다운 곳) /

that is needed to make one happy.
사람을 행복하게 만드는 데 필요한.

I have been good to the people, / and they like me;
나는 사람들에게 친절하게 대했고 / 사람들은 나를 좋아했지;

but ever since this Palace was built, / I have shut myself
하지만 이 궁궐이 세워진 후에 계속 / 나는 내 자신을 가두고 /

up / and would not see any of them.
아무도 만나려 하지 않았어.

gradually 서서히 in the midst of ~사이에, 가운데 abound 풍부하다, 많이 있다 ever since ~이래 계속

One of my greatest fears was the Witches, /
내가 가장 두려워한 것은 마녀였지 /

for while I had no magical powers at all / I soon found
왜냐하면 나는 아무런 마법의 힘이 없는 반면에 / 나는 곧 알게 되었지 /

out / that the Witches were really able to do wonderful
마녀들은 진짜로 놀라운 일을 할 수 있다는 것을.

things. There were four of them / in this country, /
네 명의 마법사가 있었고 / 이 나라에 /

and they ruled the people / who live in the North and
그 네 명이 사람들을 다스렸지 / 북쪽과 남쪽, 동쪽, 서쪽에 사는.

South and East and West.

Fortunately, / the Witches of the North and South were
다행스럽게도 / 남쪽과 북쪽 마녀는 착한 마녀였고 /

good, / and I knew / they would do me no harm; but the
나는 알고 있었지 / 그들이 나에게 해를 끼치지 않을 것을; 하지만

Witches of the East and West were terribly wicked, /
동쪽과 서쪽의 마녀는 몹시 고약했지 /

and had they not thought / I was more powerful than
만약 그들이 생각하지 않았다면 / 내가 자기들보다 더 강한 사람이라고 /

they themselves, / they would surely have destroyed me.
그들은 분명히 나를 죽이려 했을 거야.

As it was, / I lived in deadly fear of them /
그래서 / 나는 그들을 매우 두려워하며 살았지 /

for many years; so you can imagine / how pleased I was
오랜 세월 동안; 그러니 상상할 수 있겠지 / 내가 얼마나 기뻐했는지 /

/ when I heard / your house had fallen on the Wicked
내가 들었을 때 / 네 집이 동쪽 마녀 위에 떨어졌다는 소식을.

Witch of the East.

When you came to me, / I was willing to promise
너희들이 내게 왔을 때 / 나는 기꺼이 어떤 약속이라도 하려했지 /

anything / if you would only do away with the other
만약 너희들이 다른 마녀를 죽이기만 하면;

Witch; but, now that you have melted her, /
그러나 네가 마녀를 녹여버렸으니 /

I am ashamed to say / that I cannot keep my promises."
말하기가 부끄러워 / 내 약속을 지킬 수 없다는 것을"

218 The Wonderful Wizard of Oz

"I think you are a very bad man," said Dorothy.
"당신은 아주 나쁜 사람이군요" 도로시가 말했다.

"Oh, no, my dear; I'm really a very good man, /
"아니란다, 애야; 나는 사실 아주 좋은 사람이야 /

but I'm a very bad Wizard, / I must admit."
하지만 형편없는 마법사지 / 그것을 인정할 수밖에 없어."

"Can't you give me brains?" asked the Scarecrow.
"제게 두뇌를 줄 수 없나요?" 허수아비가 말했다.

"You don't need them. You are learning something every
"네겐 두뇌가 필요 없단다. 너는 매일 무언가를 배우고 있어.

day. A baby has brains, / but it doesn't know much.
아기에게는 두뇌가 있어 / 하지만 아는 게 별로 없지.

Experience is the only thing / that brings knowledge, /
경험만 유일한 것이지 / 지식을 주는 /

and the longer you are on earth / the more experience
그러니 이곳에 더 오래 머물수록 / 더 많은 경험을

you are sure to get."
분명히 너는 얻게 될 거야."

Key Expression

아래 예문의 for는 이유를 나타내는 접속사이며, while은 두 가지 상황의 차이점을 강조하거나 두 가지 상황을 대조하기 위해 사용하는 접속사로 "~인 반면에"라고 해석한다.

One of my greatest fears was the Witches, / for while I had no magical powers at all /
내가 가장 두려워한 것은 마녀였지 / 왜냐하면 나는 아무런 마법의 힘이 없는 반면에 /
I soon found out / that the Witches were really able to do wonderful things.
나는 곧 알게 되었지 / 마녀들은 진짜로 놀라운 일을 할 수 있다는 것을.

as it is 그와 같은 상황 때문에, 그래서 do away with 죽이다, 없애다 ashamed 부끄러운, 수치스러운
admit 인정하다

"That may all be true," said the Scarecrow, / "but I shall be very unhappy / unless you give me brains."

The false Wizard looked / at him carefully.

"Well," he said with a sigh, / "I'm not much of a magician, / as I said; but if you will come to me tomorrow morning, / I will stuff your head with brains. I cannot tell you / how to use them, / however; you must find / that out / for yourself."

"Oh, thank you--thank you!" cried the Scarecrow. "I'll find a way to use them, / never fear!"

carefully 주의 깊게, 신중하게

"But how about my courage?" asked the Lion anxiously.
"하지만 내 용기는요?" 사자가 걱정스럽게 물었다.

"You have plenty of courage, / I am sure," answered Oz.
"너는 많은 용기를 가지고 있어 / 분명히," 오즈가 대답했다.

"All you need is / confidence in yourself. There is no
"네게 필요한 것은 / 자신을 신뢰하는 거야(믿는 거야). 생물은 존재하지 않지 /

living thing / that is not afraid / when it faces danger.
두려워하지 않는 / 위험에 부딪치면.

The True courage/ is in facing danger / when you are
진정한 용기는 / 위험과 맞서는 거야 / 두려워할 때에도 /

afraid, / and that kind of courage / you have in plenty."
그리고 그런 용기를 / 너는 충분히 가지고 있어"

"Perhaps I have, / but I'm scared just the same,"
"그럴지도 몰라요 / 하지만 그래도 겁이 나요"

said the Lion. "I shall really be very unhappy /
사자가 말했다. "나는 정말로 불행할 거예요 /

unless you give me the sort of courage /
당신이 내게 용기를 주지 않으면 /

that makes one forget / he is afraid."
잊게 해 주는 (용기를) / 두려워한다는 사실을."

"Very well, / I will give you / that sort of courage /
"좋아 / 네게 줄게 / 그런 용기를 /

tomorrow," replied Oz.
내일" 오즈가 대답했다.

"How about my heart?" asked the Tin Woodman.
"제 심장은요?" 양철 나무꾼이 물었다.

"Why, as for that," answered Oz, /
"그것에 대해 말하면" 오즈가 대답했다 /

---

anxiously 걱정스럽게 confidence 믿음, 신뢰 just the same 마찬가지로, 그래도 as for ~에 대해 말하면

"I think you are wrong / to want a heart.
"잘못이라고 생각해 / 심장을 갖고 싶어 하는 것은.

It makes most people unhappy. If you only knew it, /
심장은 대부분 사람들을 불행하게 만들거든. 네가 그걸 알기만 하면 /

you are in luck / not to have a heart."
너는 다행인 거야 / 심장을 가지지 않은 것이."

"That must be a matter of opinion," said the Tin
"그건 의견의 차이일 뿐이야" 나무꾼이 말했다.

Woodman. "For my part, / I will bear all the unhappiness
"제 경우에는 / 모든 불행을 견딜 거야 /

/ without a murmur, / if you will give me the heart."
불평하지 않고 / 당신이 제게 심장을 준다면"

"Very well," answered Oz meekly.
"좋아" 오즈가 온화하게 말했다.

"Come to me tomorrow / and you shall have a heart.
"내일 나를 찾아와라 / 그러면 심장을 갖게 될 거야.

I have played Wizard / for so many years /
나는 마법사인척 연기했으니 / 오랫동안 /

that I may as well continue the part / a little longer."
그 역할을 계속하는 게 낫겠지 / 좀 더"

"And now," said Dorothy, /
"그럼 이제" 도로시가 말했다 /

"how am I to get back to Kansas?"
"어떻게 제가 캔자스로 돌아갈 수 있지요?"

"We shall have to think about that," replied the little
"그것에 대해서는 생각해봐야 해" 오즈가 대답했다.

man. "Give me two or three days / to consider the matter
"내게 2~3일 더 줘 / 그 문제에 대해 생각할 수 있게 /

/ and I'll try to find a way / to carry you over the desert.
그러면 방법을 찾아볼게 / 너를 사막 건너편으로 데려갈.

In the meantime / you shall all be treated /
그 동안 / 너희들은 대접을 받을 거야 /

as my guests, / and while you live in the Palace / my
내 손님으로 / 그리고 너희들이 궁궐에 있는 동안 /

people will wait upon you / and obey your slightest wish.
내 신하들이 너희들의 시중을 들고 / 원하는 것은 무엇이든 들어줄 거야.

There is only one thing / I ask in return for my help /
한 가지뿐이야 / 너희들이 도와준 대가로 내가 요구하는 것은 /

--such as it is. You must keep my secret / and tell no one
대단한 것은 아니지만. 내 비밀을 지키고 / 아무한테도 말하지 마

/ I am a humbug."
내가 사기꾼이라는 것을."

They agreed / to say nothing of what they had learned, /
그들은 동의했다 / 알게 된 사실을 말하지 않겠다고 /

and went back to their rooms / in high spirits.
그리고 방으로 돌아갔다 / 기분이 좋아서.

Even Dorothy had hope / that "The Great and Terrible
도로시조차 희망을 가졌다 / "위대하고 무서운 사기꾼'이라고"

Humbug," as she called him, / would find a way /
자신이 불렀던 사람이 / 방법을 찾아줄 것이라는 (희망을) /

to send her back to Kansas, / and if he did /
자신을 캔자스로 돌려보내 줄 (방법을) / 그렇게 해준다면 /

she was willing to forgive / him everything.
기꺼이 용서하려했다 / 그가 한 모든 짓을.

Key Expression

아래 예문의 that은 주격 관계대명사로 선행사는 thing이다. 특히 관계대명사 that만 써야하는 경우 선행사(the same, the only, the last, the very, everything, anything, all, nothing)는 제한적인 의미가 강하다.

There is no living thing / that is not afraid / when it faces danger.
생물은 존재하지 않지 / 두려워하지 않는 / 자신이 위험에 부딪치면.

for one's part ~로서는, ~에 관한 한 bear 참다 murmur 불평 meekly 온화하게
may as well ~하는 편이 낫다, 더 좋다 in the meantime 그 사이, 그러는 동안 wait on 시중을 들다
such as it is 대단한 것은 아니지만, 변변치 못하지만 humbug 사기꾼 in high spirits 기분이 좋아서
forgive 용서하다

Quiz 7

A. 단어

다음 단어의 설명을 읽고, 어떤 단어를 설명하는지 아래의 박스에서 알맞은 단어를 고르세요.

1. feeling embarrassed and guilty because of something you have done
2. to be present in large numbers or amounts
3. a young cat
4. to cry out with a long high sound, especially because you are very sad
5. to make someone annoyed
6. showing serious purpose and determination
7. to say something suddenly and loudly because you are surprised
8. to talk with someone
9. a room used for a special purpose
10. the belief that you are able to do things well

confidence	abound	exclaim	converse	chamber
solemn	ashamed	wail	vex	kitten

B. 직독직해

아래에 제시된 문장을 직독직해로 해석해보세요.

1. A few days later, / the travelers decide / to return to the Emerald City / to tell the Wizard / that they've accomplished their mission.

   →

2. The people all gathered around the travelers / and followed them / in a great crowd / to the Palace of Oz.

   →

Answer　**A. 단어**　1. ashamed　2. abound　3. kitten　4. wail　5. vex　6. solemn　7. exclaim　8. converse　9. chamber　10. confidence

B. 직독직해　1. 며칠 후에 / 여행자들은 결정한다 / 에메랄드 시로 돌아가기로 / 오즈 마법사에게 말하려고 / 자신들의 임무를 완성했다고.

2. 모든 사람들이 일행 주위에 모여들었고 / 그들을 따라갔다 / 무리를 지어 / 오즈의 궁궐까지.

3. You promised / to send me back to Kansas / when the Wicked Witch was destroyed.

    →

4. Usually / I will not see even my subjects, / and so they believe / I am something terrible.

    →

5. They agreed / to say nothing of what they had learned, / and went back to their rooms / in high spirits.

    →

C. 동시통역

아래에 제시된 직독직해를 보고, 영어로 말해보세요.

1. 날개 달린 원숭이들이 나타나서 / 하늘로 날아서 일행을 데리고 간다 / 에메랄드 시로.

    →

2. 기다리는 일은 지루하고 피곤해졌고 / 마침내 / 그들은 짜증이 났다.

    →

3. "나는 알고 있었는데 / 오즈가 무서운 짐승인줄" / 양철 나무꾼이 말했다.

    →

4. 나는 휘장 뒤에 서서 / 실을 잡아당겼어 / 눈을 움직이고 / 입을 벌리게 하려고.

    →

5. 나는 모든 불행을 견딜 거야 / 불평하지 않고 / 당신이 제게 심장을 준다면"

    →

Answer

3. 약속하셨잖아요 / 저를 캔자스로 돌려보내 준다고 / 사악한 마녀를 죽이면.
4. 보통 나는 신하들조차 만나지 않아 / 그래서 그들은 믿고 있지 / 내가 무서운 사람이라고.
5. 그들은 동의했다 / 알게 된 사실을 말하지 않겠다고 / 그리고 방으로 돌아갔다 / 기분이 좋아서.

C. 동시통역 1. The Winged Monkeys appear / and carry the travelers through the air / to the Emerald City. 2. The waiting was tiresome and wearing, / and at last / they grew vexed.
3. "And I thought / Oz was a terrible Beast," / said the Tin Woodman.
4. I stood behind the screen / and pulled a thread, / to make the eyes move / and the mouth open.
5. I will bear all the unhappiness / without a murmur, / if you will give me the heart."

Chapter 16. The Magic Art of the Great Humbug

Next morning / the Scarecrow said to his friends:

"Congratulate me. I am going to Oz / to get my brains / at last. When I return / I shall be as other men are."

"I have always liked you / as you were," said Dorothy simply.

"It is kind of you / to like a Scarecrow," he replied. "But surely / you will think more of me / when you hear the splendid thoughts / my new brain is going to turn out." Then he said good-bye to them all / in a cheerful voice / and went to the Throne Room, / where he rapped upon the door.

"Come in," said Oz.

The Scarecrow went in / and found the little man /
허수아비가 들어가서 / 오즈를 발견했다 /

sitting down by the window, / engaged in deep thought.
창가 의자에 앉아있고 / 깊은 생각에 잠겨 있는 (노인을)

"I have come for my brains," remarked the Scarecrow, /
"내 두뇌를 가지러 왔어요" 허수아비가 말했다 /

a little uneasily.
약간 불안한 목소리로

"Oh, yes; sit down in that chair, please," replied Oz.
"좋아; 그 의자에 앉게" 오즈가 대답했다.

"You must excuse me / for taking your head off, /
"양해해줘 / 네 머리를 떼어 내는 일을 /

but I shall have to do it / in order to put your brains /
하지만 그래야만 해 / 새 두뇌를 넣어주려면 /

in their proper place."
적당한 자리에"

"That's all right," said the Scarecrow.
"괜찮아요" 허수아비가 말했다.

"You are quite welcome / to take my head off, / as long
"좋아요 / 내 머리를 떼어 내도 /

as it will be a better one / when you put it on again."
더 좋은 두뇌이기만 한다면 / 당신이 다시 넣어줄 때"

Key Expression

"as you are"는 "네가 있는 그대로, 있는 모습대로"라는 의미며, as는 "~대로"라는 뜻을 지닌 접속사이다.

"I have always liked you / as you were," said Dorothy simply.
"나는 언제나 널 좋아했어 / 그대로의 모습을," 도로시가 천진난만하게 대답했다.

turn out 만들어내다, 생산하다 rap (문을) 톡톡 두드리다 engaged in ~을 하고 있는 remark 말하다
excuse 양해해주다, 너그럽게 봐주다 welcome ~해도 좋은 as long as ~하기만 하면

So the Wizard unfastened his head / and emptied out
그러자 마법사는 허수아비의 머리를 풀고 / 짚을 다 꺼냈다.

the straw. Then he entered the back room / and took up
그리고 뒷방으로 들어가 /

a measure of bran, / which he mixed with a great many
한 되 정도의 왕겨를 가져왔고 / 그것에 수많은 핀과 바늘을 넣어 섞었다.

pins and needles.

Having shaken them together thoroughly, /
그것을 흔들어 잘 섞고 /

he filled the top of the Scarecrow's head /
허수아비의 머리 위 부분에 채우고 /

with the mixture / and stuffed the rest of the space with
혼합물로 / 나머지 공간을 짚으로 채웠다 /

straw, / to hold it in place.
제 자리에 고정되도록.

When he had fastened the Scarecrow's head /
허수아비의 머리를 고정시킬 때 /

on his body again / he said to him, /
다시 몸에 / 오즈는 말했다, /

"Hereafter you will be a great man, /
"이제부터 너는 훌륭한 사람이 될 거야 /

for I have given you a lot of bran-new brains."
내가 새 두뇌를 주었으니까"

---

unfasten 풀다, 끄르다 measure 되, 도량단위 mixture 혼합물 hereafter 지금부터, 이제부터
brand-new 아주 새로운, 신품의

The Scarecrow was both pleased and proud /
허수아비는 기뻐하고 자랑스러워했다고 /

at the fulfillment of his greatest wish, / and having
자신의 간절한 소원을 성취하여 /

thanked Oz warmly / he went back to his friends.
오즈에게 따뜻하게 감사 인사를 하고 / 친구들에게 돌아왔다.

Dorothy looked at him curiously.
도로시는 허수아비를 신기한 듯이 바라보았다.

His head was quite bulged out / at the top with brains.
그의 머리는 불룩 튀어나와있다 / 머리 위 부분이.

"How do you feel?" she asked.
"기분이 어때?" 도로시가 물었다.

"I feel wise indeed," he answered earnestly.
"정말 똑똑해진 것 같아" 허수아비가 진지하게 대답했다.

"when I get used to my brains / I shall know everything."
"새 두뇌에 익숙해지면 / 모든 것을 알게 될 거야"

"Why are those needles and pins sticking / out of your
"왜 바늘과 핀이 튀어나와있지 / 머리 밖으로?"

head?" asked the Tin Woodman.
양철 나무꾼이 물었다.

"That is proof / that he is sharp," remarked the Lion.
"그건 증거야 / 허수아비의 머리가 좋다는" 사자가 말했다.

---

fulfillment 성취, 완료 bulge out 불룩해지게 하다, 부풀리다 earnestly 진심으로, 진지하게
sharp 머리가 좋은, 똑똑한

"Well, I must go to Oz / and get my heart," said the
"나도 오즈에게 가서 / 심장을 얻어야지" 나무꾼이 말했다.

Woodman. So he walked to the Throne Room /
그리고 알현실로 걸어가 /

and knocked at the door.
문을 두드렸다.

"Come in," called Oz, / and the Woodman entered /
"들어와," 오즈가 말했고 / 나무꾼은 방으로 들어가서 /

and said, / "I have come for my heart."
말했다. / "내 심장을 가지러 왔어요"

"Very well," answered the little man.
"좋아" 노인이 대답했다.

"But I shall have to cut a hole / in your breast, /
"그런데 구멍을 하나 내야 해 / 네 가슴에 /

so I can put your heart / in the right place.
그래야 네 심장을 넣을 수 있어 / 적당한 자리에.

I hope / it won't hurt you."
바란다 / 아프지 않길"

"Oh, no," answered the Woodman.
"안 아파요" 나무꾼이 대답했다.

"I shall not feel it at all."
"난 (아픔을) 전혀 느끼지 못하니까요"

So Oz brought a pair of tinsmith's shears /
그러자 오즈는 양철공의 가위를 가져와서 /

and cut a small, square hole / in the left side of the Tin
작은 사각형 모양의 구멍을 냈다 / 양철 나무꾼의 왼쪽 가슴 위에.

Woodman's breast.

230 The Wonderful Wizard of Oz

Then, / going to a chest of drawers, / he took out a pretty
그러고 나서 / 서랍이 있는 곳으로 가서 / 예쁜 심장을 꺼냈고 /

heart, / made entirely of silk / and stuffed with sawdust.
비단으로 만들어진 / 톱밥을 채워 넣었다

"Isn't it a beauty?" he asked.
"예쁘지 않아?" 오즈가 물었다.

"It is, indeed!" replied the Woodman, /
"정말 그래요!" 나무꾼이 대답했고 /

who was greatly pleased. "But is it a kind heart?"
그는 매우 기뻐했다. "그런데 그것은 친절한 심장인가요?"

"Oh, very!" answered Oz. He put the heart / in the
"물론이지!" 오즈가 대답했다. 그는 심장을 넣었다 /

Woodman's breast / and then replaced the square of tin, /
나무꾼의 가슴 속에 / 그리고 사각형 모양의 양철로 바꾸고 /

soldering it neatly together / where it had been cut.
깔끔하게 땜질해 붙였다 / 구멍이 난 자리에

"There," said he; "now you have a heart / that any man
"자," 오즈가 말했다; "이제 너는 심장을 가지게 되었다 / 누구라도 자랑스러워 할.

might be proud of. I'm sorry / I had to put a patch on
미안해 / 가슴에 (땜질할 때) 쇳조각을 붙여서 /

your breast, / but it really couldn't be helped."
하지만 그건 어쩔 수 없었지"

---

tinsmith 양철공 shears 큰 가위 a chest of drawers 서랍, 장롱 replace 바꾸다 solder 납땜하다 patch 쇳조각

"Never mind the patch," exclaimed the happy Woodman.
"땜질한 쇳조각은 신경 쓰지 마세요" 행복해진 나무꾼이 큰소리로 말했다.

"I am very grateful to you, / and shall never forget your kindness."
"정말 고맙습니다 / 베풀어주신 친절을 절대 잊지 않을게요"

"Don't speak of it," replied Oz.
"그런 말은 하지도 마" 오즈가 대답했다.

Then the Tin Woodman went back to his friends, / who
그리고 양철 나무꾼은 친구들에게 돌아갔고 /

wished him every joy on account of his good fortune.
친구들은 그에게 행운을 빌어 주었다.

The Lion now walked to the Throne Room /
이번에는 사자가 알현실로 걸어가서 /

and knocked at the door.
문을 두드렸다.

"Come in," said Oz.
"들어와" 오즈가 말했다

"I have come for my courage," announced the Lion, /
"용기를 얻으러 왔어요" 사자가 큰소리로 말했다 /

entering the room.
방으로 들어가면서

"Very well," answered the little man;
"좋아" 작은 남자(오즈)가 말했다;

"I will get it for you."
"너에게 용기를 줄게"

He went to a cupboard / and reaching up to a high shelf /
오즈는 찬장으로 가서 /   높은 선반에 팔을 뻗고 /

took down a square green bottle, / the contents of which
네모난 초록색 유리병을 꺼냈다 /   병 안에 있던 내용물을 /

/ he poured into a green-gold dish, / beautifully carved.
황록색 접시에 따랐다 /   아름답게 조각이 새겨져 있는(접시에).

Placing this / before the Cowardly Lion, / who sniffed at
이것을 놓자 /   겁쟁이 사자 앞에 /   사자는 킁킁 냄새를 맡았

it / as if he did not like it, / the Wizard said:
고 /   좋아하지 않는 듯이 /   마법사가 말했다:

"Drink."
"마시게"

"What is it?" asked the Lion.
"그게 뭔데요?"   사자가 물었다.

"Well," answered Oz, / "if it were inside of you, /
"음,"   오즈가 대답했다 /   "이것이 네 몸속에 들어가면 /

it would be courage. You know, / of course, /
용기로 변할 거야.   알다시피 /   물론 /

that courage is always inside one; so that this really
용기란 항상 몸속에 있는 거란다;   그래서 이것을 진정한

cannot be called courage / until you have swallowed it.
용기라 부를 수는 없어 /   네가 삼키기 전에.

Therefore I advise you / to drink it / as soon as possible."
그래서 너에게 권하지 /   마시라고 /   되도록 빨리.

The Lion hesitated no longer, / but drank /
사자는 더 이상 주저하지 않고 /   마셨다 /

till the dish was empty.
접시에 아무것도 없을 때까지.

exclaim 외치다, 큰소리로 말하다 grateful 고마워하는, 감사하고 있는 wish (행운을) 빌어주다
announce 큰소리로 알리다(말하다) content 내용물 advise 권하다, 충고하다

"How do you feel now?" asked Oz.

"Full of courage," replied the Lion, who went joyfully back to his friends to tell them of his good fortune.

Oz, left to himself, smiled to think of his success in giving the Scarecrow and the Tin Woodman and the Lion exactly what they thought they wanted. "How can I help being a humbug," he said, "when all these people make me do things that everybody knows can't be done? It was easy to make the Scarecrow and the Lion and the Woodman happy, because they imagined I could do anything. But it will take more than imagination to carry Dorothy back to Kansas, and I'm sure I don't know how it can be done."

Key Expression

"in+동명사"는 "~할 때"라는 의미로 사용된다. 아래 예문의 "his success in giving the Scarecrow ~"을 해석하면, "오즈가 허수아비, 나무꾼, 사자에게 그들이 원하는 것을 줄 때 자신이 성공한 것"이다.

Oz, left to himself, / smiled to think of his success / in giving the Scarecrow
홀로 남겨진 오즈는 /　　　자신이 성공한 것을 생각하며 미소 지었다 / 허수아비와

and the Tin Woodman and the Lion / exactly what they thought they wanted.
양철 나무꾼과 사자에게 주는 일에 /　　　정확히 그들이 원한 것을

Chapter 17. How the Balloon Was Launched

For three days Dorothy heard nothing from Oz. These were sad days for the little girl, although her friends were all quite happy and contented. The Scarecrow told them there were wonderful thoughts in his head; but he would not say what they were because he knew no one could understand them but himself. When the Tin Woodman walked about he felt his heart rattling around in his breast; and he told Dorothy he had discovered it to be a kinder and more tender heart than the one he had owned when he was made of flesh. The Lion declared he was afraid of nothing on earth, and would gladly face an army or a dozen of the fierce Kalidahs.

Thus each of the little party was satisfied /
이렇게 일행의 각자는 만족하고 있었다 /

except Dorothy, / who longed more than ever /
도로시를 제외하고 / 그녀는 전보다 더 간절해졌다 /

to get back to Kansas.
캔자스로 돌아가길.

On the fourth day, / to her great joy, / Oz sent for her, /
나흘째 되는 날 / 기쁘게도 / 오즈가 도로시를 불렀고 /

and when she entered the Throne Room /
그녀가 알현실로 들어갔을 때 /

he greeted her pleasantly:
오즈가 반갑게 맞아 주었다:

"Sit down, my dear; I think I have found the way /
"앉으렴, 애야; 내가 방법을 찾은 것 같구나 /

to get you out of this country."
너를 이 나라 밖으로 데려갈 수 있는."

"And back to Kansas?" she asked eagerly.
"그리고 캔자스로 돌아가는 건가?" 도로시가 간절하게 물었다.

"Well, I'm not sure about Kansas," said Oz, /
"글쎄, 캔자스로 갈 수 있을 지 잘 모르겠어" 오즈가 말했다 /

"for I haven't the faintest notion / which way it lies.
"왜냐하면 도저히 알 수 없으니까 / 캔자스가 어느 쪽인지.

But the first thing to do / is to cross the desert, /
하지만 우선 해야 할 일은 / 사막을 건너는 거야 /

and then it should be easy / to find your way home."
그러면 쉬워질 거야 / 네 집으로 가는 길을 찾는 것은"

long (간절히) 바라다 haven't the faintest notion 도저히 모르다, 알 수 없다

"How can I cross the desert?" she inquired.
"어떻게 사막을 건너나요?" 도로시가 물었다.

"Well, I'll tell you what I think," said the little man.
"내가 생각한 것을 말해줄게" 오즈가 말했다.

"You see, / when I came to this country / it was in a
"알다시피 / 내가 이 나라에 왔을 때 / 기구를 타고 왔지.

balloon. You also came through the air, / being carried
너도 하늘을 날아 왔지 / 회오리바람에 휩쓸려.

by a cyclone. So I believe / the best way to get across the
그러니 내 생각에 / 사막을 건너는 가장 좋은 방법은 /

desert / will be through the air.
하늘을 날아가는 거야.

Now, / it is quite beyond my powers / to make a cyclone;
그런데 / 내 힘을 넘어서는 일이야(나는 도저히 불가능하지) / 회오리바람을 만들어내는 것은;

but I've been thinking the matter over, /
하지만 그 문제에 대해 곰곰이 생각해 보았고 /

and I believe I can make a balloon."
기구를 만들 수 있을 것 같구나"

Key Expression

would가 부정문에 사용되면, "강한 주장이나 거절"을 의미한다. 그래서 "would not say"를 "말하려 하지 않았다"라고 해석한다.

He would not say / what they were ~.
그는 말하려 하지 않았다 / 그게 무엇인지

think over 곰곰이 생각하다

"How?" asked Dorothy.
"어떻게요?" 도로시가 물었다.

"A balloon," said Oz, / "is made of silk, / which is coated with glue / to keep the gas in it. I have plenty of silk in the Palace, / so it will be no trouble / to make the balloon. But in all this country / there is no gas / to fill the balloon with, / to make it float."
"기구는" 오즈가 말했다 / "비단 천으로 만들고 / 천에 풀을 칠하지 / 가스가 새지 않도록. 이 궁전에 비단천이 잔뜩 있지 / 그러니 문제가 되지 않을 거야 / 기구를 만드는 것은. 하지만 이 나라 어디에도 / 가스가 없지 / 기구에 채워 넣을 / 기구를 떠있게 하기 위해."

"If it won't float," remarked Dorothy,
"기구가 떠오르지 않으면" 도로시가 말했다.

"it will be of no use to us."
"기구는 소용없잖아요"

"True," answered Oz. "But there is another way / to make it float, / which is to fill it with hot air. Hot air isn't as good as gas, / for if the air should get cold / the balloon would come down in the desert, / and we should be lost."
"맞아" 오즈가 대답했다. "하지만 다른 방법이 있어 / 기구를 띄울 수 있는 / 그것은 뜨거운 공기를 채우는 거야. 뜨거운 공기는 가스처럼 좋진 않아 / 왜냐하면 공기가 차가워지면 / 기구는 사막에 내려앉아버리고 / 우리는 길을 잃게 될 테니까"

"We!" exclaimed the girl. "Are you going with me?"
"우리라고요!" 도로시가 소리쳤다. "저랑 같이 가실 건가요?"

float 떠오르다, 뜨다

"Yes, of course," replied Oz.
"물론이지" 오즈가 대답했다.

"I am tired of being such a humbug. If I should go out of this Palace / my people would soon discover / I am not a Wizard, / and then they would be vexed with me / for having deceived them. So I have to stay / shut up in these rooms / all day, / and it gets tiresome. I'd much rather / go back to Kansas / with you / and be in a circus again."
"사기꾼 노릇도 지쳤어. 내가 이 궁궐을 나간다면 / 부하들이 곧 알게 될 거야 / 내가 마법사가 아니란 것을 / 그리고 내게 화를 낼 거야 / 자신들을 속인 것에. 그래서 나는 있어야 했지 / 이 방안에 갇혀 / 하루 종일 / 그런 일에 싫증이 났어. 훨씬 더 좋지 / 캔자스로 돌아가서 / 너와 함께 / 서커스에 다시 들어가는 것이"

"I shall be glad to have your company," said Dorothy.
"함께 가신다면 저도 좋아요" 도로시가 말했다.

"Thank you," he answered.
"고맙구나" 오즈가 대답했다.

"Now, / if you will help / me sew the silk together, / we will begin to work on our balloon."
"이제 / 네가 도와주면 / 비단을 꿰매는 일을 / 우리는 기구 만드는 일을 당장 시작할거야"

So Dorothy took a needle and thread, / and as fast as Oz cut / the strips of silk into proper shape / the girl sewed them neatly together.
그러자 도로시는 바늘과 실을 가져왔고 / 오즈가 자료자마자 / 비단 천 조각을 적당한 모양으로 / 도로시는 천들을 깔끔하게 꿰맸다.

First there was a strip of light green silk, /
처음에는 밝은 초록색 천 조각이 있었고 /

then a strip of dark green / and then a strip of emerald
다음에는 어두운 초록색 천 조각 / 그 다음은 에메랄드 빛 초록색 천이 있었다;

green; for Oz had a fancy / to make the balloon /
오즈는 생각했기 때문에 / 기구를 만들겠다고 /

in different shades of the color about them.
다른 색의 천으로.

It took three days / to sew all the strips together, /
3일이 걸렸다 / 모든 천 조각을 꿰매는 일은 /

but when it was finished / they had a big bag of green
하지만 그 일이 끝났을 때 / 그들은 초록색 비단의 커다란 주머니를 갖게

silk / more than twenty feet long.
되었다 / 길이가 20피트가 넘는.

Then Oz painted it on the inside / with a coat of thin
그 다음에 오즈는 주머니 안쪽에 칠했고 / 풀로 /

glue, / to make it airtight, / after which he announced /
공기가 새지 않도록 / 그 일을 마치고 오즈는 말했다 /

that the balloon was ready.
기구가 완성되었다고

---

be tired of ~에 지친, ~에 싫증이 나다 vex 화나게 하다, 짜증나게 하다 deceive 속이다 get tiresome 싫증이 나다
would much rather ~하는 것이 훨씬 더 좋다 strip (가늘고 긴) 조각 airtight 공기가 새지 않는, 밀폐한

"But we must have a basket to ride in," he said.
"하지만 우리가 탈 바구니가 있어야 해" 오즈가 말했다.

So he sent the soldier with the green whiskers /
그래서 그는 초록색 수염 병사를 보냈다 /

for a big clothes basket, / which he fastened /
커다란 바구니를 가져오라고 / 그것을 매달았다 /

with many ropes / to the bottom of the balloon.
여러 개의 끈으로 / 기구의 밑 부분에.

When it was all ready, / Oz sent word to his people /
기구가 준비되었을 때 / 오즈는 부하들에게 소식을 전했다 /

that he was going to make a visit / to a great brother
자신은 방문할 예정이라고 / 위대한 동생 마법사를 /

Wizard / who lived in the clouds.
구름 속에 살고 있는.

The news spread rapidly throughout the city /
이 소식은 순식간에 도시 전체로 퍼졌고 /

and everyone came to see / the wonderful sight.
모든 사람들이 구경하러 왔다 / 놀라운 광경을.

Oz ordered the balloon carried out / in front of the
오즈는 기구를 옮기라고 명령했고 / 궁궐 앞으로 /

Palace, / and the people gazed upon it / with much
사람들은 기구를 쳐다보았다 / 호기심에 가득차서.

curiosity. The Tin Woodman had chopped a big pile of
양철 나무꾼이 큰 장작더미로 나무를 쪼갰고 /

wood, / and now he made a fire of it, / and Oz held the
이제 그는 불을 피웠고 / 오즈는 기구 아래 부분을

bottom of the balloon over the fire / so that the hot air
모닥불 위에 놓았다 / 모닥불에서 나온 뜨거운 공기가 /

that arose from it / would be caught in the silken bag.
비단 주머니 안에 있도록.

---

fasten 묶다, 매달다 gaze 지켜보다, 쳐다보다 curiosity 호기심

Gradually the balloon swelled out / and rose into the air,
점점 기구가 부풀어 오르고 / 궁중으로 떠올랐다 /

/ until finally the basket just touched the ground.
마침내 바구니만 간신히 땅에 닿아있게 될 때 까지.

Then Oz got into the basket / and said to all the people /
그러자 오즈는 바구니에 올라타고 / 사람들에게 말했다 /

in a loud voice:
큰 소리로:

"I am now going away to make a visit. While I am gone
"나는 이제 먼 곳을 방문하려고 떠날 것이다. 내가 없는 동안 /

/ the Scarecrow will rule over you. I command you to
허수아비가 너희를 통치할 것이다. 너희들이 그를 따르라고 명령한다 /

obey him / as you would me."
나를 따르듯이."

The balloon was by this time tugging hard / at the rope /
기구는 이제 팽팽히 당기고 있었다 / 밧줄을 /

that held it to the ground, / for the air within it was hot, /
땅에 매어놓은 (밧줄을) / 왜냐하면 기구 속 공기가 뜨겁고 /

and this made it so much lighter in weight / than the air
기구가 훨씬 더 가벼워져서 / 바깥 공기보다 /

without / that it pulled hard to rise into the sky.
기구는 세게 당기면 하늘로 떠올랐다.

"Come, Dorothy!" cried the Wizard.
'이리 와, 도로시!" 마법사가 외쳤다.

"Hurry up, / or the balloon will fly away."
"서둘러 / 그렇지 않으면 기구가 날아가 버릴 거야"

swell out 부풀어 오르다 tug 당기다, 세게 잡아당기다

"I can't find Toto anywhere," replied Dorothy, /
"토토가 어디에도 안보여요" 도로시가 대답했다 /

who did not wish to leave / her little dog behind.
그녀는 떠나고 싶지 않았다 / 토토를 남겨두고.

Toto had run into the crowd / to bark at a kitten, /
토토는 군중 안으로 뛰어 들어갔고 / 새끼고양이를 쫓아다니며 짖기 위해 /

and Dorothy at last found him. She picked him up /
마침내 도로시가 토토를 발견했다. 도로시는 토토를 들어올리고 /

and ran towards the balloon.
기구로 뛰어왔다.

She was within a few steps of it, / and Oz was holding
도로시가 몇 발자국 떨어진 곳으로 왔고 / 오즈가 손을 뻗고 있었다 /

out his hands / to help her into the basket, / when, /
그녀가 바구니에 들어오는 것을 도우려고 / 그때 /

crack! went the ropes, / and the balloon rose into the air /
밧줄이 날카롭게 툭 끊어졌고 / 기구가 하늘로 떠올라 버렸다 /

without her.
도로시 없이.

"Come back!" she screamed. "I want to go, too!"
"돌아와요!" 도로시가 소리쳤다. "나도 같이 가고 싶어요!"

"I can't come back, my dear," called Oz from the basket.
"돌아갈 수 없어, 애야" 오즈가 바구니에서 외쳤다.

"Good-bye!"
"안녕!"

"Good-bye!" shouted everyone, / and all eyes were
"안녕!" 모두가 소리쳤다 / 그리고 모두의 눈이 하늘을 향했고 /

turned upward / to where the Wizard was riding in the
하늘에서 마법사는 바구니에 타고 /

basket, / rising every moment / farther and farther into
계속 하늘로 떠올라갔다 / 하늘 속으로 점점 더 멀어지면서.

the sky.

And that was the last / any of them ever saw of Oz,
그것이 마지막 순간이었다 / 놀라운 마법사 오즈를 보았던 /

the Wonderful Wizard, / though he may have reached
오즈는 오마하에 안전하게 도착했고 /

Omaha safely, / and be there now, / for all we know.
지금 그곳에 있을지도 모르지만 / 아마

But the people remembered him lovingly, / and said to
하지만 사람들은 그가 다정스러운 사람이었다고 기억했고 / 서로에게 말했다:

one another:

"Oz was always our friend. When he was here / he built for us / this beautiful Emerald City, / and now he is gone / he has left the Wise Scarecrow / to rule over us."

Still, for many days / they grieved over / the loss of the Wonderful Wizard, / and would not be comforted.

crack (밧줄이 끊어지는) 날카로운 소리 for all we know 아마, 우리가 알기로는
grieve over ~에 대해 몹시 슬퍼하다 comfort 위로하다, 안심시키다

Quiz 8

A. 단어

다음 단어의 설명을 읽고, 어떤 단어를 설명하는지 아래의 박스에서 알맞은 단어를 고르세요.

1. to say something
2. to join two metal surfaces together
3. the subject contained in something
4. to make short sharp knocking sounds as something moves or shakes
5. to want something very much
6. to attach something firmly to another object
7. to pull something quickly with force
8. to make someone feel less worried
9. to move slowly on the surface of a liquid and not sink
10. to have or possess something

tug	own	long	comfort	float
rattle	remark	solder	content	fasten

B. 직독직해

아래에 제시된 문장을 직독직해로 해석해보세요.

1. You will think more of me / when you hear the splendid thoughts / my new brain is going to turn out.

   →

2. So / the Wizard unfastened his head / and emptied out the straw.

   →

Answer A. 단어 1. remark 2. solder 3. content 4. rattle 5. long 6. fasten 7. tug 8. comfort 9. float 10. own
B. 직독직해 1. 너는 나를 더 소중히 여길 거야 / 멋진 생각들을 듣게 되면 / 내 새로운 두뇌가 생각해 낸.
2. 그러자 / 마법사는 허수아비의 머리를 풀고 / 짚을 다 꺼냈다.

3. Placing this / before the Cowardly Lion, / who sniffed at it / as if he did not like it.

   →

4. "I can't find Toto anywhere," / replied Dorothy, / who did not wish to leave / her little dog behind.

   →

5. She was within a few steps of it, / and Oz was holding out his hands / to help her into the basket.

   →

C. 동시통역

아래에 제시된 직독직해를 보고, 영어로 말해보세요.

1. 정말 친절하구나 / 네가 허수아비를 좋아하다니 / 그가 대답했다.

   →

2. 이제 너는 심장을 가지게 되었다 / 누구라도 자랑스러워 할.

   →

3. 그는 알게 되었다 / 그것은 훨씬 친절하고 상냥한 심장이라는 것을 / 전에 가지고 있던 것보다.

   →

4. 그것이(기구가) 준비되었을 때 / 오즈는 부하들에게 소식을 전했다 / 자신은 방문할 예정이라고 / 위대한 동생 마법사를 / 구름 속에 살고 있는.

   →

5. 오즈는 항상 우리의 친구였어. 여기 있을 때 / 그는 우리에게 만들어줬고 / 이 아름다운 에메랄드 시를.

   →

Answer

3. 이것을 놓자 / 겁쟁이 사자 앞에 / 사자는 킁킁 냄새를 맡았다 / 좋아하지 않는 듯이.
4. "토토를 어디에서도 찾을 수 없어요" / 도로시가 대답했다 / 그녀는 떠나고 싶지 않았다 / 자신의 작은 강아지를 남겨두고.   5. 도로시가 몇 발자국 떨어진 곳으로 왔고 / 오즈가 자신의 손을 뻗고 있었다 / 그녀가 바구니에 들어오는 것을 도우려고.

C. 동시통역   1. It is kind / of you to like a Scarecrow," / he replied.   2. Now you have a heart / that any man might be proud of.   3. He had discovered / it to be a kinder and more tender heart / than the one he had owned.   4. When it was all ready, / Oz sent word to his people / that he was going to make a visit / to a great brother Wizard / who lived in the clouds.
5. Oz was always our friend. When he was here / he built for us / this beautiful Emerald City.

Chapter 18. Away to the South
남쪽으로 (줄거리)

In the eighteenth chapter, / the Scarecrow suggests /
18장에서 / 허수아비는 제안한다 /

that Dorothy have the Winged Monkeys / take her back
도로시가 날개 달린 원숭이에게 명령할 것을 / 캔자스로 데려가라고.

to Kansas. Dorothy accepts the suggestion.
도로시는 그 제안을 받아들인다.

But the King of the Winged Monkeys declares /
하지만 날개 달린 원숭이의 왕은 말한다 /

that this is impossible. The Winged Monkeys never have
그런 일은 불가능하다고. 날개 달린 원숭이들은 캔자스에 가본 적이 없고 /

been in Kansas, / and they can't leave / the land of Oz.
자신들은 떠날 수 없다고 (말한다) / 오즈의 나라를.

The Soldier with the Green Whiskers then is called
그러자 초록색 수염이 있는 병사를 불러온다.

for. He suggests / that Glinda, the Good Witch of the
그는 제안한다 / 남쪽의 착한 마녀인 글린다가 /

South, / may be able to help. He explains / that Quadling
도와줄 수도 있다고. 그는 설명한다 /

inhabitants of the southern part of Oz / never visit the
오즈 남쪽 지방의 쿼들링 주민들은 / 에메랄드 시를 방문하지

Emerald City / on account of the dangers in the way.
못한다고 / (에메랄드 시로 오는) 길이 위험하기 때문에.

The Scarecrow decides / that Dorothy's best course is to
허수아비는 판단한다 / 도로시에게 가장 좋은 방법은 글린다를 방문하는 것

visit Glinda. He, the Tin Woodman, and the Cowardly
이라고. 허수아비, 양철 나무꾼, 겁쟁이 사자 모두가 결심한다 /

Lion all decide / to accompany her there.
그녀와 함께 그곳에 가기로

have (누군가에게) 명령하다, 설득하다 declare 확실하게 말하다, 주장하다 inhabitant 주민, 거주자
on account of 때문에

Chapter 19. Attacked by the Fighting Tree
싸움꾼 나무의 공격을 받는다(줄거리)

In the nineteenth chapter, / the travelers head straight south / from the Emerald City. On the second day of their trip, / they come across / a large, dense forest. The Scarecrow takes the lead / and tries to enter the forest. But the first tree that he passes / grabs him and throws him back.

The Tin Woodman then tries to enter the forest. The tree, which is one of the Fighting Trees, / tries to grab him too. But the Woodman chops off the branch / that the tree is using. While the tree is shaking from pain, / the other travelers pass by it. The other trees don't resist them. But at the far end of the forest, / they meet up with a high wall / made of china. There apparently is no doorway in the wall.

come across 우연히 마주치다 dense (나무가) 빽빽이 들어찬 resist 방해하다, 저항하다
apparently 명백히, 언뜻 보기에

Chapter 20. The Dainty China Country
아름다운 도자기 나라(줄거리)

In the twentieth chapter, / the Tin Woodman fashions a ladder. The travelers climb the ladder / to reach the top of the wall. There they notice / that everything below them and beyond the wall / is made of china. But the ladder is too heavy / to pull up and over the top of the wall.

The ground below is made of china. So the Scarecrow falls off the wall, / and the others jump onto him / so he can cushion them against the hard ground. They then walk carefully through the China Country. But on the way, / a cow that's being milked / suddenly kicks over the pail, / breaking both her leg and the pail.

The travelers therefore become extra careful. They do whatever they can / to make sure that no further damage is done / to the China Country or its inhabitants.

Presently they reach the wall / marking the boundary of
곧 일행들은 담장에 도착한다 / 부서지기 쉬운 도자기 나라의 경계를

this fragile domain.
표시하는.

It isn't as high as the first wall. By standing on the back
이번의 담장은 처음에 만난 담장만큼 높지 않다.   겁쟁이 사자의 등에 서서 /

of the Cowardly Lion, / the other travelers all reach the
                        나머지 일행들은 담장 꼭대기로 올라간다.

top. The Cowardly Lion then jumps onto the wall top /
그리고 겁쟁이 사자는 담장 꼭대기를 뛰어넘는다 /

and accidentally destroys a china church / with his tail.
우연히 도자기 교회가 부서진다 /   꼬리로.

---

fashion 만들다, 제조하다 cushion 충격을 완화하다 damage 손해, 피해 inhabitant 주민, 거주자 presently 곧 boundary 경계, 분계선 fragile 부서지기 쉬운, 손상되기 쉬운 domain 영토 accidently 우연히

Chapter 21. The Lion becomes the King of Beasts
사자가 맹수의 왕이 된다(줄거리)

In the twenty-first chapter, / the travelers descend from the wall.
21장에서 / 여행자들은 담장에서 내려온다.

They pass through an area of bogs.
그들은 습지로 된 지역을 통과한다.

They then enter another forest, / where the beasts are having a meeting.
그러고 나서 그들은 또 다른 숲속으로 들어가는데 / 그곳에서 짐승들은 회의를 하고 있다.

The Cowardly Lion discovers / that a most tremendous monster like a great spider / has been attacking and eating them.
겁쟁이 사자는 알게 된다 / 큰 거미같이 생긴 아주 거대한 괴물이 / 짐승들을 공격하고 잡아먹는다는 것을

He finds the giant spider asleep, / jumps onto the monster's back, / and beheads it with a single blow of his paw.
그는 거대한 거미가 잠들어 있는 것을 발견하고 / 괴물의 등에 올라타고 / 앞발로 한번 걷어차자 목이 떨어져나간다.

When the other beasts find out / what has happened, / they acknowledge / the Cowardly Lion as their King.
다른 동물들이 알았을 때 / 어떤 일이 일어나는지 / 그들은 인정한다 / 겁쟁이 사자를 자신들의 왕의 자격이 있다고

---

descend 내려오다, 내려가다 bog 습지, 소택지 behead 목을 베다, 참수하다 paw 동물의 발
acknowledge (자격을) 인정하다

Chapter 22. The Country of Quadlings
쿼들링 나라(줄거리)

Beyond the forest, in the twenty-second chapter, /
숲을 지나자, 22장에서 /

the travelers come across the land of the Hammerheads.
여행자들은 우연히 망치대가리의 나라를.

The Hammerheads have no arms.
망치대가리는 팔이 없다.

But their stretchable necks / allow them to use their
하지만 그들의 마음대로 뻗을 수 있는 목 때문에 / 머리를 이용할 수 있다 /

heads / to butt anyone who tries to enter their country.
자신들의 나라에 들어오려는 누구든지 머리로 떠밀어 낼 수 있는 (머리를)

The Scarecrow and the Cowardly Lion both defy /
허수아비와 겁쟁이 사자는 무시한다 /

the Hammerheads' order to keep out. Both of them are
들어오지 말라는 망치대가리의 명령을   허수아비와 겁쟁이 사자 모두가

butted down the hill / that marks the boundary of the
언덕 아래로 밀려난다 /   망치대가리 나라의 영역을 표시하는 (언덕)

Hammerhead country. So Dorothy uses the Golden Cap /
그래서 도로시가 황금모자를 사용한다 /

to summon the Winged Monkeys, /
날개 달린 원숭이를 부르기 위해 /

who carry the travelers through the air / and far beyond
원숭이들이 여행자들을 하늘로 데리고 가서 /   망치대가리의 공격범위

the shooting range of the Hammerheads' heads.
밖으로 벗어난다.

The Winged Monkeys point out / that this is the last time
날개 달린 원숭이들은 말한다 /   이번이 마지막 기회였다고 /

/ that Dorothy can call them.
도로시가 그들을 부를 수 있는

The travelers meet with no further difficulties.
여행자들은 더 이상 역경을 만나지 않는다.

Presently they arrive at Glinda's castle.
곧 그들은 글린다의 성에 도착한다.

There, they obtain immediate admittance.
그곳(성)으로, 그들은 즉시 들어간다.

---

hammerhead 망치대가리 stretchable 뻗을 수 있는, 펼 수 있는 butt (머리로) 밀쳐내다, 떠밀다
defy 무시하다, 반항하다 boundary 영역, 경계 summon 부르다, 호출하다 range 범위
point out 알려주다, 언급하다 presently 곧 admittance 입장(허가)

Chapter 23.

Glinda The Good Witch Grants Dorothy's Wish
선한 마녀 글린다가 도로시의 소원을 들어주다

Before they went to see Glinda, / however, / they were
도로시 일행이 글린다를 만나러 가기 전에 / 그러나 / 그들을

taken to a room of the Castle, / where Dorothy washed
성 안의 방으로 데리고 갔다 / 그곳에서 도로시는 세수를 하고 /

her face / and combed her hair, / and the Lion shook the
머리를 빗었으며 / 사자는 갈기의 먼지를 털어냈고 /

dust out of his mane, / and the Scarecrow patted himself
허수아비는 자신의 몸을 두드려 적절한 모습이 되었고 /

into his best shape, / and the Woodman polished his tin /
나무꾼은 양철 몸을 닦아 윤을 내고 /

and oiled his joints.
이음매에 기름칠을 했다.

When they were all quite presentable / they followed
모두가 단정한 모습이 되었을 때 / 그들은 소녀 병사를 따라

the soldier girl into a big room / where the Witch Glinda
큰 방으로 들어갔고 / 그곳에 마녀 글린다는

sat upon a throne of rubies. She was both beautiful and
루비로 만든 옥좌에 앉아있었다. 그녀는 아름답고 젊어 보였다 /

young / to their eyes. Her hair was a rich red in color /
그들의 눈에. 그녀의 머리는 강렬한 붉은 색이었고 /

and fell in flowing ringlets / over her shoulders.
머리에서 곱슬머리가 흘러내렸다 / 어깨 위로.

Her dress was pure white / but her eyes were blue, /
옷은 새하얀 색이었고 / 눈은 파란 색이었는데 /

and they looked kindly upon the little girl.
그 눈으로 도로시를 다정하게 바라보았다.

"What can I do for you, / my child?" she asked.
"내가 무엇을 도와줄까 / 얘야?" 글린다가 물었다

Dorothy told the Witch all her story:
도로시는 마녀에게 자신의 이야기를 했다:

how the cyclone had brought her / to the Land of Oz, /
어떻게 회오리바람이 자신을 데려왔는지 / 오즈의 나라로 /

how she had found her companions, /
어떻게 자신이 친구들을 찾았는지 /

and of the wonderful adventures / they had met with.
그리고 놀라운 모험에 대해 / 자신들이 겪은.

"My greatest wish now," she added, / "is to get back
"지금 제 가장 큰 소원은" 도로시가 말했다 / "캔자스로 돌아가는 것이에요 /

to Kansas, / for Aunt Em will surely think / something
엠 숙모는 분명히 생각하실 것이기에 / 제게 무서운 일이

dreadful has happened to me, / and that will make her
생겼다고 / 그래서 상복을 입고 계실 거예요;

put on mourning; and unless the crops are better this
그런데 올해 수확이 더 많지 않으면 /

year / than they were last, / I am sure / Uncle Henry
작년보다 / 분명히 / 헨리 아저씨는

cannot afford it." Glinda leaned forward and kissed /
상복을 입을 여유도 없을 거예요" 글린다는 몸을 숙이고 입맞춤을 했다 /

the sweet, upturned face of the loving little girl.
위를 쳐다보는 사랑스러운 소녀의 얼굴에

"Bless your dear heart," she said, / "I am sure / I can tell
"네 아름다운 마음씨에 축복을" 마녀가 말했다 / "분명히 / 나는 네게 방법을

you of a way / to get back to Kansas." Then she added, /
알려 줄 수 있을 거야 / 캔자스로 돌아가는" 그리고 덧붙였다 /

"But, / if I do, / you must give me the Golden Cap."
"하지만 / 그렇게 하면 / 너는 내게 그 황금 모자를 줘야 해"

polish 윤을 내다, 닦다 presentable 남 앞에 내놓을 만한, 외모가 단정한 ringlet 곱슬머리
put on mourning 상복을 입다 upturned 위로 향한

259

"Willingly!" exclaimed Dorothy; "indeed, / it is of no use to me now, / and when you have it / you can command the Winged Monkeys / three times."

"And I think I shall need their service / just those three times," answered Glinda, / smiling.

Dorothy then gave her the Golden Cap, / and the Witch said to the Scarecrow, / "What will you do / when Dorothy has left us?"

"I will return to the Emerald City," he replied, / "for Oz has made me its ruler / and the people like me. The only thing that worries me is / how to cross the hill of the Hammer-Heads."

"By means of the Golden Cap / I shall command the Winged Monkeys / to carry you to the gates of the Emerald City," said Glinda, / "for it would be a shame /

to deprive the people of so wonderful a ruler."
사람들에게서 너처럼 뛰어난 통치자를 빼앗는 것은

"Am I really wonderful?" asked the Scarecrow.
"제가 그렇게 대단한가요?" 허수아비가 말했다.

"You are unusual," replied Glinda.
"너는 비범해" 글린다가 대답했다.

Turning to the Tin Woodman, / she asked, / "What will
양철 나무꾼을 돌아보며 / 글린다가 물었다 / "너는 어떻게 할 거니 /

become of you / when Dorothy leaves this country?"
도로시가 이 나라를 떠나면?"

He leaned on his axe / and thought a moment.
그는 도끼에 기댄 채 / 잠시 생각에 잠겼다.

Then he said, / "The Winkies were very kind to me, /
그러고 나서 말했다 / "윙키들은 나한테 매우 친절했고

and wanted me to rule over them / after the Wicked
그들을 통치해주길 원했어요 / 사악한 마녀가 죽은 후.

Witch died. I am fond of the Winkies, / and if I could get
나도 윙키들을 좋아해요 / 그래서 다시 돌아갈 수만

back again / to the Country of the West, / I should like
있다면 / 서쪽 나라로 / 더 이상 바라는 게

nothing better than / to rule over them forever."
없을 거예요 / 영원히 그들을 다스리는 일보다"

Key Expression

"of+추상명사(of no use)"는 형용사(useless)와 같은 의미로 사용된다. 비슷한 예로 of importance는 important와, of value는 valuable, of help는 helpful와 같은 의미로 사용된다.

Indeed, / it is of no use to me now ~.
사실 / 이 모자는 이제 제게 쓸모없어요.

by means of ~을 이용하여, ~의 도움으로 shame 심한 일, 애석한 일 deprive ~에게서 빼앗다
unusual 비범한, 보통이 아닌 what will become of ~ 어떻게 될 것인가

"My second command to the Winged Monkeys," /
"날개 달린 원숭이들에게 하는 두 번째 명령은" /

said Glinda / "will be that they carry you safely /
글린다가 말했다 / "너를 안전하게 보내 주는 것이야 /

to the land of the Winkies. Your brain may not be so
윙키들의 나라로. 네 두뇌는 그다지 크지 않지 /

large / to look at / as those of the Scarecrow, /
보기에 / 허수아비의 두뇌보다 /

but you are really brighter / than he is /
하지만 너는 정말로 더 똑똑해 / 그보다 /

--when you are well polished-- / and I am sure /
잘 닦기만 하면 / 틀림없이 /

you will rule the Winkies wisely and well."
너는 윙키들을 현명하게 잘 다스릴 거야"

Then the Witch looked at the big, shaggy Lion / and
그러고 나서 마녀는 덩치가 크고 털이 수북한 사자를 보며 /

asked, / "When Dorothy has returned to her own home, /
물었다 / "도로시가 자기 집으로 돌아가면 /

what will become of you?"
너는 어떻게 할 거니?"

"Over the hill of the Hammer-Heads," he answered, /
"망치대가리 언덕 너머에" 그가 대답했다 /

"lies a grand old forest, / and all the beasts /
"오래된 넓은 숲이 있고 / 모든 짐승들이 /

that live there / have made me their King.
그곳에 사는 / 저를 왕으로 삼았어요.

If I could only get back to this forest, / I would pass my
그 숲으로 돌아갈 수만 있으면 / 여생을 보내겠어요 /

life / very happily there."
그곳에서 아주 행복하게."

"My third command to the Winged Monkeys,"
"날개 달린 원숭이에게 하는 세 번째 명령은"

said Glinda, / "shall be to carry you to your forest.
글린다가 말했다 / "너를 네 숲으로 보내 주는 것이야.

Then, / having used up the powers of the Golden Cap, /
그리고 / 황금 모자의 힘을 사용한 후에 /

I shall give it to the King of the Monkeys, / that he and
그 모자를 원숭이들의 왕에게 돌려줄 거야 / 원숭이들 무리가

his band may / thereafter / be free for evermore."
앞으로 / 영원히 자유롭게 살 수 있도록"

The Scarecrow and the Tin Woodman and the Lion /
허수아비와 양철 나무꾼과 사자는 /

now thanked the Good Witch earnestly /
이제 착한 마녀에게 진심으로 고마워했다 /

for her kindness; and Dorothy exclaimed:
친절한 행동에; 그리고 도로시가 소리쳤다:

"You are certainly as good / as you are beautiful! But
"정말로 친절하시군요 / 아름다운 것만큼! 하지만

you have not yet told me / how to get back to Kansas."
제게 아직 가르쳐 주지 않았어요 / 캔자스로 돌아가는 방법을"

"Your Silver Shoes will carry you over the desert,"
"네 은 구두가 너를 사막 너머로 데려다 줄 거야"

replied Glinda. "If you had known their power /
글린다가 대답했다. "네가 은 구두의 힘을 알았다면 /

Key Expression

"I/we shall"은 앞으로 주어가 어떤 일을 하겠다는 의향을 표현한다. 한편 "Shall I/we ~?" 상대방의 의향을 물어볼 때 사용한다.

I shall give it to the King of the Monkeys, / that he and his band
나는 그 모자를 원숭이들의 왕에게 돌려줄 거야 / 원숭이들 무리가

may ~ be free for evermore."
영원히 자유롭게 살 수 있도록"

band 무리 thereafter 그 후에, 그로부터

you could have gone back to your Aunt Em /
엠 숙모에게 돌아갈 수 있었을 거야 /

the very first day / you came to this country."
첫 날에 /   이 나라에 온."

"But then I should not have had my wonderful brains!"
"하지만 그랬다면 나는 훌륭한 두뇌를 얻지 못했을 거예요!"

cried the Scarecrow.
허수아비가 외쳤다.

"I might have passed my whole life / in the farmer's
"나는 평생을 보냈을지도 몰라요 /   농부의 옥수수 밭에서"

cornfield."

"And I should not have had my lovely heart,"
"그리고 나는 내 사랑스런 심장을 얻지 못했을 거예요"

said the Tin Woodman.
양철 나무꾼이 말했다.

"I might have stood and rusted in the forest /
"나는 숲속에 서서 녹슬고 말았을 거예요 /

till the end of the world."
이 세상이 끝날 때까지"

"And I should have lived a coward forever,"
"그리고 나는 영원히 겁쟁이로 살았을 거예요"

declared the Lion, / "and no beast in all the forest would
사자가 말했다 /   "그리고 숲속의 어떤 짐승도 나를 칭찬하지 않았겠지요."

have had a good word to say to me."

"This is all true," said Dorothy, / "and I am glad /
"모두 사실이에요"   도로시가 말했다 /   "그래서 기뻐요 /

I was of use to these good friends. But now that each of
이 착한 친구들에게 도움이 될 수 있어서.   하지만 그들 모두 얻었고 /

them has had / what he most desired, / and each is happy
각자가 가장 원하는 것을 / 행복해 하고 있으니 /

/ in having a kingdom to rule / besides, / I think I should
다스릴 나라를 갖게 되어 / 게다가 / 저는 캔자스로

like to go back to Kansas."
돌아가고 싶어요"

"The Silver Shoes," said the Good Witch, /
"그 은 구두는" 착한 마녀가 말했다 /

"have wonderful powers. And one of the most curious
"놀라운 힘을 가지고 있단다. 그리고 그 구두가 가진 가장 신비로운 힘은 /

things about them / is that they can carry you /
너를 데려다 줄 수 있다는 것이지 /

to any place in the world / in three steps, /
세상 어느 곳이든 / 세 걸음 만에 /

and each step will be made / in the wink of an eye.
그리고 각 걸음을 내딛게 되지 / 눈 깜짝할 사이에 .

All you have to do / is to knock the heels together /
네가 해야 할 일은 / 구두 뒤꿈치를 부딪치고 /

three times / and command the shoes / to carry you /
세 번 / 구두에게 명령하는 것뿐이지 / 너를 데려다 달라고 /

wherever you wish to go."
원하는 곳으로"

rust 녹슬다 coward 겁쟁이 curious 진기한, 호기심을 끄는 heel (구두의) 굽, 뒤꿈치

"If that is so," said the child joyfully, /
"그렇다면" 도로시가 기뻐하며 말했다 /

"I will ask them / to carry me back to Kansas / at once."
"구두에게 부탁할 거야 / 나를 캔자스로 보내 달라고 / 즉시"

She threw her arms around the Lion's neck /
도로시는 사자의 목을 끌어안고 /

and kissed him, / patting his big head tenderly.
사자에게 입을 맞추었다 / 큰 머리를 상냥하게 토닥이면서.

Then she kissed the Tin Woodman, / who was weeping /
그런 다음 양철 나무꾼에게 입을 맞추었다 / 울고 있는 /

in a way most dangerous to his joints.
이음매에 매우 위험하게.

But she hugged the soft, stuffed body of the Scarecrow /
하지만 그녀는 부드러운 허수아비의 몸을 끌어안았다 /

in her arms / instead of kissing his painted face, /
팔로 / 색칠한 얼굴에 입 맞추는 대신 /

and found she was crying herself / at this sorrowful
그리고 자신도 울고 있는 것을 알았다 / 슬픈 이별 때문에 /

parting / from her loving comrades.
사랑하는 친구들과 헤어지는

Glinda the Good stepped down from her ruby throne /
글린다는 자신의 루비 옥좌에서 내려왔고 /

to give the little girl a good-bye kiss, /
도로시에게 작별의 입맞춤을 하려고 /

and Dorothy thanked her for all the kindness
도로시는 글린다의 친절함에 고마워했다 /

she had shown to her friends and herself.
글린다가 자신과 친구들에게 보여준.

Dorothy now took Toto up solemnly / in her arms,
도로시는 이제 토토를 꽉 진지하게 끌어안고 / 자신의 팔에 /

and having said one last good-bye / she clapped the heels
마지막 작별인사를 하고 / 구두 굽을 맞부딪쳤다 /

of her shoes together / three times, / saying:
세 번 / 말하면서:

"Take me home to Aunt Em!"
"나를 엠 숙모에게 데려다 주렴!"

Instantly she was whirling through the air, / so swiftly /
곧 그녀는 하늘을 빙빙 돌며 날아가고 있었다 / 매우 빨라서 /

that all she could see or feel / was the wind whistling
도로시가 보거나 느낄 수 있는 것이란 / 귓가를 스치며 소리를 내는 바람이었다.

past her ears.

The Silver Shoes took but three steps, / and then she
은 구두는 딱 세 걸음을 걸었고 / 갑자기 멈추었다 /

stopped so suddenly / that she rolled over upon the grass
그래서 그녀는 풀밭에 굴렀다 /

/ several times / before she knew / where she was.
몇 번이나 / 알아채기도 전에 / 자신이 어디에 있는지.

At length, / however, / she sat up / and looked about her.
마침내 / 그러나 / 그녀는 일어나 앉고 / 주변을 둘러보았다.

"Good gracious!" she cried.
"어머나!" 도로시가 소리쳤다.

For she was sitting on the broad Kansas prairie, / and
왜냐하면 그녀는 캔자스의 넓은 들판에 앉아 있었고 /

just before her / was the new farmhouse / Uncle Henry
그 앞에 / 새 집이 있었기 때문에 / 헨리 아저씨가 지은 /

joyfully 기뻐서, 기쁜 듯이 tenderly 상냥하게, 친절하게 parting 이별, 고별 comrade 친구, 동료
solemnly 진진하게, 엄숙하게 instantly 즉시, 당장에 whirl 빙빙 돌며 가다, 선회하다 whistle 휘파람 소리를 내다
Good gracious! 어머나, 맙소사

built / after the cyclone had carried away the old one.
회오리바람이 옛 집을 날려 버린 후에.

Uncle Henry was milking the cows / in the barnyard, /
헨리 아저씨는 암소의 젖을 짜고 있었고 /   앞뜰에서 /

and Toto had jumped out of her arms / and was running
토토는 도로시의 팔에서 뛰어 내려 /   헛간으로 달려가고 있었다 /

toward the barn, / barking furiously.
세차게 짖어대며.

Dorothy stood up and found / she was in her stocking-
도로시는 자리에서 일어나자 알게 되었다 /   자신이 양말만 신고 있음을.

feet. For the Silver Shoes had fallen off / in her flight
은 구두는 벗겨졌고 /   하늘을 나는 동안 /

through the air, / and were lost forever / in the desert.
영원히 잃어버렸다 /   사막에.

---

barnyard 앞마당, 농가의 안뜰 furiously 맹렬히, 세차게 flight 날기, 비행

Chapter 24. Home Again
다시 집으로

Aunt Em had just come out of the house /
엠 숙모가 막 집에서 나왔다 /

to water the cabbages / when she looked up and saw /
양배추에 물을 주려고 / 고개를 들고 발견했을 때 /

Dorothy running toward her.
자신이 있는 곳으로 도로시가 달려오는 것을.

"My darling child!" she cried, / folding the little girl in
"아가야!" 엠 숙모가 외쳤다 / 어린 조카를 팔에 끌어안고 /

her arms / and covering her face with kisses.
얼굴에 입맞춤을 퍼부으며.

"Where in the world did you come from?"
"도대체 어디에서 온 거니?"

"From the Land of Oz," said Dorothy gravely.
"오즈의 나라에서 왔어요" 도로시가 진지하게 대답했다.

"And here is Toto, too. And oh, Aunt Em!
"토토도 있어요. 아, 엠 숙모!

I'm so glad to be at home again!"
집에 돌아와서 정말 기뻐요!"

gravely 진지하게

Quiz 9

A. 단어

다음 단어의 설명을 읽고, 어떤 단어를 설명하는지 아래의 박스에서 알맞은 단어를 고르세요.

1. an occasion when two people leave each other
2. a friend, especially someone you have worked with
3. someone who is not brave, is easily frightened, or tries to avoid difficulties
4. a group of people formed because of a common purpose
5. to take something away from someone
6. to make something smooth and shiny by rubbing
7. to refuse to do what someone in authority tells you to do
8. to officially order someone to come to a place
9. to go down or come down something
10. an area of low wet muddy ground

coward	comrade	polish	defy	bog
band	descend	parting	deprive	summon

B. 직독직해

아래에 제시된 문장을 직독직해로 해석해보세요.

1. The Scarecrow decides / that Dorothy's best course is to visit Glinda.
   →

2. The tree, / which is one of the Fighting Trees, / tries to grab him too.
   →

Answer A. 단어 1. parting 2. comrade 3. coward 4. band 5. deprive 6. polish 7. defy 8. summon 9. descend 10. bog

B. 직독직해 1. 허수아비는 판단한다 / 도로시에게 가장 좋은 방법은 글린다를 방문하는 것이라고.
2. 나무가 / 싸움꾼인 / 그도 잡으려 한다.

3. The ladder is too heavy / to pull up and over the top of the wall.
   →

4. They enter another forest, / where the beasts are having a meeting.
   →

5. When they were all quite presentable / they followed the soldier girl into a big room / where the Witch Glinda sat upon a throne of rubies.
   →

C. 동시통역

아래에 제시된 직독직해를 보고, 영어로 말해보세요.

1. 양철 나무꾼이 숲으로 들어가려 한다.
   →

2. 그곳에서 그들은 알게 된다 / 그들 밑과 담장 너머 있는 모든 것이 / 도자기로 만들어졌다는 것을.
   →

3. 그들은 습지로 된 지역을 통과한다.
   →

4. 나는 평생을 보냈을지도 몰라요 / 농부의 옥수수 밭에서.
   →

5. 그녀는 하늘을 빙빙 돌며 날아가고 있었다 / 매우 빨라서 / 도로시가 보거나 느낄 수 있는 것은 / 귓가를 스치며 소리를 내는 바람이었다.
   →

Answer

3. 사다리가 지나치게 무거워 / 담장 위로 끌어올려 담장을 넘을 수 없다.
4. 그들은 또 다른 숲속으로 들어가는데 / 그곳에서 짐승들은 회의를 하고 있다.
5. 모두가 단정한 모습이 되었을 때 / 그들은 소녀 병사를 따라 큰 방으로 들어갔고 / 그곳에 마녀 글린다는 루비로 만든 옥좌에 앉아 있었다.

C. 동시통역   1. The Tin Woodman then tries to enter the forest.
2. There they notice / that everything below them and beyond the wall / is made of china.
3. They pass through an area of bogs.
4. I might have passed my whole life / in the farmer's cornfield.
5. She was whirling through the air, / so swiftly / that all she could see or feel / was the wind whistling past her ears.

〈The Wonderful Wizard of OZ〉를 다시 읽어 보세요.

Chapter 1. The Cyclone

Dorothy lived in the midst of the great Kansas prairies, with Uncle Henry, who was a farmer, and Aunt Em, who was the farmer's wife. Their house was small, for the lumber to build it had to be carried by wagon many miles. There were four walls, a floor and a roof, which made one room; and this room contained a rusty looking cookstove, a cupboard for the dishes, a table, three or four chairs, and the beds. Uncle Henry and Aunt Em had a big bed in one corner, and Dorothy a little bed in another corner. There was no garret at all, and no cellar--except a small hole dug in the ground, called a cyclone cellar, where the family could go in case one of those great whirlwinds arose, mighty enough to crush any building in its path. It was reached by a trap door in the middle of the floor, from which a ladder led down into the small, dark hole.

When Dorothy stood in the doorway and looked around, she could see nothing but the great gray prairie on every side. Not a tree nor a house broke the broad sweep of flat country that reached to the edge of the sky in all directions. The sun had baked the plowed land into a gray mass, with little cracks running through it. Even the grass was not green, for the sun had burned the tops of the long blades until they were the same gray color to be seen everywhere. Once the house had been painted, but the sun blistered the paint and the rains washed it away, and now the house was as dull and gray as everything else.

When Aunt Em came there to live she was a young, pretty wife. The sun and wind had changed her, too. They had taken the sparkle from her eyes and left them a sober gray; they had taken the red from her cheeks and lips, and they were gray also. She was thin and gaunt, and never smiled now. When Dorothy, who was an orphan, first came to her, Aunt Em had been so startled by the child's laughter that she would scream and press her hand upon her heart whenever Dorothy's merry voice reached her ears; and she still looked at the little girl with wonder that she could find anything to laugh at.

Uncle Henry never laughed. He worked hard from morning till night and did not know what joy was. He was gray also, from his long beard to his rough boots, and he looked stern and solemn, and rarely spoke.

It was Toto that made Dorothy laugh, and saved her from growing as gray as her other surroundings. Toto was not gray; he was a little black dog, with long silky hair and small black eyes that twinkled merrily on either side of his funny, wee nose. Toto played all day long, and Dorothy played with him, and loved him dearly.

Today, however, they were not playing. Uncle Henry sat upon the doorstep and looked anxiously at the sky, which was even grayer than usual. Dorothy stood in the door with Toto in her arms, and looked at the sky too. Aunt Em was washing the dishes.

From the far north they heard a low wail of the wind, and Uncle Henry and Dorothy could see where the long grass bowed in waves before the coming storm. There now came a sharp whistling in the air from the south, and as they turned their eyes that way they saw ripples in the grass coming from that direction also.

Suddenly Uncle Henry stood up.

"There's a cyclone coming, Em," he called to his wife. "I'll go look after the stock." Then he ran toward the sheds where the cows and horses were kept.

Aunt Em dropped her work and came to the door. One glance told her of the danger close at hand.

"Quick, Dorothy!" she screamed. "Run for the cellar!"

Toto jumped out of Dorothy's arms and hid under the bed, and the girl started to get him. Aunt Em, badly frightened, threw open the trap door in the floor and climbed down the ladder into the small, dark hole. Dorothy caught Toto at last and started to follow her aunt. When she was halfway across the room there came a great shriek from the wind, and the house shook so hard that she lost her footing and sat down suddenly upon the floor.

Then a strange thing happened.

The house whirled around two or three times and rose slowly through the air. Dorothy felt as if she were going up in a balloon.

The north and south winds met where the house stood, and made it the exact center of the cyclone. In the middle of a cyclone the air is generally still, but the great pressure of the wind on every side of the house raised it up higher and higher, until it was at the very top of the cyclone; and there it remained and was carried miles and miles away as easily as you could carry a feather.

It was very dark, and the wind howled horribly around her, but Dorothy found she was riding quite easily. After the first few whirls around, and one other time when the house tipped badly, she felt as if she were being rocked gently, like a baby in a cradle.

Toto did not like it. He ran about the room, now here, now there, barking loudly; but Dorothy sat quite still on the floor and waited to see what would happen.

Once Toto got too near the open trap door, and fell in; and at first the little girl thought she had lost him. But soon she saw one of his ears sticking up through the hole, for the strong pressure of the air was keeping him up so that he could not fall. She crept to the hole, caught Toto by the ear, and dragged him into the room again, afterward closing the trap door so that no more accidents could happen.

Hour after hour passed away, and slowly Dorothy got over her fright; but she felt quite lonely, and the wind shrieked so loudly all about her that she nearly became deaf. At first she had wondered if she would be dashed to pieces when the house fell again; but as the hours passed and nothing terrible happened, she stopped worrying and resolved to wait calmly and see what the future would bring. At last she crawled over the swaying floor to her bed, and lay down upon it; and Toto followed and lay down beside her.

In spite of the swaying of the house and the wailing of the wind, Dorothy soon closed her eyes and fell fast asleep.

Chapter 2. The Council with the Munchkins

She was awakened by a shock, so sudden and severe that if Dorothy had not been lying on the soft bed she might have been hurt. As it was, the jar made her catch her breath and wonder what had happened; and Toto put his cold little nose into her face and whined dismally. Dorothy sat up and noticed that the house was not moving; nor was it dark, for the bright sunshine came in at the window, flooding the little room. She sprang from her bed and with Toto at her heels ran and opened the door.

The little girl gave a cry of amazement and looked about her, her eyes growing bigger and bigger at the wonderful sights she saw.

The cyclone had set the house down very gently--for a cyclone--in the midst of a country of marvelous beauty. There were lovely patches of greensward all about, with stately trees bearing rich and luscious fruits. Banks of gorgeous flowers were on every hand, and birds with rare and brilliant plumage sang and fluttered in the trees and bushes. A little way off was a small brook, rushing and sparkling along between green banks, and murmuring in a voice very grateful to a little girl who had lived so long on the dry, gray prairies.

While she stood looking eagerly at the strange and beautiful sights, she noticed coming toward her a group of the queerest people she had ever seen. They were not as big as the grown folk she had always been used to; but neither were they very small. In fact, they seemed about as tall as Dorothy, who was a well-grown child for her age, although they were, so far as looks go, many years older.

Three were men and one a woman, and all were oddly dressed. They wore round hats that rose to a small point a foot above their heads, with little bells around the brims that tinkled sweetly as they moved. The hats of the men were blue; the little woman's hat was white, and she wore a white gown that hung in pleats from her shoulders. Over it were sprinkled little stars that glistened in the sun like diamonds. The men were dressed in blue, of the same shade as their hats, and wore well-polished boots with a deep roll of blue at the tops. The men, Dorothy thought, were about as old as Uncle Henry, for two of them had beards. But the little woman was doubtless much older. Her face was covered with wrinkles, her hair was nearly white, and she walked rather stiffly.

When these people drew near the house where Dorothy was standing in the doorway, they paused and whispered among themselves, as if afraid to come farther. But the little old woman walked up to Dorothy, made a low bow and said, in a sweet voice:

"You are welcome, most noble Sorceress, to the land of the Munchkins. We are so grateful to you for having killed the Wicked Witch of the East, and for setting our people free from bondage."

Dorothy listened to this speech with wonder. What could the little woman possibly mean by calling her a sorceress, and saying she had killed the Wicked Witch of the East? Dorothy was an innocent, harmless little girl, who had been carried by a cyclone many miles from home; and she had never killed anything in all her life.

But the little woman evidently expected her to answer; so Dorothy said, with hesitation, "You are very kind, but there must be some mistake. I have not killed anything."

"Your house did, anyway," replied the little old woman, with a laugh, "and that is the same thing. See!" she continued, pointing to the corner of the house. "There are her two feet, still sticking out from under a block of wood."

Dorothy looked, and gave a little cry of fright. There, indeed, just under the corner of the great beam the house rested on, two feet were sticking out, shod in silver shoes with pointed toes.

"Oh, dear! Oh, dear!" cried Dorothy, clasping her hands together in dismay. "The house must have fallen on her. Whatever shall we do?"

"There is nothing to be done," said the little woman calmly.

"But who was she?" asked Dorothy.

"She was the Wicked Witch of the East, as I said," answered the little woman. "She has held all the Munchkins in bondage for many years, making them slave for her night and day. Now they are all set free, and are grateful to you for the favor."

"Who are the Munchkins?" inquired Dorothy.

"They are the people who live in this land of the East where the Wicked Witch ruled."

"Are you a Munchkin?" asked Dorothy.

"No, but I am their friend, although I live in the land of the North. When they saw the Witch of the East was dead the Munchkins sent a swift messenger to me, and I came at once. I am the Witch of the North."

"Oh, gracious!" cried Dorothy. "Are you a real witch?"

"Yes, indeed," answered the little woman. "But I am a good witch, and the people love me. I am not as powerful as the Wicked Witch was who ruled here, or I should have set the people free myself."

"But I thought all witches were wicked," said the girl, who was half frightened at facing a real witch. "Oh, no, that is a great mistake. There were only four witches in all the Land of Oz, and two of them, those who live in the North and the South, are good witches. I know this is true, for I am one of them myself, and cannot be mistaken. Those who dwelt in the East and the West were, indeed, wicked witches; but now that you have killed one of them, there is but one Wicked Witch in all the Land of Oz--the one who lives in the West."

"But," said Dorothy, after a moment's thought, "Aunt Em has told me that the witches were all dead--years and years ago."

"Who is Aunt Em?" inquired the little old woman.

"She is my aunt who lives in Kansas, where I came from."

The Witch of the North seemed to think for a time, with her head bowed and her eyes upon the ground. Then she looked up and said, "I do not know where Kansas is, for I have never heard that country mentioned before. But tell me, is it a civilized country?"

"Oh, yes," replied Dorothy.

"Then that accounts for it. In the civilized countries I believe there are no witches left, nor wizards, nor sorceresses, nor magicians. But, you see, the Land of Oz has never been civilized, for we are cut off from all the rest of the world. Therefore we still have witches and wizards amongst us."

"Who are the wizards?" asked Dorothy.

"Oz himself is the Great Wizard," answered the Witch, sinking her voice to a whisper. "He is more powerful than all the rest of us together. He lives in the City of Emeralds."

Dorothy was going to ask another question, but just then the Munchkins, who had been standing silently by, gave a loud shout and pointed to the corner of the house where the Wicked Witch had been lying.

"What is it?" asked the little old woman, and looked, and began to laugh. The feet of the dead Witch had disappeared entirely, and nothing was left but the silver shoes.

"She was so old," explained the Witch of the North, "that she dried up quickly in the sun. That is the end of her. But the silver shoes are yours, and you shall have them to wear." She reached down and picked up the shoes, and after shaking the dust out of them handed them to Dorothy.

"The Witch of the East was proud of those silver shoes," said one of the Munchkins, "and there is some charm connected with them; but what it is we never knew."

Dorothy carried the shoes into the house and placed them on the table. Then she came out again to the Munchkins and said:

"I am anxious to get back to my aunt and uncle, for I am sure they will worry about me. Can you help me find my way?"

The Munchkins and the Witch first looked at one another, and then at Dorothy, and then shook their heads.

"At the East, not far from here," said one, "there is a great desert, and none could live to cross it."

"It is the same at the South," said another, "for I have been there and seen it. The South is the country of the Quadlings."

"I am told," said the third man, "that it is the same at the West. And that country, where the Winkies live, is ruled by the Wicked Witch of the West, who would make you her slave if you passed her way."

"The North is my home," said the old lady, "and at its edge is the same great desert that surrounds this Land of Oz. I'm afraid, my dear, you will have to live with us."

Dorothy began to sob at this, for she felt lonely among all these strange people. Her tears seemed to grieve the kind-hearted Munchkins, for they immediately took out their handkerchiefs and began to weep also. As for the little old woman, she took off her cap and balanced the point on the end of her nose, while she counted "One, two, three" in a solemn voice. At once the cap changed to a slate, on which was written in big, white chalk marks:

"LET DOROTHY GO TO THE CITY OF EMERALDS"

The little old woman took the slate from her nose, and having read the words on it, asked, "Is your name Dorothy, my dear?"

"Yes," answered the child, looking up and drying her tears.

"Then you must go to the City of Emeralds. Perhaps Oz will help you."

"Where is this city?" asked Dorothy.

"It is exactly in the center of the country, and is ruled by Oz, the Great Wizard I told you of."

"Is he a good man?" inquired the girl anxiously.

"He is a good Wizard. Whether he is a man or not I cannot tell, for I have never seen him."

"How can I get there?" asked Dorothy.

"You must walk. It is a long journey, through a country that is sometimes pleasant and sometimes dark and terrible. However, I will use all the magic arts I know of to keep you from harm."

"Won't you go with me?" pleaded the girl, who had begun to look upon the little old woman as her only friend.

"No, I cannot do that," she replied, "but I will give you my kiss, and no one will dare injure a person who has been kissed by the Witch of the North."

She came close to Dorothy and kissed her gently on the forehead. Where her lips touched the girl they left a round, shining mark, as Dorothy found out soon after.

"The road to the City of Emeralds is paved with yellow brick," said the Witch, "so you cannot miss it. When you get to Oz do not be afraid of him, but tell your story and ask him to help you. Good-bye, my dear."

The three Munchkins bowed low to her and wished her a pleasant journey, after which they walked away through the trees. The Witch gave Dorothy a friendly little nod, whirled around on her left heel three times, and straightway disappeared, much to the surprise of little Toto, who barked after her loudly enough when she had gone, because he had been afraid even to growl while she stood by.

But Dorothy, knowing her to be a witch, had expected her to disappear in just that way, and was not surprised in the least.

Chapter 3. How Dorothy Saved the Scarecrow

When Dorothy was left alone she began to feel hungry. So she went to the cupboard and cut herself some bread, which she spread with butter. She gave some to Toto, and taking a pail from the shelf she carried it down to the little brook and filled it with clear, sparkling water. Toto ran over to the trees and began to bark at the birds sitting there. Dorothy went to get him, and saw such delicious fruit hanging from the branches that she gathered some of it, finding it just what she wanted to help out her breakfast.

Then she went back to the house, and having helped herself and Toto to a good drink of the cool, clear water, she set about making ready for the journey to the City of Emeralds.

Dorothy had only one other dress, but that happened to be clean and was hanging on a peg beside her bed. It was gingham, with checks of white and blue; and although the blue was somewhat faded with many washings, it was still a pretty frock. The girl washed herself carefully, dressed herself in the clean gingham, and tied her pink sunbonnet on her head. She took a little basket and filled it with bread from the cupboard, laying a white cloth over the top. Then she looked down at her feet and noticed how old and worn her shoes were.

"They surely will never do for a long journey, Toto," she said. And Toto looked up into her face with his little black eyes and wagged his tail to show he knew what she meant.

At that moment Dorothy saw lying on the table the silver shoes that had belonged to the Witch of the East.

"I wonder if they will fit me," she said to Toto. "They would be just the thing to take a long walk in, for they could not wear out."

She took off her old leather shoes and tried on the silver ones, which fitted her as well as if they had been made for her.

Finally she picked up her basket.

"Come along, Toto," she said. "We will go to the Emerald City and ask the Great Oz how to get back to Kansas again."

She closed the door, locked it, and put the key carefully in the pocket of her dress. And so, with Toto trotting along soberly behind her, she started on her journey.

There were several roads near by, but it did not take her long to find the one paved with yellow bricks. Within a short time she was walking briskly toward the Emerald City, her silver shoes tinkling merrily on the hard, yellow road-bed. The sun shone bright and the birds sang sweetly, and Dorothy did not feel nearly so bad as you might think a little girl would who had been suddenly whisked away from her own country and set down in the midst of a strange land.

She was surprised, as she walked along, to see how pretty the country was about her. There were neat fences at the sides of the road, painted a dainty blue color, and beyond them were fields of grain and vegetables in abundance. Evidently the Munchkins were good farmers and able to raise large crops. Once in a while she would pass a house, and the people came out to look at her and bow low as she went by; for everyone knew she had been the means of destroying the Wicked Witch and setting them free from bondage. The houses of the Munchkins were odd-looking dwellings, for each was round, with a big dome for a roof. All were painted blue, for in this country of the East blue was the favorite color.

Toward evening, when Dorothy was tired with her long walk and began to wonder where she should pass the night, she came to a house rather larger than the rest. On the green lawn before it many men and women were dancing. Five little fiddlers played as loudly as possible, and the people were laughing and singing, while a big table near by was loaded with delicious fruits and nuts, pies and cakes, and many other good things to eat.

The people greeted Dorothy kindly, and invited her to supper and to pass the night with them; for this was the home of one of the richest Munchkins in the land, and his friends were gathered with him to celebrate their freedom from the bondage of the Wicked Witch. Dorothy ate a hearty supper and was waited upon by the rich Munchkin himself, whose name was Boq. Then she sat upon a settee and watched the people dance.

When Boq saw her silver shoes he said, "You must be a great sorceress."

"Why?" asked the girl.

"Because you wear silver shoes and have killed the Wicked Witch. Besides, you have white in your frock, and only witches and sorceresses wear white."

"My dress is blue and white checked," said Dorothy, smoothing out the wrinkles in it.

"It is kind of you to wear that," said Boq. "Blue is the color of the Munchkins, and white is the witch color. So we know you are a friendly witch."

Dorothy did not know what to say to this, for all the people seemed to think her a witch, and she knew very well she was only an ordinary little girl who had come by the chance of a cyclone into a strange land.

When she had tired watching the dancing, Boq led her into the house, where he gave her a room with a pretty bed in it. The sheets were made of blue cloth, and Dorothy slept soundly in them till morning, with Toto curled up on the blue rug beside her.

She ate a hearty breakfast, and watched a wee Munchkin baby, who played with Toto and pulled his tail and crowed and laughed in a way that greatly amused Dorothy. Toto was a fine curiosity to all the people, for they had never seen a dog before.

"How far is it to the Emerald City?" the girl asked.

"I do not know," answered Boq gravely, "for I have never been there. It is better for people to keep away from Oz, unless they have business with him. But it is a long way to the Emerald City, and it will take you many days. The country here is rich and pleasant, but you must pass through rough and dangerous places before you reach the end of your journey."

This worried Dorothy a little, but she knew that only the Great Oz could help her get to Kansas again, so she bravely resolved not to turn back. She bade her friends good-bye, and again started along the road of yellow brick. When she had gone several miles she thought she would stop to rest, and so climbed to the top of the fence beside the road and sat down. There was a great cornfield beyond the fence, and not far away she saw a Scarecrow, placed high on a pole to keep the birds from the ripe corn.

Dorothy leaned her chin upon her hand and gazed thoughtfully at the Scarecrow. Its head was a small sack stuffed with straw, with eyes, nose, and mouth painted on it to represent a face. An old, pointed blue hat, that had belonged to some Munchkin, was perched on his head, and the rest of the figure was a blue suit of clothes, worn and faded, which had also been stuffed with straw. On the feet were some old boots with blue tops, such as every man wore in this country, and the figure was raised above the stalks of corn by means of the pole stuck up its back.

While Dorothy was looking earnestly into the queer, painted face of the Scarecrow, she was surprised to see one of the eyes slowly wink at her. She thought she must have been mistaken at first, for none of the scarecrows in Kansas ever wink; but presently the figure nodded its head to her in a friendly way. Then she climbed down from the fence and walked up to it, while Toto ran around the pole and barked.

"Good day," said the Scarecrow, in a rather husky voice.

"Did you speak?" asked the girl, in wonder.

"Certainly," answered the Scarecrow. "How do you do?"

"I'm pretty well, thank you," replied Dorothy politely. "How do you do?"

"I'm not feeling well," said the Scarecrow, with a smile, "for it is very tedious being perched up here night and day to scare away crows."

"Can't you get down?" asked Dorothy.

"No, for this pole is stuck up my back. If you will please take away the pole I shall be greatly obliged to you."

Dorothy reached up both arms and lifted the figure off the pole, for, being stuffed with straw, it was quite light.

"Thank you very much," said the Scarecrow, when he had been set down on the ground. "I feel like a new man."

Dorothy was puzzled at this, for it sounded queer to hear a stuffed man speak, and to see him bow and walk along beside her.

"Who are you?" asked the Scarecrow when he had stretched himself and yawned. "And where are you going?"

"My name is Dorothy," said the girl, "and I am going to the Emerald City, to ask the Great Oz to send me back to Kansas."

"Where is the Emerald City?" he inquired. "And who is Oz?"

"Why, don't you know?" she returned, in surprise.

"No, indeed. I don't know anything. You see, I am stuffed, so I have no brains at all," he answered sadly.

"Oh," said Dorothy, "I'm awfully sorry for you."

"Do you think," he asked, "if I go to the Emerald City with you, that Oz would give me some brains?"

"I cannot tell," she returned, "but you may come with me, if you like. If Oz will not give you any brains you will be no worse off than you are now."

"That is true," said the Scarecrow. "You see," he continued confidentially, "I don't mind my legs and arms and body being stuffed, because I cannot get hurt. If anyone treads on my toes or sticks a pin into me, it doesn't matter, for I can't feel it. But I do not want people to call me a fool, and if my head stays stuffed with straw instead of with brains, as yours is, how am I ever to know anything?"

"I understand how you feel," said the little girl, who was truly sorry for him. "If you will come with me I'll ask Oz to do all he can for you."

"Thank you," he answered gratefully.

They walked back to the road. Dorothy helped him over the fence, and they started along the path of yellow brick for the Emerald City.

Toto did not like this addition to the party at first. He smelled around the stuffed man as if he suspected there might be a nest of rats in the straw, and he often growled in an unfriendly way at the Scarecrow.

"Don't mind Toto," said Dorothy to her new friend. "He never bites."

"Oh, I'm not afraid," replied the Scarecrow. "He can't hurt the straw. Do let me carry that basket for you. I shall not mind it, for I can't get tired. I'll tell you a secret," he continued, as he walked along. "There is only one thing in the world I am afraid of."

"What is that?" asked Dorothy; "the Munchkin farmer who made you?"

"No," answered the Scarecrow; "it's a lighted match."

Chapter 4. The Road Through the Forest

In this short chapter Dorothy and the Scarecrow tell each other their stories. When Dorothy tells the Scarecrow about Kansas, he wonders why anyone would want go back to such a gray place.

We learn that the Scarecrow was made just two days ago and that he has seen little in his short life. When the farmer first set him in the in field, the Scarecrow effectively fooled the crows. Soon, however, an old crow discovered the Scarecrow for what he was. The old crow told the Scarecrow that brains would make him just as good as a man.

By the time Dorothy and the Scarecrow finish their stories, the road paved in yellow bricks has lead to the edge of a dark forest. They decide to go into the forest because it is the only way to Oz. They spend the night in a small cabin.

Chapter 5. The Rescue of the Tin Woodman

When Dorothy awoke the sun was shining through the trees and Toto had long been out chasing birds around him and squirrels. She sat up and looked around her. Scarecrow, still standing patiently in his corner, was waiting for her.

"We must go and search for water," she said to him.

"Why do you want water?" he asked.

"To wash my face clean after the dust of the road, and to drink, so the dry bread will not stick in my throat."

"It must be inconvenient to be made of flesh," said the Scarecrow thoughtfully, "for you must sleep, and eat and drink. However, you have brains, and it is worth a lot of bother to be able to think properly."

They left the cottage and walked through the trees until they found a little spring of clear water, where Dorothy drank and bathed and ate her breakfast. She saw there was not much bread left in the basket, and the girl was thankful the Scarecrow did not have to eat anything, for there was scarcely enough for herself and Toto for the day.

When she had finished her meal, and was about to go back to the road of yellow brick, she was startled to hear a deep groan near by.

"What was that?" she asked timidly.

"I cannot imagine," replied the Scarecrow; "but we can go and see."

Just then another groan reached their ears, and the sound seemed to come from behind them. They turned and walked through the forest a few steps, when Dorothy discovered something shining in a ray of sunshine that fell between the trees. She ran to the place and then stopped short, with a little cry of surprise.

One of the big trees had been partly chopped through, and standing beside it, with an uplifted axe in his hands, was a man made entirely of tin. His head and arms and legs were jointed upon his body, but he stood perfectly motionless, as if he could not stir at all.

Dorothy looked at him in amazement, and so did the Scarecrow, while Toto barked sharply and made a snap at the tin legs, which hurt his teeth.

"Did you groan?" asked Dorothy.

"Yes," answered the tin man, "I did. I've been groaning for more than a year, and no one has ever heard me before or come to help me."

"What can I do for you?" she inquired softly, for she was moved by the sad voice in which the man spoke.

"Get an oil-can and oil my joints," he answered. "They are rusted so badly that I cannot move them at all; if I am well oiled I shall soon be all right again. You will find an oil-can on a shelf in my cottage."

Dorothy at once ran back to the cottage and found the oil-can, and then she returned and asked anxiously, "Where are your joints?"

"Oil my neck, first," replied the Tin Woodman. So she oiled it, and as it was quite badly rusted the Scarecrow took hold of the tin head and moved it gently from side to side until it worked freely, and then the man could turn it himself.

"Now oil the joints in my arms," he said. And Dorothy oiled them and the Scarecrow bent them carefully until they were quite free from rust and as good as new.

The Tin Woodman gave a sigh of satisfaction and lowered his axe, which he leaned against the tree.

"This is a great comfort," he said. "I have been holding that axe in the air ever since I rusted, and I'm glad to be able to put it down at last. Now, if you will oil the joints of my legs, I shall be all right once more."

So they oiled his legs until he could move them freely; and he thanked them again and again for his release, for he seemed a very polite creature, and very grateful.

"I might have stood there always if you had not come along," he said; "so you have certainly saved my life. How did you happen to be here?"

"We are on our way to the Emerald City to see the Great Oz," she answered, "and we stopped at your cottage to pass the night."

"Why do you wish to see Oz?" he asked.

"I want him to send me back to Kansas, and the Scarecrow wants him to put a few brains into his head," she replied.

The Tin Woodman appeared to think deeply for a moment. Then he said: "Do you suppose Oz could give me a heart?"

"Why, I guess so," Dorothy answered. "It would be as easy as to give the Scarecrow brains."

"True," the Tin Woodman returned. "So, if you will allow me to join your party, I will also go to the Emerald City and ask Oz to help me."

"Come along," said the Scarecrow heartily, and Dorothy added that she would be pleased to have his company. So the Tin Woodman shouldered his axe and they all passed through the forest until they came to the road that was paved with yellow brick.

The Tin Woodman had asked Dorothy to put the oil-can in her basket. "For," he said, "if I should get caught in the rain, and rust again, I would need the oil-can badly."

It was a bit of good luck to have their new comrade join the party, for soon after they had begun their journey again they came to a place where the trees and branches grew so thick over the road that the travelers could not pass. But the Tin Woodman set to work with his axe and chopped so well that soon he cleared a passage for the entire party. Dorothy was thinking so earnestly as they walked along that she did not notice when the Scarecrow stumbled into a hole and rolled over to the side of the road. Indeed he was obliged to call to her to help him up again.

"Why didn't you walk around the hole?" asked the Tin Woodman.

"I don't know enough," replied the Scarecrow cheerfully. "My head is stuffed with straw, you know, and that is why I am going to Oz to ask him for some brains."

"Oh, I see," said the Tin Woodman. "But, after all, brains are not the best things in the world."

"Have you any?" inquired the Scarecrow.

"No, my head is quite empty," answered the Woodman. "But once I had brains, and a heart also; so, having tried them both, I should much rather have a heart."

"And why is that?" asked the Scarecrow.

"I will tell you my story, and then you will know."

So, while they were walking through the forest, the Tin Woodman told the following story:

"I was born the son of a woodman who chopped down trees in the forest and sold the wood for a living. When I grew up, I too became a woodchopper, and after my father died I took care of my old mother as long as she lived. Then I made up my mind that instead of living alone I would marry, so that I might not become lonely.

"There was one of the Munchkin girls who was so beautiful that I soon grew to love her with all my heart. She, on her part, promised to marry me as soon as I could earn enough money to build a better house for her; so I set to work harder than ever. But the girl lived with an old woman who did not want her to marry anyone, for she was so lazy she wished the girl to remain with her and do the cooking and the housework. So the old woman went to the Wicked Witch of the East, and promised her two sheep and a cow if she would prevent the marriage. Thereupon the Wicked Witch enchanted my axe, and when I was chopping away at my best one day, for I was anxious to get the new house and my wife as soon as possible, the axe slipped all at once and cut off my left leg.

"This at first seemed a great misfortune, for I knew a one-legged man could not do very well as a wood-chopper. So I went to a tinsmith and had him make me a new leg out of tin. The leg worked very well, once I was used to it. But my action angered the Wicked Witch of the East, for she had promised the old woman I should not marry the pretty Munchkin girl. When I began chopping again, my axe slipped and cut off my right leg. Again I went to the tinsmith, and again he made me a leg out of tin. After this the enchanted axe cut off my arms, one after the other; but, nothing daunted, I had them replaced with tin ones. The Wicked Witch then made the axe slip and cut off my head, and at first I thought that was the end of me. But the tinsmith happened to come along, and he made me a new head out of tin.

"I thought I had beaten the Wicked Witch then, and I worked harder than ever; but I little knew how cruel my enemy could be. She thought of a new way to kill my love for the beautiful Munchkin maiden, and made my axe slip again, so that it cut right through my body, splitting me into two halves. Once more the tinsmith came to my help and made me a body of tin, fastening my tin arms and legs and head to it, by means of joints, so that I could move around as well as ever. But, alas! I had now no heart, so that I lost all my love for the Munchkin girl, and did not care whether I married her or not. I suppose she is still living with the old woman, waiting for me to come after her.

"My body shone so brightly in the sun that I felt very proud of it and it did not matter now if my axe slipped, for it could not cut me. There was only one danger--that my joints would rust; but I kept an oil-can in my cottage and took care to oil myself whenever I needed it. However, there came a day when I forgot to do this, and, being caught in a rainstorm, before I thought of the danger my joints had rusted, and I was left to stand in the woods until you came to help me. It was a terrible thing to undergo, but during the year I stood there I had time to think that the greatest loss I had known was the loss of my heart. While I was in love I was the happiest man on earth; but no one can love who has not a heart, and so I am resolved to ask Oz to give me one. If he does, I will go back to the Munchkin maiden and marry her."

Both Dorothy and the Scarecrow had been greatly interested in the story of the Tin Woodman, and now they knew why he was so anxious to get a new heart.

"All the same," said the Scarecrow, "I shall ask for brains instead of a heart; for a fool would not know what to do with a heart if he had one."

"I shall take the heart," returned the Tin Woodman; "for brains do not make one happy, and happiness is the best thing in the world."

Dorothy did not say anything, for she was puzzled to know which of her two friends was right, and she decided if she could only get back to Kansas and Aunt Em, it did not matter so much whether the Woodman had no brains and the Scarecrow no heart, or each got what he wanted. What worried her most was that the bread was nearly gone, and another meal for herself and Toto would empty the basket. To be sure neither the

Woodman nor the Scarecrow ever ate anything, but she was not made of tin nor straw, and could not live unless she was fed.

Chapter 6. The Cowardly Lion

All this time Dorothy and her companions had been walking through the thick woods. The road was still paved with yellow brick, but these were much covered by dried branches and dead leaves from the trees, and the walking was not at all good.

There were few birds in this part of the forest, for birds love the open country where there is plenty of sunshine. But now and then there came a deep growl from some wild animal hidden among the trees. These sounds made the little girl's heart beat fast, for she did not know what made them; but Toto knew, and he walked close to Dorothy's side, and did not even bark in return.

"How long will it be," the child asked of the Tin Woodman, "before we are out of the forest?"

"I cannot tell," was the answer, "for I have never been to the Emerald City. But my father went there once, when I was a boy, and he said it was a long journey through a dangerous country, although nearer to the city where Oz dwells the country is beautiful. But I am not afraid so long as I have my oil-can, and nothing can hurt the Scarecrow, while you bear upon your forehead the mark of the Good Witch's kiss, and that will protect you from harm."

"But Toto!" said the girl anxiously. "What will protect him?"

"We must protect him ourselves if he is in danger," replied the Tin Woodman.

Just as he spoke there came from the forest a terrible roar, and the next moment a great Lion bounded into the road. With one blow of his paw he sent the Scarecrow spinning over and over to the edge of the road, and then he struck at the Tin Woodman with his sharp claws. But, to the Lion's surprise, he could make no impression on the tin, although the Woodman fell over in the road and lay still.

Little Toto, now that he had an enemy to face, ran barking toward the Lion, and the great beast had opened his mouth to bite the dog, when Dorothy, fearing Toto would be killed, and heedless of danger, rushed forward and slapped the Lion upon his nose as hard as she could, while she cried out:

"Don't you dare to bite Toto! You ought to be ashamed of yourself, a big beast like you, to bite a poor little dog!"

"I didn't bite him," said the Lion, as he rubbed his nose with his paw where Dorothy had hit it.

"No, but you tried to," she retorted. "You are nothing but a big coward."

"I know it," said the Lion, hanging his head in shame. "I've always known it. But how can I help it?"

"I don't know, I'm sure. To think of your striking a stuffed man, like the poor Scarecrow!"

"Is he stuffed?" asked the Lion in surprise, as he watched her pick up the Scarecrow and set him upon his feet, while she patted him into shape again.

"Of course he's stuffed," replied Dorothy, who was still angry.

"That's why he went over so easily," remarked the Lion. "It astonished me to see him whirl around so. Is the other one stuffed also?"

"No," said Dorothy, "he's made of tin." And she helped the Woodman up again.

"That's why he nearly blunted my claws," said the Lion. "When they scratched against the tin it made a cold shiver run down my back. What is that little animal you are so tender of?"

"He is my dog, Toto," answered Dorothy.

"Is he made of tin, or stuffed?" asked the Lion.

"Neither. He's a--a--a meat dog," said the girl.

"Oh! He's a curious animal and seems remarkably small, now that I look at him. No one would think of biting such a little thing, except a coward like me," continued the Lion sadly.

"What makes you a coward?" asked Dorothy, looking at the great beast in wonder, for he was as big as a small horse.

"It's a mystery," replied the Lion. "I suppose I was born that way. All the other animals in the forest naturally expect me to be brave, for the Lion is everywhere thought to be the King of Beasts. I learned that if I roared very loudly every living thing was frightened and got out of my way. Whenever I've met a man I've been awfully scared; but I just roared at him, and he has always run away as fast as he could go. If the elephants and the tigers and the bears had ever tried to fight me, I should have run myself--I'm such a coward; but just as soon as they hear me roar they all try to get away from me, and of course I let them go."

"But that isn't right. The King of Beasts shouldn't be a coward," said the Scarecrow.

"I know it," returned the Lion, wiping a tear from his eye with the tip of his tail. "It is my great sorrow, and makes my life very unhappy. But whenever there is danger, my heart begins to beat fast."

"Perhaps you have heart disease," said the Tin Woodman.

"It may be," said the Lion.

"If you have," continued the Tin Woodman, "you ought to be glad, for it proves you have a heart. For my part, I have no heart; so I cannot have heart disease."

"Perhaps," said the Lion thoughtfully, "if I had no heart I should not be a coward."

"Have you brains?" asked the Scarecrow.

"I suppose so. I've never looked to see," replied the Lion.

"I am going to the Great Oz to ask him to give me some," remarked the Scarecrow, "for my head is stuffed with straw."

"And I am going to ask him to give me a heart," said the Woodman.

"And I am going to ask him to send Toto and me back to Kansas," added Dorothy.

"Do you think Oz could give me courage?" asked the Cowardly Lion.

"Just as easily as he could give me brains," said the Scarecrow.

"Or give me a heart," said the Tin Woodman.

"Or send me back to Kansas," said Dorothy.

"Then, if you don't mind, I'll go with you," said the Lion, "for my life is simply unbearable without a bit of courage."

"You will be very welcome," answered Dorothy, "for you will help to keep away the other wild beasts. It seems to me they must be more cowardly than you are if they allow you to scare them so easily."

"They really are," said the Lion, "but that doesn't make me any braver, and as long as I know myself to be a coward I shall be unhappy."

So once more the little company set off upon the journey, the Lion walking with stately strides at Dorothy's side. Toto did not approve this new comrade at first, for he could not forget how nearly he had been crushed between the Lion's great jaws. But after a time he became more at ease, and presently Toto and the Cowardly Lion had grown to be good friends.

During the rest of that day there was no other adventure to mar the peace of their journey. Once, indeed, the Tin Woodman stepped upon a beetle that was crawling along the road, and killed the poor little thing. This made the Tin Woodman very unhappy, for he was always careful not to hurt any living creature; and as he walked along he wept several tears of sorrow and regret. These tears ran slowly down his face and over the hinges of his jaw, and there they rusted. When Dorothy presently asked him a question the Tin Woodman could not open his mouth, for his jaws were tightly rusted together. He became greatly frightened at this and made many motions to Dorothy to relieve him, but she could not understand. The Lion was also puzzled to know what was wrong. But the Scarecrow seized the oil-can from Dorothy's basket and oiled the Woodman's jaws, so that after a few moments he could talk as well as before.

"This will serve me a lesson," said he, "to look where I step. For if I should kill another bug or beetle I should surely cry again, and crying rusts my jaws so that I cannot speak."

Thereafter he walked very carefully, with his eyes on the road, and when he saw a tiny ant toiling by he would step over it, so as not to harm it. The Tin Woodman knew very well he had no heart, and therefore he took great care never to be cruel or unkind to anything.

"You people with hearts," he said, "have something to guide you, and need never do wrong; but I have no heart, and so I must be very careful. When Oz gives me a heart of course I needn't mind so much."

Chapter 7. The Journey to the Great Oz

They were obliged to camp out that night under a large tree in the forest, for there were no houses near. The tree made a good, thick covering to protect them from the dew, and the Tin Woodman chopped a great pile of wood with his axe and Dorothy built a splendid fire that warmed her and made her feel less lonely. She and Toto ate the last of their bread, and now she did not know what they would do for breakfast.

"If you wish," said the Lion, "I will go into the forest and kill a deer for you. You can roast it by the fire, since your tastes are so peculiar that you prefer cooked food, and then you will have a very good breakfast."

"Don't! Please don't," begged the Tin Woodman. "I should certainly weep if you killed a poor deer, and then my jaws would rust again."

But the Lion went away into the forest and found his own supper, and no one ever knew what it was, for he didn't mention it. And the Scarecrow found a tree full of nuts and filled Dorothy's basket with them, so that she would not be hungry for a long time. She thought this was very kind and thoughtful of the Scarecrow, but she laughed heartily at the awkward way in which the poor creature picked up the nuts. His padded hands were so clumsy and the nuts were so small that he dropped almost as many as he put in the basket. But the Scarecrow did not mind how long it took him to fill the basket, for it enabled him to keep away from the fire, as he feared a spark might get into his straw and burn him up. So he kept a good distance away from the flames, and only came near to cover Dorothy with dry leaves when she lay down to sleep. These kept her very snug and warm, and she slept soundly until morning.

When it was daylight, the girl bathed her face in a little rippling brook, and soon after they all started toward the Emerald City.

This was to be an eventful day for the travelers. They had hardly been walking an hour when they saw before them a great ditch that crossed the road and divided the forest as far as they could see on either side. It was a very wide ditch, and when they crept up to the edge and looked into it they could see it was also very deep, and there were many big, jagged rocks at the bottom. The sides were so steep that none of them could climb down, and for a moment it seemed that their journey must end.

"What shall we do?" asked Dorothy despairingly.

"I haven't the faintest idea," said the Tin Woodman, and the Lion shook his shaggy mane and looked thoughtful.

But the Scarecrow said, "We cannot fly, that is certain. Neither can we climb down into this great ditch. Therefore, if we cannot jump over it, we must stop where we are."

"I think I could jump over it," said the Cowardly Lion, after measuring the distance carefully in his mind.

"Then we are all right," answered the Scarecrow, "for you can carry us all over on your back, one at a time."

"Well, I'll try it," said the Lion. "Who will go first?"

"I will," declared the Scarecrow, "for, if you found that you could not jump over the gulf, Dorothy would be killed, or the Tin Woodman badly dented on the rocks below. But if I am on your back it will not matter so much, for the fall would not hurt me at all."

"I am terribly afraid of falling, myself," said the Cowardly Lion, "but I suppose there is nothing to do but try it. So get on my back and we will make the attempt."

The Scarecrow sat upon the Lion's back, and the big beast walked to the edge of the gulf and crouched down.

"Why don't you run and jump?" asked the Scarecrow.

"Because that isn't the way we Lions do these things," he replied. Then giving a great spring, he shot through the air and landed safely on the other side. They were all greatly pleased to see how easily he did it, and after the Scarecrow had got down from his back the Lion sprang across the ditch again.

Dorothy thought she would go next; so she took Toto in her arms and climbed on the Lion's back, holding tightly to his mane with one hand. The next moment it seemed as if she were flying through the air; and then, before she had time to think about it, she was safe on the other side. The Lion went back a third time and got the Tin Woodman, and then they all sat down for a few moments to give the beast a chance to rest, for his great leaps had made his breath short, and he panted like a big dog that has been running too long.

They found the forest very thick on this side, and it looked dark and gloomy. After the Lion had rested they started along the road of yellow brick, silently wondering, each in his own mind, if ever they would come to the end of the woods and reach the bright sunshine again. To add to their discomfort, they soon heard strange noises in the depths of the forest, and the Lion whispered to them that it was in this part of the country that the Kalidahs lived.

"What are the Kalidahs?" asked the girl.

"They are monstrous beasts with bodies like bears and heads like tigers," replied the Lion, "and with claws so long and sharp that they could tear me in two as easily as I could kill Toto. I'm terribly afraid of the Kalidahs."

"I'm not surprised that you are," returned Dorothy. "They must be dreadful beasts."

The Lion was about to reply when suddenly they came to another gulf across the road. But this one was so broad and deep that the Lion knew at once he could not leap across it.

So they sat down to consider what they should do, and after serious thought the Scarecrow said:

"Here is a great tree, standing close to the ditch. If the Tin Woodman can chop it down, so that it will fall to the other side, we can walk across it easily."

"That is a first-rate idea," said the Lion. "One would almost suspect you had brains in your head, instead of straw."

The Woodman set to work at once, and so sharp was his axe that the tree was soon chopped nearly through. Then the Lion put his strong front legs against the tree and pushed with all his might, and slowly the big tree tipped and fell with a crash across the ditch, with its top branches on the other side.

They had just started to cross this queer bridge when a sharp growl made them all look up, and to their horror they saw running toward them two great beasts with bodies like bears and heads like tigers.

"They are the Kalidahs!" said the Cowardly Lion, beginning to tremble.

"Quick!" cried the Scarecrow. "Let us cross over."

So Dorothy went first, holding Toto in her arms, the Tin Woodman followed, and the Scarecrow came next. The Lion, although he was certainly afraid, turned to face the Kalidahs, and then he gave so loud and terrible a roar that Dorothy screamed and the Scarecrow fell over backward, while even the fierce beasts stopped short and looked at him in surprise.

But, seeing they were bigger than the Lion, and remembering that there were two of them and only one of him, the Kalidahs again rushed forward, and the Lion crossed over the tree and turned to see what they would do next. Without stopping an instant the fierce beasts also began to cross the tree. And the Lion said to Dorothy:

"We are lost, for they will surely tear us to pieces with their sharp claws.

But stand close behind me, and I will fight them as long as I am alive."

"Wait a minute!" called the Scarecrow. He had been thinking what was best to be done, and now he asked the Woodman to chop away the end of the tree that rested on their side of the ditch. The Tin Woodman began to use his axe at once, and, just as the two Kalidahs were nearly across, the tree fell with a crash into the gulf, carrying the ugly, snarling brutes with it, and both were dashed to pieces on the sharp rocks at the bottom.

"Well," said the Cowardly Lion, drawing a long breath of relief, "I see we are going to live a little while longer, and I am glad of it, for it must be a very uncomfortable thing not to be alive. Those creatures frightened me so badly that my heart is beating yet."

"Ah," said the Tin Woodman sadly, "I wish I had a heart to beat."

This adventure made the travelers more anxious than ever to get out of the forest, and they walked so fast that Dorothy became tired, and had to ride on the Lion's back. To their great joy the trees became thinner the farther they advanced, and in the afternoon they suddenly came upon a broad river, flowing swiftly just before them. On the other side of the water they could see the road of yellow brick running through a beautiful country, with green meadows dotted with bright flowers and all the road bordered with trees hanging full of delicious fruits. They were greatly pleased to see this delightful country before them.

"How shall we cross the river?" asked Dorothy.

"That is easily done," replied the Scarecrow. "The Tin Woodman must build us a raft, so we can float to the other side."

So the Woodman took his axe and began to chop down small trees to make a raft, and while he was busy at this the Scarecrow found on the riverbank a tree full of fine fruit. This pleased Dorothy, who had eaten nothing but nuts all day, and she made a hearty meal of the ripe fruit.

But it takes time to make a raft, even when one is as industrious and untiring as the Tin Woodman, and when night came the work was not done. So they found a cozy place under the trees where they slept well until the morning; and Dorothy dreamed of the Emerald City, and of the good Wizard Oz, who would soon send her back to her own home again.

Chapter 8. The Deadly Poppy Field

The next morning, in the eighth chapter, the raft is completed. But the strong current soon sweeps the raft far away from the Yellow Brick Road. In an effort to bring the raft to the far bank, the Scarecrow pushes the pole that he is using as a propulsive instrument so deep into the river bottom that it sticks fast. The pole and the Scarecrow soon are left far behind by the raft as a result of the strong current.

The Cowardly Lion jumps into the river. The Tin Woodman grabs hold of the Lion's tail. The two get the raft to shore. The travelers walk back along the river bank until they can see the Scarecrow perched on his pole in the middle of the river. A Stork comes to the rescue and carries the Scarecrow back to his comrades.

Before the travelers can get back to the Yellow Brick Road, they enter a field of poppies. The poppies cause Dorothy, Toto, and the Cowardly Lion to fall asleep. The Scarecrow and the Tin Woodman realize the need to pull their three comrades out of the poppy field. They pick up Dorothy and Toto and carry them out of the field. But the Lion is too big and heavy to be carried. So he is left sleeping among the poppies.

Chapter 9. The Queen of the Field Mice

In the ninth chapter, the Tin Woodman is beyond the poppy field, but short of the Yellow Brick Road. He discovers a field mouse being pursued by a ravenous wildcat. To save the mouse, he beheads the wildcat with his ax. He then discovers that the mouse whose life he just has saved is the Queen of the Field Mice. The Queen's subjects find out what has happened, and one of them asks how the mice can repay the Tin Woodman. The Woodman can't think of anything.

The Scarecrow suggests that the Field Mice rescue the Cowardly Lion from the poppy field. At the Scarecrow's suggestion, the Tin Woodman cuts down several nearby trees and makes a truck out of them, complete with wheels. Thousands of Field Mice attach strings to the truck and pull the truck into the poppy field. The Scarecrow and the Tin Woodman help load the Lion onto the truck. The mice pull the truck, Lion and all, out of the poppy field. During this time, Dorothy and Toto wake up and find out that they are no longer among the poppies.

Chapter 10. The Guardian of the Gates

In the tenth chapter, the Cowardly Lion awakes and finds that he has been pulled out of the deadly poppy field. The travelers resume their quest for the Yellow Brick Road. It isn't long before they find and follow it all the way to the gates of the Emerald City.

Along the way, the travelers have to make an overnight stop at a farmhouse. Their host tells them that the Wizard never permits anyone to see him face to face. The Wizard in fact takes on whatever form he pleases. So no one knows what the Wizard's natural form is.

This doesn't deter Dorothy or her companions. The next morning, they resume their trip and arrive at the Emerald City. There, the Guardian of the Gate puts spectacles with green lenses on them so the splendor of the city won't blind them. After that, he leads them into the Emerald City proper.

Chapter 11. The Wonderful City of Oz

Even with eyes protected by the green spectacles, Dorothy and her friends were at first dazzled by the brilliancy of the wonderful City. The streets were lined with beautiful houses all built of green marble and studded everywhere with sparkling emeralds. They walked over a pavement of the same green marble, and where the blocks were joined together were rows of emeralds, set closely, and glittering in the brightness of the sun. The window panes were of green glass; even the sky above the City had a green tint, and the rays of the sun were green. There were many people--men, women, and children--walking about, and these were all dressed in green clothes and had greenish skins. They looked at Dorothy and her strangely assorted company with wondering eyes, and the children all ran away and hid behind their mothers when they saw the Lion; but no one spoke to them. Many shops stood in the street, and Dorothy saw that everything in them was green. Green candy and green pop corn were offered for sale, as well as green shoes, green hats, and green clothes of all sorts. At one place a man was selling green lemonade, and when the children bought it Dorothy could see that they paid for it with green pennies.

There seemed to be no horses nor animals of any kind; the men carried things around in little green carts, which they pushed before them. Everyone seemed happy and contented and prosperous.

The Guardian of the Gates led them through the streets until they came to a big building, exactly in the middle of the City, which was the Palace of Oz, the Great Wizard. There was a soldier before the door, dressed in a green uniform and wearing a long green beard.

"Here are strangers," said the Guardian of the Gates to him, "and they demand to see the Great Oz."

"Step inside," answered the soldier, "and I will carry your message to him."

So they passed through the Palace Gates and were led into a big room with a green carpet and lovely green furniture set with emeralds. The soldier made them all wipe their feet upon a green mat before entering this room, and when they were seated he said politely:

"Please make yourselves comfortable while I go to the door of the Throne Room and tell Oz you are here."

They had to wait a long time before the soldier returned. When, at last, he came back, Dorothy asked:

"Have you seen Oz?"

"Oh, no," returned the soldier; "I have never seen him. But I spoke to him as he sat behind his screen and gave him your message. He said he will grant you an audience, if you so desire; but each one of you must enter his presence alone, and he will admit but one each day. Therefore, as you must remain in the Palace for several days, I will have you shown to rooms where you may rest in comfort after your journey."

"Thank you," replied the girl; "that is very kind of Oz."

The soldier now blew upon a green whistle, and at once a young girl, dressed in a pretty green silk gown, entered the room. She had lovely green hair and green eyes, and she bowed low before Dorothy as she said, "Follow me and I will show you your room."

So Dorothy said good-bye to all her friends except Toto, and taking the dog in her arms followed the green girl through seven passages and up three flights of stairs until they came to a room at the front of the Palace. It was the sweetest little room in the world, with a soft comfortable bed that had sheets of green silk and a green velvet counterpane. There was a tiny fountain in the middle of the room, that shot a spray of green perfume into the air, to fall back into a beautifully carved green marble basin. Beautiful green flowers stood in the windows, and there was a shelf with a row of little green books. When Dorothy had time to open these books she found them full of queer green pictures that made her laugh, they were so funny.

In a wardrobe were many green dresses, made of silk and satin and velvet; and all of them fitted Dorothy exactly.

"Make yourself perfectly at home," said the green girl, "and if you wish for anything ring the bell. Oz will send for you tomorrow morning."

She left Dorothy alone and went back to the others. These she also led to rooms, and each one of them found himself lodged in a very pleasant part of the Palace. Of course this politeness was wasted on the Scarecrow; for when he found himself alone in his room he stood stupidly in one spot, just within the doorway, to wait till morning. It would not rest him to lie down, and he could not close his eyes; so he remained all night staring at a little spider which was weaving its web in a corner of the room, just as if it were not one of the most wonderful rooms in the world. The Tin Woodman lay down on his bed from force of habit, for he remembered when he was made of flesh; but not being able to sleep, he passed the night moving his joints up and down to make sure they kept in good working order. The Lion would have preferred a bed of dried leaves in the forest, and did not like being shut up in a room;

but he had too much sense to let this worry him, so he sprang upon the bed and rolled himself up like a cat and purred himself asleep in a minute.

The next morning, after breakfast, the green maiden came to fetch Dorothy, and she dressed her in one of the prettiest gowns, made of green brocaded satin. Dorothy put on a green silk apron and tied a green ribbon around Toto's neck, and they started for the Throne Room of the Great Oz.

First they came to a great hall in which were many ladies and gentlemen of the court, all dressed in rich costumes. These people had nothing to do but talk to each other, but they always came to wait outside the Throne Room every morning, although they were never permitted to see Oz. As Dorothy entered they looked at her curiously, and one of them whispered:

"Are you really going to look upon the face of Oz the Terrible?"

"Of course," answered the girl, "if he will see me."

"Oh, he will see you," said the soldier who had taken her message to the Wizard, "although he does not like to have people ask to see him. Indeed, at first he was angry and said I should send you back where you came from. Then he asked me what you looked like, and when I mentioned your silver shoes he was very much interested. At last I told him about the mark upon your forehead, and he decided he would admit you to his presence."

Just then a bell rang, and the green girl said to Dorothy, "That is the signal. You must go into the Throne Room alone."

She opened a little door and Dorothy walked boldly through and found herself in a wonderful place. It was a big, round room with a high arched roof, and the walls and ceiling and floor were covered with large emeralds set closely together. In the center of the roof was a great light, as bright as the sun, which made the emeralds sparkle in a wonderful manner.

But what interested Dorothy most was the big throne of green marble that stood in the middle of the room. It was shaped like a chair and sparkled with gems, as did everything else. In the center of the chair was an enormous Head, without a body to support it or any arms or legs whatever. There was no hair upon this head, but it had eyes and a nose and mouth, and was much bigger than the head of the biggest giant.

As Dorothy gazed upon this in wonder and fear, the eyes turned slowly and looked at her sharply and steadily. Then the mouth moved, and Dorothy heard a voice say:

"I am Oz, the Great and Terrible. Who are you, and why do you seek me?"

It was not such an awful voice as she had expected to come from the big Head; so she took courage and answered:

"I am Dorothy, the Small and Meek. I have come to you for help."

The eyes looked at her thoughtfully for a full minute. Then said the voice:

"Where did you get the silver shoes?"

"I got them from the Wicked Witch of the East, when my house fell on her and killed her," she replied.

"Where did you get the mark upon your forehead?" continued the voice.

"That is where the Good Witch of the North kissed me when she bade me good-bye and sent me to you," said the girl.

Again the eyes looked at her sharply, and they saw she was telling the truth. Then Oz asked, "What do you wish me to do?"

"Send me back to Kansas, where my Aunt Em and Uncle Henry are," she answered earnestly. "I don't like your country, although it is so beautiful. And I am sure Aunt Em will be dreadfully worried over my being away so long."

The eyes winked three times, and then they turned up to the ceiling and down to the floor and rolled around so queerly that they seemed to see every part of the room. And at last they looked at Dorothy again.

"Why should I do this for you?" asked Oz.

"Because you are strong and I am weak; because you are a Great Wizard and I am only a little girl."

"But you were strong enough to kill the Wicked Witch of the East," said Oz.

"That just happened," returned Dorothy simply; "I could not help it."

"Well," said the Head, "I will give you my answer. You have no right to expect me to send you back to Kansas unless you do something for me in return. In this country everyone must pay for everything he gets. If you wish me to use my magic power to send you home again you must do something for me first. Help me and I will help you."

"What must I do?" asked the girl.

"Kill the Wicked Witch of the West," answered Oz.

"But I cannot!" exclaimed Dorothy, greatly surprised.

"You killed the Witch of the East and you wear the silver shoes, which bear a powerful charm. There is now but one Wicked Witch left in all this land, and when you can tell me she is dead I will send you back to Kansas--but not before."

The little girl began to weep, she was so much disappointed; and the eyes winked again and looked upon her anxiously, as if the Great Oz felt that she could help him if she would.

"I never killed anything, willingly," she sobbed. "Even if I wanted to, how could I kill the Wicked Witch? If you, who are Great and Terrible, cannot kill her yourself, how do you expect me to do it?"

"I do not know," said the Head; "but that is my answer, and until the Wicked Witch dies you will not see your uncle and aunt again. Remember that the Witch is Wicked--tremendously Wicked--and ought to be killed. Now go, and do not ask to see me again until you have done your task."

Sorrowfully Dorothy left the Throne Room and went back where the Lion and the Scarecrow and the Tin Woodman were waiting to hear what Oz had said to her. "There is no hope for me," she said sadly, "for Oz will not send me home until I have killed the Wicked Witch of the West; and that I can never do."

Her friends were sorry, but could do nothing to help her; so Dorothy went to her own room and lay down on the bed and cried herself to sleep. The next morning the soldier with the green whiskers came to the Scarecrow and said:

"Come with me, for Oz has sent for you."

So the Scarecrow followed him and was admitted into the great Throne Room, where he saw, sitting in the emerald throne, a most lovely Lady. She was dressed in green silk gauze and wore upon her flowing green locks a crown of jewels. Growing from her shoulders were wings, gorgeous in color and so light that they fluttered if the slightest breath of air reached them.

When the Scarecrow had bowed, as prettily as his straw stuffing would let him, before this beautiful creature, she looked upon him sweetly, and said:

"I am Oz, the Great and Terrible. Who are you, and why do you seek me?"

Now the Scarecrow, who had expected to see the great Head Dorothy had told him of, was much astonished; but he answered her bravely.

"I am only a Scarecrow, stuffed with straw. Therefore I have no brains, and I come to you praying that you will put brains in my head instead of straw, so that I may become as much a man as any other in your dominions."

"Why should I do this for you?" asked the Lady.

"Because you are wise and powerful, and no one else can help me," answered the Scarecrow.

"I never grant favors without some return," said Oz; "but this much I will promise. If you will kill for me the Wicked Witch of the West, I will bestow upon you a great many brains, and such good brains that you will be the wisest man in all the Land of Oz."

"I thought you asked Dorothy to kill the Witch," said the Scarecrow, in surprise.

"So I did. I don't care who kills her. But until she is dead I will not grant your wish. Now go, and do not seek me again until you have earned the brains you so greatly desire."

The Scarecrow went sorrowfully back to his friends and told them what Oz had said; and Dorothy was surprised to find that the Great Wizard was not a Head, as she had seen him, but a lovely Lady.

"All the same," said the Scarecrow, "she needs a heart as much as the Tin Woodman."

On the next morning the soldier with the green whiskers came to the Tin Woodman and said:

"Oz has sent for you. Follow me."

So the Tin Woodman followed him and came to the great Throne Room. He did not know whether he would find Oz a lovely Lady or a Head, but he hoped it would be the lovely Lady. "For," he said to himself, "if it is the head, I am sure I shall not be given a heart, since a head has no heart of its own and therefore cannot feel for me. But if it is the lovely Lady I shall beg hard for a heart, for all ladies are themselves said to be kindly hearted."

But when the Woodman entered the great Throne Room he saw neither the Head nor the Lady, for Oz had taken the shape of a most terrible Beast. It was nearly as big as an elephant, and the green throne seemed hardly strong enough to hold its weight. The Beast had a head like that of a rhinoceros, only there were five eyes in its face. There were five long arms growing out of its body, and it also had five long, slim legs. Thick, woolly hair covered every part of it, and a more dreadful-looking monster could not be imagined. It was fortunate the Tin Woodman had no heart at that moment, for it would have beat loud and fast from terror. But being only tin, the Woodman was not at all afraid, although he was much disappointed.

"I am Oz, the Great and Terrible," spoke the Beast, in a voice that was one great roar. "Who are you, and why do you seek me?"

"I am a Woodman, and made of tin. Therefore I have no heart, and cannot love. I pray you to give me a heart that I may be as other men are."

"Why should I do this?" demanded the Beast.

"Because I ask it, and you alone can grant my request," answered the Woodman.

Oz gave a low growl at this, but said, gruffly: "If you indeed desire a heart, you must earn it."

"How?" asked the Woodman.

"Help Dorothy to kill the Wicked Witch of the West," replied the Beast.

"When the Witch is dead, come to me, and I will then give you the biggest and kindest and most loving heart in all the Land of Oz."

So the Tin Woodman was forced to return sorrowfully to his friends and tell them of the terrible Beast he had seen. They all wondered greatly at the many forms the Great Wizard could take upon himself, and the Lion said:

"If he is a Beast when I go to see him, I shall roar my loudest, and so frighten him that he will grant all I ask. And if he is the lovely Lady, I shall pretend to spring upon her, and so compel her to do my bidding. And if he is the great Head, he will be at my mercy; for I will roll this head all about the room until he promises to give us what we desire. So be of good cheer, my friends, for all will yet be well."

The next morning the soldier with the green whiskers led the Lion to the great Throne Room and bade him enter the presence of Oz.

The Lion at once passed through the door, and glancing around saw, to his surprise, that before the throne was a Ball of Fire, so fierce and glowing he could scarcely bear to gaze upon it. His first thought was that Oz had by accident caught on fire and was burning up; but when he tried to go nearer, the heat was so intense that it singed his whiskers, and he crept back tremblingly to a spot nearer the door.

Then a low, quiet voice came from the Ball of Fire, and these were the words it spoke:

"I am Oz, the Great and Terrible. Who are you, and why do you seek me?"

And the Lion answered, "I am a Cowardly Lion, afraid of everything. I came to you to beg that you give me courage, so that in reality I may become the King of Beasts, as men call me."

"Why should I give you courage?" demanded Oz.

"Because of all Wizards you are the greatest, and alone have power to grant my request," answered the Lion.

The Ball of Fire burned fiercely for a time, and the voice said, "Bring me proof that the Wicked Witch is dead, and that moment I will give you courage. But as long as the Witch lives, you must remain a coward."

The Lion was angry at this speech, but could say nothing in reply, and while he stood silently gazing at the Ball of Fire it became so furiously hot that he turned tail and rushed from the room. He was glad to find his friends waiting for him, and told them of his terrible interview with the Wizard.

"What shall we do now?" asked Dorothy sadly.

"There is only one thing we can do," returned the Lion, "and that is to go to the land of the Winkies, seek out the Wicked Witch, and destroy her."

"But suppose we cannot?" said the girl.

"Then I shall never have courage," declared the Lion.

"And I shall never have brains," added the Scarecrow.

"And I shall never have a heart," spoke the Tin Woodman.

"And I shall never see Aunt Em and Uncle Henry," said Dorothy, beginning to cry.

"Be careful!" cried the green girl. "The tears will fall on your green silk gown and spot it."

So Dorothy dried her eyes and said, "I suppose we must try it; but I am sure I do not want to kill anybody, even to see Aunt Em again."

"I will go with you; but I'm too much of a coward to kill the Witch," said the Lion.

"I will go too," declared the Scarecrow; "but I shall not be of much help to you, I am such a fool."

"I haven't the heart to harm even a Witch," remarked the Tin Woodman;

"but if you go I certainly shall go with you."

Therefore it was decided to start upon their journey the next morning, and the Woodman sharpened his axe on a green grindstone and had all his joints properly oiled. The Scarecrow stuffed himself with fresh straw and Dorothy put new paint on his eyes that he might see better. The green girl, who was very kind to them, filled Dorothy's basket with good things to eat, and fastened a little bell around Toto's neck with a green ribbon.

They went to bed quite early and slept soundly until daylight, when they were awakened by the crowing of a green cock that lived in the back yard of the Palace, and the cackling of a hen that had laid a green egg.

Chapter 12. The Search for the Wicked Witch

The soldier with the green whiskers led them through the streets of the Emerald City until they reached the room where the Guardian of the Gates lived. This officer unlocked their spectacles to put them back in his great box, and then he politely opened the gate for our friends.

"Which road leads to the Wicked Witch of the West?" asked Dorothy.

"There is no road," answered the Guardian of the Gates. "No one ever wishes to go that way."

"How, then, are we to find her?" inquired the girl.

"That will be easy," replied the man, "for when she knows you are in the country of the Winkies she will find you, and make you all her slaves."

"Perhaps not," said the Scarecrow, "for we mean to destroy her."

"Oh, that is different," said the Guardian of the Gates. "No one has ever destroyed her before, so I naturally thought she would make slaves of you, as she has of the rest. But take care; for she is wicked and fierce, and may not allow you to destroy her. Keep to the West, where the sun sets, and you cannot fail to find her."

They thanked him and bade him good-bye, and turned toward the West, walking over fields of soft grass dotted here and there with daisies and buttercups. Dorothy still wore the pretty silk dress she had put on in the palace, but now, to her surprise, she found it was no longer green, but pure white. The ribbon around Toto's neck had also lost its green color and was as white as Dorothy's dress.

The Emerald City was soon left far behind. As they advanced the ground became rougher and hillier, for there were no farms nor houses in this country of the West, and the ground was untilled.

In the afternoon the sun shone hot in their faces, for there were no trees to offer them shade; so that before night Dorothy and Toto and the Lion were tired, and lay down upon the grass and fell asleep, with the Woodman and the Scarecrow keeping watch.

Now the Wicked Witch of the West had but one eye, yet that was as powerful as a telescope, and could see everywhere. So, as she sat in the door of her castle, she happened to look around and saw Dorothy lying asleep, with her friends all about her. They were a long distance off, but the Wicked Witch was angry to find them in her country; so she blew upon a silver whistle that hung around her neck.

At once there came running to her from all directions a pack of great wolves. They had long legs and fierce eyes and sharp teeth.

"Go to those people," said the Witch, "and tear them to pieces."

"Are you not going to make them your slaves?" asked the leader of the wolves.

"No," she answered, "one is of tin, and one of straw; one is a girl and another a Lion. None of them is fit to work, so you may tear them into small pieces."

"Very well," said the wolf, and he dashed away at full speed, followed by the others.

It was lucky the Scarecrow and the Woodman were wide awake and heard the wolves coming.

"This is my fight," said the Woodman, "so get behind me and I will meet them as they come."

He seized his axe, which he had made very sharp, and as the leader of the wolves came on the Tin Woodman swung his arm and chopped the wolf's head from its body, so that it immediately died. As soon as he could raise his axe another wolf came up, and he also fell under the sharp edge of the Tin Woodman's weapon. There were forty wolves, and forty times a wolf was killed, so that at last they all lay dead in a heap before the Woodman.

Then he put down his axe and sat beside the Scarecrow, who said, "It was a good fight, friend."

They waited until Dorothy awoke the next morning. The little girl was quite frightened when she saw the great pile of shaggy wolves, but the Tin Woodman told her all. She thanked him for saving them and sat down to breakfast, after which they started again upon their journey.

Now this same morning the Wicked Witch came to the door of her castle and looked out with her one eye that could see far off. She saw all her wolves lying dead, and the strangers still traveling through her country. This made her angrier than before, and she blew her silver whistle twice. Straightway a great flock of wild crows came flying toward her, enough to darken the sky.

And the Wicked Witch said to the King Crow, "Fly at once to the strangers; peck out their eyes and tear them to pieces."

The wild crows flew in one great flock toward Dorothy and her companions. When the little girl saw them coming she was afraid. But the Scarecrow said, "This is my battle, so lie down beside me and you will not be harmed."

So they all lay upon the ground except the Scarecrow, and he stood up and stretched out his arms. And when the crows saw him they were frightened, as these birds always are by scarecrows, and did not dare to come any nearer. But the King Crow said:

"It is only a stuffed man. I will peck his eyes out."

The King Crow flew at the Scarecrow, who caught it by the head and twisted its neck until it died. And then another crow flew at him, and the Scarecrow twisted its neck also. There were forty crows, and forty times the Scarecrow twisted a neck, until at last all were lying dead beside him. Then he called to his companions to rise, and again they went upon their journey.

When the Wicked Witch looked out again and saw all her crows lying in a heap, she got into a terrible rage, and blew three times upon her silver whistle.

Forthwith there was heard a great buzzing in the air, and a swarm of black bees came flying toward her.

"Go to the strangers and sting them to death!" commanded the Witch, and the bees turned and flew rapidly until they came to where Dorothy and her friends were walking. But the Woodman had seen them coming, and the Scarecrow had decided what to do.

"Take out my straw and scatter it over the little girl and the dog and the Lion," he said to the Woodman, "and the bees cannot sting them." This the Woodman did, and as Dorothy lay close beside the Lion and held Toto in her arms, the straw covered them entirely.

The bees came and found no one but the Woodman to sting, so they flew at him and broke off all their stings against the tin, without hurting the Woodman at all. And as bees cannot live when their stings are broken that was the end of the black bees, and they lay scattered thick about the Woodman, like little heaps of fine coal.

Then Dorothy and the Lion got up, and the girl helped the Tin Woodman put the straw back into the Scarecrow again, until he was as good as ever. So they started upon their journey once more.

The Wicked Witch was so angry when she saw her black bees in little heaps like fine coal that she stamped her foot and tore her hair and gnashed her teeth. And then she called a dozen of her slaves, who were the Winkies, and gave them sharp spears, telling them to go to the strangers and destroy them.

The Winkies were not a brave people, but they had to do as they were told. So they marched away until they came near to Dorothy. Then the Lion gave a great roar and sprang towards them, and the poor Winkies were so frightened that they ran back as fast as they could.

When they returned to the castle the Wicked Witch beat them well with a strap, and sent them back to their work, after which she sat down to think what she should do next. She could not understand how all her plans to destroy these strangers had failed; but she was a powerful Witch, as well as a wicked one, and she soon made up her mind how to act.

There was, in her cupboard, a Golden Cap, with a circle of diamonds and rubies running round it. This Golden Cap had a charm. Whoever owned it could call three times upon the Winged Monkeys, who would obey any order they were given. But no person could command these strange creatures more than three times. Twice already the Wicked Witch had used the charm of the Cap. Once was when she had made the Winkies her slaves, and set herself to rule over their country. The Winged Monkeys had helped her do this. The second time was when she had fought against the Great Oz himself, and driven him out of the land of the West. The Winged Monkeys had also helped her in doing this. Only once more could she use this Golden Cap, for which reason she did not like to do so until all her other powers were exhausted. But now that her fierce wolves and her wild crows and her stinging bees were gone, and her slaves had been scared away by the Cowardly Lion, she saw there was only one way left to destroy Dorothy and her friends.

So the Wicked Witch took the Golden Cap from her cupboard and placed it upon her head. Then she stood upon her left foot and said slowly:

"Ep-pe, pep-pe, kak-ke!"

Next she stood upon her right foot and said:

"Hil-lo, hol-lo, hel-lo!"

After this she stood upon both feet and cried in a loud voice:

"Ziz-zy, zuz-zy, zik!"

Now the charm began to work. The sky was darkened, and a low rumbling sound was heard in the air. There was a rushing of many wings, a great chattering and laughing, and the sun came out of the dark sky to show the Wicked Witch surrounded by a crowd of monkeys, each with a pair of immense and powerful wings on his shoulders.

One, much bigger than the others, seemed to be their leader. He flew close to the Witch and said, "You have called us for the third and last time. What do you command?"

"Go to the strangers who are within my land and destroy them all except the Lion," said the Wicked Witch. "Bring that beast to me, for I have a mind to harness him like a horse, and make him work."

"Your commands shall be obeyed," said the leader. Then, with a great deal of chattering and noise, the Winged Monkeys flew away to the place where Dorothy and her friends were walking.

Some of the Monkeys seized the Tin Woodman and carried him through the air until they were over a country thickly covered with sharp rocks. Here they dropped the poor Woodman, who fell a great distance to the rocks, where he lay so battered and dented that he could neither move nor groan.

Others of the Monkeys caught the Scarecrow, and with their long fingers pulled all of the straw out of his clothes and head. They made his hat and boots and clothes into a small bundle and threw it into the top branches of a tall tree.

The remaining Monkeys threw pieces of stout rope around the Lion and wound many coils about his body and head and legs, until he was unable to bite or scratch or struggle in any way. Then they lifted him up and flew away with him to the Witch's castle, where he was placed in a small yard with a high iron fence around it, so that he could not escape.

But Dorothy they did not harm at all. She stood, with Toto in her arms, watching the sad fate of her comrades and thinking it would soon be her turn. The leader of the Winged Monkeys flew up to her, his long, hairy arms stretched out and his ugly face grinning terribly; but he saw the mark of the Good Witch's kiss upon her forehead and stopped short, motioning the others not to touch her.

"We dare not harm this little girl," he said to them, "for she is protected by the Power of Good, and that is greater than the Power of Evil. All we can do is to carry her to the castle of the Wicked Witch and leave her there."

So, carefully and gently, they lifted Dorothy in their arms and carried her swiftly through the air until they came to the castle, where they set her down upon the front doorstep. Then the leader said to the Witch:

"We have obeyed you as far as we were able. The Tin Woodman and the Scarecrow are destroyed, and the Lion is tied up in your yard. The little girl we dare not harm, nor the dog she carries in her arms. Your power over our band is now ended, and you will never see us again."

Then all the Winged Monkeys, with much laughing and chattering and noise, flew into the air and were soon out of sight.

The Wicked Witch was both surprised and worried when she saw the mark on Dorothy's forehead, for she knew well that neither the Winged Monkeys nor she, herself, dare hurt the girl in any way. She looked down at Dorothy's feet, and seeing the Silver Shoes, began to tremble with fear, for she knew what a powerful charm belonged to them. At first the Witch was tempted to run away from Dorothy; but she happened to look into the child's eyes and saw how simple the soul behind them was, and that the little girl did not know of the wonderful power the Silver Shoes gave her. So the Wicked Witch laughed to herself, and thought, "I can still make her my slave, for she does not know how to use her power." Then she said to Dorothy, harshly and severely:

"Come with me; and see that you mind everything I tell you, for if you do not I will make an end of you, as I did of the Tin Woodman and the Scarecrow."

Dorothy followed her through many of the beautiful rooms in her castle until they came to the kitchen, where the Witch bade her clean the pots and kettles and sweep the floor and keep the fire fed with wood.

Dorothy went to work meekly, with her mind made up to work as hard as she could; for she was glad the Wicked Witch had decided not to kill her. With Dorothy hard at work, the Witch thought she would go into the courtyard and harness the Cowardly Lion like a horse; it would amuse her, she was sure, to make him draw her chariot whenever she wished to go to drive. But as she opened the gate the Lion gave a loud roar and bounded at her so fiercely that the Witch was afraid, and ran out and shut the gate again.

"If I cannot harness you," said the Witch to the Lion, speaking through the bars of the gate, "I can starve you. You shall have nothing to eat until you do as I wish."

So after that she took no food to the imprisoned Lion; but every day she came to the gate at noon and asked, "Are you ready to be harnessed like a horse?"

And the Lion would answer, "No. If you come in this yard, I will bite you."

The reason the Lion did not have to do as the Witch wished was that every night, while the woman was asleep, Dorothy carried him food from the cupboard. After he had eaten he would lie down on his bed of straw, and Dorothy would lie beside him and put her head on his soft, shaggy mane, while they talked of their troubles and tried to plan some way to escape. But they could find no way to get out of the castle, for it was constantly guarded by the yellow Winkies, who were the slaves of the Wicked Witch and too afraid of her not to do as she told them.

The girl had to work hard during the day, and often the Witch threatened to beat her with the same old umbrella she always carried in her hand. But, in truth, she did not dare to strike Dorothy, because of the mark upon her forehead. The child did not know this, and was full of fear for herself and Toto. Once the Witch struck Toto a blow with her umbrella and the brave little dog flew at her and bit her leg in return. The Witch did not bleed where she was bitten, for she was so wicked that the blood in her had dried up many years before.

Dorothy's life became very sad as she grew to understand that it would be harder than ever to get back to Kansas and Aunt Em again. Sometimes she would cry bitterly for hours, with Toto sitting at her feet and looking into her face, whining dismally to show how sorry he was for his little mistress. Toto did not really care whether he was in Kansas or the Land of Oz so long as Dorothy was with him; but he knew the little girl was unhappy, and that made him unhappy too.

Now the Wicked Witch had a great longing to have for her own the Silver Shoes which the girl always wore. Her bees and her crows and her wolves were lying in heaps and drying up, and she had used up all the power of the Golden Cap; but if she could only get hold of the Silver Shoes, they would give her more power than all the other things she had lost. She watched Dorothy carefully, to see if she ever took off her shoes, thinking she might steal them. But the child was so proud of her pretty shoes that she never took them off except at night and when she took her bath. The Witch was too much afraid of the dark to dare go in Dorothy's room at night to take the shoes, and her dread of water was greater than her fear of the dark, so she never came near when Dorothy was bathing. Indeed, the old Witch never touched water, nor ever let water touch her in any way.

But the wicked creature was very cunning, and she finally thought of a trick that would give her what she wanted. She placed a bar of iron in the middle of the kitchen floor, and then by her magic arts made the iron invisible to human eyes. So that when Dorothy walked across the floor she stumbled over the bar, not being able to see it, and fell at full length. She was not much hurt, but in her fall one of the Silver Shoes came off; and before she could reach it, the Witch had snatched it away and put it on her own skinny foot.

The wicked woman was greatly pleased with the success of her trick, for as long as she had one of the shoes she owned half the power of their charm, and Dorothy could not use it against her, even had she known how to do so.

The little girl, seeing she had lost one of her pretty shoes, grew angry, and said to the Witch, "Give me back my shoe!"

"I will not," retorted the Witch, "for it is now my shoe, and not yours."

"You are a wicked creature!" cried Dorothy. "You have no right to take my shoe from me."

"I shall keep it, just the same," said the Witch, laughing at her, "and someday I shall get the other one from you, too."

This made Dorothy so very angry that she picked up the bucket of water that stood near and dashed it over the Witch, wetting her from head to foot.

Instantly the wicked woman gave a loud cry of fear, and then, as Dorothy looked at her in wonder, the Witch began to shrink and fall away.

"See what you have done!" she screamed. "In a minute I shall melt away."

"I'm very sorry, indeed," said Dorothy, who was truly frightened to see the Witch actually melting away like brown sugar before her very eyes.

"Didn't you know water would be the end of me?" asked the Witch, in a wailing, despairing voice.

"Of course not," answered Dorothy. "How should I?"

"Well, in a few minutes I shall be all melted, and you will have the castle to yourself. I have been wicked in my day, but I never thought a little girl like you would ever be able to melt me and end my wicked deeds. Look out--here I go!"

With these words the Witch fell down in a brown, melted, shapeless mass and began to spread over the clean boards of the kitchen floor. Seeing that she had really melted away to nothing, Dorothy drew another bucket of water and threw it over the mess. She then swept it all out the door. After picking out the silver shoe, which was all that was left of the old woman, she cleaned and dried it with a cloth, and put it on her foot again. Then, being at last free to do as she chose, she ran out to the courtyard to tell the Lion that the Wicked Witch of the West had come to an end, and that they were no longer prisoners in a strange land.

Chapter 13. The Rescue

In the thirteenth chapter, Dorothy sets the Lion free from his prison. She calls the Winkies together to tell them that they now are free from the Witch's tyranny. She asks them to rescue the Scarecrow and the Tin Woodman. The Winkies restuff the Scarecrow and solder together and repair the Tin Woodman.

A few days later, the travelers decide to return to the Emerald City to tell the Wizard that they've accomplished their mission. On this occasion, Dorothy notices the Golden Cap. She doesn't know what it's supposed to be used for. But she decides to take it with her. The travelers all bid farewell to the Winkies and start off for the Emerald City.

Chapter 14. The Winged Monkeys

In the fourteenth chapter, the travelers soon become lost because of the lack of a road between the Witch's castle and the Emerald City. Dorothy summons the Queen of the Field Mice. The Queen tells the travelers that they have traveled in the wrong direction. She then notices the Golden Cap and suggests that Dorothy use it to summon the Winged Monkeys. The Queen tells Dorothy of the charm that's on the inside of the Cap and that summons the Winged Monkeys.

Dorothy uses the charm. The Winged Monkeys appear and carry the travelers through the air to the Emerald City. On the way there, the King explains why his Winged Monkeys must obey the commands of the possessor of the Golden Cap. He also explains why the Cap can be used by any given person only three times.

Chapter 15. The Discovery of Oz, the Terrible

The four travelers walked up to the great gate of Emerald City and rang the bell. After ringing several times, it was opened by the same Guardian of the Gates they had met before.

"What! are you back again?" he asked, in surprise.

"Do you not see us?" answered the Scarecrow.

"But I thought you had gone to visit the Wicked Witch of the West."

"We did visit her," said the Scarecrow.

"And she let you go again?" asked the man, in wonder.

"She could not help it, for she is melted," explained the Scarecrow.

"Melted! Well, that is good news, indeed," said the man. "Who melted her?"

"It was Dorothy," said the Lion gravely.

"Good gracious!" exclaimed the man, and he bowed very low indeed before her.

Then he led them into his little room and locked the spectacles from the great box on all their eyes, just as he had done before. Afterward they passed on through the gate into the Emerald City. When the people heard from the Guardian of the Gates that Dorothy had melted the Wicked Witch of the West, they all gathered around the travelers and followed them in a great crowd to the Palace of Oz.

The soldier with the green whiskers was still on guard before the door, but he let them in at once, and they were again met by the beautiful green girl, who showed each of them to their old rooms at once, so they might rest until the Great Oz was ready to receive them.

The soldier had the news carried straight to Oz that Dorothy and the other travelers had come back again, after destroying the Wicked Witch; but Oz made no reply. They thought the Great Wizard would send for them at once, but he did not. They had no word from him the next day, nor the next, nor the next. The waiting was tiresome and wearing, and at last they grew vexed that Oz should treat them in so poor a fashion, after sending them to undergo hardships and slavery. So the Scarecrow at last asked the green girl to take another message to Oz, saying if he did not let them in to see him at once they would call the Winged Monkeys to help them, and find out whether he kept his promises or not. When the Wizard was given this message he was so frightened that he sent word for them to come to the Throne Room at four minutes after nine o'clock the next morning. He had once met the Winged Monkeys in the Land of the West, and he did not wish to meet them again.

The four travelers passed a sleepless night, each thinking of the gift Oz had promised to bestow on him. Dorothy fell asleep only once, and then she dreamed she was in Kansas, where Aunt Em was telling her how glad she was to have her little girl at home again.

Promptly at nine o'clock the next morning the green-whiskered soldier came to them, and four minutes later they all went into the Throne Room of the Great Oz.

Of course each one of them expected to see the Wizard in the shape he had taken before, and all were greatly surprised when they looked about and saw no one at all in the room. They kept close to the door and closer to one another, for the stillness of the empty room was more dreadful than any of the forms they had seen Oz take.

Presently they heard a solemn Voice, that seemed to come from somewhere near the top of the great dome, and it said:

"I am Oz, the Great and Terrible. Why do you seek me?"

They looked again in every part of the room, and then, seeing no one, Dorothy asked, "Where are you?"

"I am everywhere," answered the Voice, "but to the eyes of common mortals I am invisible. I will now seat myself upon my throne, that you may converse with me." Indeed, the Voice seemed just then to come straight from the throne itself; so they walked toward it and stood in a row while Dorothy said:

"We have come to claim our promise, O Oz."

"What promise?" asked Oz.

"You promised to send me back to Kansas when the Wicked Witch was destroyed," said the girl.

"And you promised to give me brains," said the Scarecrow.

"And you promised to give me a heart," said the Tin Woodman.

"And you promised to give me courage," said the Cowardly Lion.

"Is the Wicked Witch really destroyed?" asked the Voice, and Dorothy thought it trembled a little.

"Yes," she answered, "I melted her with a bucket of water."

"Dear me," said the Voice, "how sudden! Well, come to me tomorrow, for I must have time to think it over."

"You've had plenty of time already," said the Tin Woodman angrily.

"We shan't wait a day longer," said the Scarecrow.

"You must keep your promises to us!" exclaimed Dorothy.

The Lion thought it might as well frighten the Wizard, so he gave a large, loud roar, which was so fierce and dreadful that Toto jumped away from him in alarm and tipped over the screen that stood in a corner. As it fell with a crash they looked that way, and the next moment all of them were filled with wonder. For they saw, standing in just the spot the screen had hidden, a little old man, with a bald head and a wrinkled face, who seemed to be as much surprised as they were. The Tin Woodman, raising his axe, rushed toward the little man and cried out, "Who are you?"

"I am Oz, the Great and Terrible," said the little man, in a trembling voice. "But don't strike me--please don't--and I'll do anything you want me to."

Our friends looked at him in surprise and dismay.

"I thought Oz was a great Head," said Dorothy.

"And I thought Oz was a lovely Lady," said the Scarecrow.

"And I thought Oz was a terrible Beast," said the Tin Woodman.

"And I thought Oz was a Ball of Fire," exclaimed the Lion.

"No, you are all wrong," said the little man meekly. "I have been making believe."

"Making believe!" cried Dorothy. "Are you not a Great Wizard?"

"Hush, my dear," he said. "Don't speak so loud, or you will be overheard--and I should be ruined. I'm supposed to be a Great Wizard."

"And aren't you?" she asked.

"Not a bit of it, my dear; I'm just a common man."

"You're more than that," said the Scarecrow, in a grieved tone; "you're a humbug."

"Exactly so!" declared the little man, rubbing his hands together as if it pleased him. "I am a humbug."

"But this is terrible," said the Tin Woodman. "How shall I ever get my heart?"

"Or I my courage?" asked the Lion.

"Or I my brains?" wailed the Scarecrow, wiping the tears from his eyes with his coat sleeve.

"My dear friends," said Oz, "I pray you not to speak of these little things. Think of me, and the terrible trouble I'm in at being found out."

"Doesn't anyone else know you're a humbug?" asked Dorothy.

"No one knows it but you four--and myself," replied Oz. "I have fooled everyone so long that I thought I should never be found out. It was a great mistake my ever letting you into the Throne Room. Usually I will not see even my subjects, and so they believe I am something terrible."

"But, I don't understand," said Dorothy, in bewilderment. "How was it that you appeared to me as a great Head?"

"That was one of my tricks," answered Oz. "Step this way, please, and I will tell you all about it."

He led the way to a small chamber in the rear of the Throne Room, and they all followed him. He pointed to one corner, in which lay the great Head, made out of many thicknesses of paper, and with a carefully painted face.

"This I hung from the ceiling by a wire," said Oz. "I stood behind the screen and pulled a thread, to make the eyes move and the mouth open."

"But how about the voice?" she inquired.

"Oh, I am a ventriloquist," said the little man. "I can throw the sound of my voice wherever I wish, so that you thought it was coming out of the Head. Here are the other things I used to deceive you." He showed the Scarecrow the dress and the mask he had worn when he seemed to be the lovely Lady. And the Tin Woodman saw that his terrible Beast was nothing but a lot of skins, sewn together, with slats to keep their sides out. As for the Ball of Fire, the false Wizard had hung that also from the ceiling. It was really a ball of cotton, but when oil was poured upon it the ball burned fiercely.

"Really," said the Scarecrow, "you ought to be ashamed of yourself for being such a humbug."

"I am--I certainly am," answered the little man sorrowfully; "but it was the only thing I could do. Sit down, please, there are plenty of chairs; and I will tell you my story."

So they sat down and listened while he told the following tale.

"I was born in Omaha--"

"Why, that isn't very far from Kansas!" cried Dorothy.

"No, but it's farther from here," he said, shaking his head at her sadly. "When I grew up I became a ventriloquist, and at that I was very well trained by a great master. I can imitate any kind of a bird or beast."

Here he mewed so like a kitten that Toto pricked up his ears and looked everywhere to see where she was. "After a time," continued Oz, "I tired of that, and became a balloonist."

"What is that?" asked Dorothy.

"A man who goes up in a balloon on circus day, so as to draw a crowd of people together and get them to pay to see the circus," he explained.

"Oh," she said, "I know."

"Well, one day I went up in a balloon and the ropes got twisted, so that I couldn't come down again. It went way up above the clouds, so far that a current of air struck it and carried it many, many miles away. For a day and a night I traveled through the air, and on the morning of the second day I awoke and found the balloon floating over a strange and beautiful country.

"It came down gradually, and I was not hurt a bit. But I found myself in the midst of a strange people, who, seeing me come from the clouds, thought I was a great Wizard. Of course I let them think so, because they were afraid of me, and promised to do anything I wished them to.

"Just to amuse myself, and keep the good people busy, I ordered them to build this City, and my Palace; and they did it all willingly and well. Then I thought, as the country was so green and beautiful, I would call it the Emerald City; and to make the name fit better I put green spectacles on all the people, so that everything they saw was green."

"But isn't everything here green?" asked Dorothy.

"No more than in any other city," replied Oz; "but when you wear green spectacles, why of course everything you see looks green to you. The Emerald City was built a great many years ago, for I was a young man when the balloon brought me here, and I am a very old man now. But my people have worn green glasses on their eyes so long that most of them think it really is an Emerald City, and it certainly is a beautiful place, abounding in jewels and precious metals, and every good thing that is needed to make one happy. I have been good to the people, and they like me; but ever since this Palace was built, I have shut myself up and would not see any of them.

"One of my greatest fears was the Witches, for while I had no magical powers at all I soon found out that the Witches were really able to do wonderful things. There were four of them in this country, and they ruled the people who live in the North and South and East and West.

Fortunately, the Witches of the North and South were good, and I knew they would do me no harm; but the Witches of the East and West were terribly wicked, and had they not thought I was more powerful than they themselves, they would surely have destroyed me. As it was, I lived in deadly fear of them for many years; so you can imagine how pleased I was when I heard your house had fallen on the Wicked Witch of the East. When you came to me, I was willing to promise anything if you would only do away with the other Witch; but, now that you have melted her, I am ashamed to say that I cannot keep my promises."

"I think you are a very bad man," said Dorothy.

"Oh, no, my dear; I'm really a very good man, but I'm a very bad Wizard, I must admit."

"Can't you give me brains?" asked the Scarecrow.

"You don't need them. You are learning something every day. A baby has brains, but it doesn't know much. Experience is the only thing that brings knowledge, and the longer you are on earth the more experience you are sure to get."

"That may all be true," said the Scarecrow, "but I shall be very unhappy unless you give me brains."

The false Wizard looked at him carefully.

"Well," he said with a sigh, "I'm not much of a magician, as I said; but if you will come to me tomorrow morning, I will stuff your head with brains. I cannot tell you how to use them, however; you must find that out for yourself."

"Oh, thank you--thank you!" cried the Scarecrow. "I'll find a way to use them, never fear!"

"But how about my courage?" asked the Lion anxiously.

"You have plenty of courage, I am sure," answered Oz. "All you need is confidence in yourself. There is no living thing that is not afraid when it faces danger. The True courage is in facing danger when you are afraid, and that kind of courage you have in plenty."

"Perhaps I have, but I'm scared just the same," said the Lion. "I shall really be very unhappy unless you give me the sort of courage that makes one forget he is afraid."

"Very well, I will give you that sort of courage tomorrow," replied Oz.

"How about my heart?" asked the Tin Woodman.

"Why, as for that," answered Oz, "I think you are wrong to want a heart. It makes most people unhappy. If you only knew it, you are in luck not to have a heart."

"That must be a matter of opinion," said the Tin Woodman. "For my part, I will bear all the unhappiness without a murmur, if you will give me the heart."

"Very well," answered Oz meekly. "Come to me tomorrow and you shall have a heart. I have played Wizard for so many years that I may as well continue the part a little longer."

"And now," said Dorothy, "how am I to get back to Kansas?"

"We shall have to think about that," replied the little man. "Give me two or three days to consider the matter and I'll try to find a way to carry you over the desert. In the meantime you shall all be treated as my guests, and while you live in the Palace my people will wait upon you and obey your slightest wish. There is only one thing I ask in return for my help--such as it is. You must keep my secret and tell no one I am a humbug."

They agreed to say nothing of what they had learned, and went back to their rooms in high spirits. Even Dorothy had hope that "The Great and Terrible Humbug," as she called him, would find a way to send her back to Kansas, and if he did she was willing to forgive him everything.

Chapter 16. The Magic Art of the Great Humbug

Next morning the Scarecrow said to his friends:

"Congratulate me. I am going to Oz to get my brains at last. When I return I shall be as other men are."

"I have always liked you as you were," said Dorothy simply.

"It is kind of you to like a Scarecrow," he replied. "But surely you will think more of me when you hear the splendid thoughts my new brain is going to turn out." Then he said good-bye to them all in a cheerful voice and went to the Throne Room, where he rapped upon the door.

"Come in," said Oz.

The Scarecrow went in and found the little man sitting down by the window, engaged in deep thought.

"I have come for my brains," remarked the Scarecrow, a little uneasily.

"Oh, yes; sit down in that chair, please," replied Oz. "You must excuse me for taking your head off, but I shall have to do it in order to put your brains in their proper place."

"That's all right," said the Scarecrow. "You are quite welcome to take my head off, as long as it will be a better one when you put it on again."

So the Wizard unfastened his head and emptied out the straw. Then he entered the back room and took up a measure of bran, which he mixed with a great many pins and needles. Having shaken them together thoroughly, he filled the top of the Scarecrow's head with the mixture and stuffed the rest of the space with straw, to hold it in place.

When he had fastened the Scarecrow's head on his body again he said to him, "Hereafter you will be a great man, for I have given you a lot of bran-new brains."

The Scarecrow was both pleased and proud at the fulfillment of his greatest wish, and having thanked Oz warmly he went back to his friends.

Dorothy looked at him curiously. His head was quite bulged out at the top with brains.

"How do you feel?" she asked.

"I feel wise indeed," he answered earnestly. "When I get used to my brains I shall know everything."

"Why are those needles and pins sticking out of your head?" asked the Tin Woodman.

"That is proof that he is sharp," remarked the Lion.

"Well, I must go to Oz and get my heart," said the Woodman. So he walked to the Throne Room and knocked at the door.

"Come in," called Oz, and the Woodman entered and said, "I have come for my heart."

"Very well," answered the little man. "But I shall have to cut a hole in your breast, so I can put your heart in the right place. I hope it won't hurt you."

"Oh, no," answered the Woodman. "I shall not feel it at all."

So Oz brought a pair of tinsmith's shears and cut a small, square hole in the left side of the Tin Woodman's breast. Then, going to a chest of drawers, he took out a pretty heart, made entirely of silk and stuffed with sawdust.

"Isn't it a beauty?" he asked.

"It is, indeed!" replied the Woodman, who was greatly pleased. "But is it a kind heart?"

"Oh, very!" answered Oz. He put the heart in the Woodman's breast and then replaced the square of tin, soldering it neatly together where it had been cut.

"There," said he; "now you have a heart that any man might be proud of. I'm sorry I had to put a patch on your breast, but it really couldn't be helped."

"Never mind the patch," exclaimed the happy Woodman. "I am very grateful to you, and shall never forget your kindness."

"Don't speak of it," replied Oz.

Then the Tin Woodman went back to his friends, who wished him every joy on account of his good fortune.

The Lion now walked to the Throne Room and knocked at the door.

"Come in," said Oz.

"I have come for my courage," announced the Lion, entering the room.

"Very well," answered the little man; "I will get it for you."

He went to a cupboard and reaching up to a high shelf took down a square green bottle, the contents of which he poured into a green-gold dish, beautifully carved. Placing this before the Cowardly Lion, who sniffed at it as if he did not like it, the Wizard said:

"Drink."

"What is it?" asked the Lion.

"Well," answered Oz, "if it were inside of you, it would be courage. You know, of course, that courage is always inside one; so that this really cannot be called courage until you have swallowed it. Therefore I advise you to drink it as soon as possible."

The Lion hesitated no longer, but drank till the dish was empty.

"How do you feel now?" asked Oz.

"Full of courage," replied the Lion, who went joyfully back to his friends to tell them of his good fortune.

Oz, left to himself, smiled to think of his success in giving the Scarecrow and the Tin Woodman and the Lion exactly what they thought they wanted. "How can I help being a humbug," he said, "when all these people make me do things that everybody knows can't be done? It was easy to make the Scarecrow and the Lion and the Woodman happy, because they imagined I could do anything. But it will take more than imagination to carry Dorothy back to Kansas, and I'm sure I don't know how it can be done."

Chapter 17. How the Balloon Was Launched

For three days Dorothy heard nothing from Oz. These were sad days for the little girl, although her friends were all quite happy and contented. The Scarecrow told them there were wonderful thoughts in his head; but he would not say what they were because he knew no one could understand them but himself. When the Tin Woodman walked about he felt his heart rattling around in his breast; and he told Dorothy he had discovered it to be a kinder and more tender heart than the one he had owned when he was made of flesh. The Lion declared he was afraid of nothing on earth, and would gladly face an army or a dozen of the fierce Kalidahs.

Thus each of the little party was satisfied except Dorothy, who longed more than ever to get back to Kansas.

On the fourth day, to her great joy, Oz sent for her, and when she entered the Throne Room he greeted her pleasantly:

"Sit down, my dear; I think I have found the way to get you out of this country."

"And back to Kansas?" she asked eagerly.

"Well, I'm not sure about Kansas," said Oz, "for I haven't the faintest notion which way it lies. But the first thing to do is to cross the desert, and then it should be easy to find your way home."

"How can I cross the desert?" she inquired.

"Well, I'll tell you what I think," said the little man. "You see, when I came to this country it was in a balloon. You also came through the air, being carried by a cyclone. So I believe the best way to get across the desert will be through the air. Now, it is quite beyond my powers to make a cyclone; but I've been thinking the matter over, and I believe I can make a balloon."

"How?" asked Dorothy.

"A balloon," said Oz, "is made of silk, which is coated with glue to keep the gas in it. I have plenty of silk in the Palace, so it will be no trouble to make the balloon. But in all this country there is no gas to fill the balloon with, to make it float."

"If it won't float," remarked Dorothy, "it will be of no use to us."

"True," answered Oz. "But there is another way to make it float, which is to fill it with hot air. Hot air isn't as good as gas, for if the air should get cold the balloon would come down in the desert, and we should be lost."

"We!" exclaimed the girl. "Are you going with me?"

"Yes, of course," replied Oz. "I am tired of being such a humbug. If I should go out of this Palace my people would soon discover I am not a Wizard, and then they would be vexed with me for having deceived them. So I have to stay shut up in these rooms all day, and it gets tiresome. I'd much rather go back to Kansas with you and be in a circus again."

"I shall be glad to have your company," said Dorothy.

"Thank you," he answered. "Now, if you will help me sew the silk together, we will begin to work on our balloon."

So Dorothy took a needle and thread, and as fast as Oz cut the strips of silk into proper shape the girl sewed them neatly together. First there was a strip of light green silk, then a strip of dark green and then a strip of emerald green; for Oz had a fancy to make the balloon in different shades of the color about them. It took three days to sew all the strips together, but when it was finished they had a big bag of green silk more than twenty feet long.

Then Oz painted it on the inside with a coat of thin glue, to make it airtight, after which he announced that the balloon was ready.

"But we must have a basket to ride in," he said. So he sent the soldier with the green whiskers for a big clothes basket, which he fastened with many ropes to the bottom of the balloon.

When it was all ready, Oz sent word to his people that he was going to make a visit to a great brother Wizard who lived in the clouds. The news spread rapidly throughout the city and everyone came to see the wonderful sight.

Oz ordered the balloon carried out in front of the Palace, and the people gazed upon it with much curiosity. The Tin Woodman had chopped a big pile of wood, and now he made a fire of it, and Oz held the bottom of the balloon over the fire so that the hot air that arose from it would be caught in the silken bag. Gradually the balloon swelled out and rose into the air, until finally the basket just touched the ground.

Then Oz got into the basket and said to all the people in a loud voice: "I am now going away to make a visit. While I am gone the Scarecrow will rule over you. I command you to obey him as you would me."

The balloon was by this time tugging hard at the rope that held it to the ground, for the air within it was hot, and this made it so much lighter in weight than the air without that it pulled hard to rise into the sky.

"Come, Dorothy!" cried the Wizard. "Hurry up, or the balloon will fly away."

"I can't find Toto anywhere," replied Dorothy, who did not wish to leave her little dog behind. Toto had run into the crowd to bark at a kitten, and Dorothy at last found him. She picked him up and ran towards the balloon.

She was within a few steps of it, and Oz was holding out his hands to help her into the basket, when, crack! went the ropes, and the balloon rose into the air without her.

"Come back!" she screamed. "I want to go, too!"

"I can't come back, my dear," called Oz from the basket. "Good-bye!"

"Good-bye!" shouted everyone, and all eyes were turned upward to where the Wizard was riding in the basket, rising every moment farther and farther into the sky.

And that was the last any of them ever saw of Oz, the Wonderful Wizard, though he may have reached Omaha safely, and be there now, for all we know. But the people remembered him lovingly, and said to one another:

"Oz was always our friend. When he was here he built for us this beautiful Emerald City, and now he is gone he has left the Wise Scarecrow to rule over us."

Still, for many days they grieved over the loss of the Wonderful Wizard, and would not be comforted.

Chapter 18. Away to the South

In the eighteenth chapter, the Scarecrow suggests that Dorothy have the Winged Monkeys take her back to Kansas. Dorothy accepts the suggestion. But the King of the Winged Monkeys declares that this is impossible. The Winged Monkeys never have been in Kansas, and they can't leave the land of Oz.

The Soldier with the Green Whiskers then is called for. He suggests that Glinda, the Good Witch of the South, may be able to help. He explains that Quadling inhabitants of the southern part of Oz never visit the Emerald City on account of the dangers in the way.

The Scarecrow decides that Dorothy's best course is to visit Glinda. He, the Tin Woodman, and the Cowardly Lion all decide to accompany her there.

Chapter 19. Attacked by the Fighting Tree

In the nineteenth chapter, the travelers head straight south from the Emerald City. On the second day of their trip, they come across a large, dense forest. The Scarecrow takes the lead and tries to enter the forest. But the first tree that he passes grabs him and throws him back.

The Tin Woodman then tries to enter the forest. The tree, which is one of the Fighting Trees, tries to grab him too. But the Woodman chops off the branch that the tree is using. While the tree is shaking from pain, the other travelers pass by it. The other trees don't resist them.

But at the far end of the forest, they meet up with a high wall made of china. There apparently is no doorway in the wall.

Chapter 20. The Dainty China Country

In the twentieth chapter, the Tin Woodman fashions a ladder. The travelers climb the ladder to reach the top of the wall. There they notice that everything below them and beyond the wall is made of china. But the ladder is too heavy to pull up and over the top of the wall. The ground below is made of china. So the Scarecrow falls off the wall, and the others jump onto him so he can cushion them against the hard ground. They then walk carefully through the China Country. But on the way, a cow that's being milked suddenly kicks over the pail, breaking both her leg and the pail.

The travelers therefore become extra careful. They do whatever they can to make sure that no further damage is done to the China Country or its inhabitants.

Presently they reach the wall marking the boundary of this fragile domain. It isn't as high as the first wall. By standing on the back of the Cowardly Lion, the other travelers all reach the top. The Cowardly Lion then jumps onto the wall top and accidentally destroys a china church with his tail.

Chapter 21. The Lion becomes the King of Beasts

In the twenty-first chapter, the travelers descend from the wall. They pass through an area of bogs. They then enter another forest, where the beasts are having a meeting. The Cowardly Lion discovers that a most tremendous monster like a great spider has been attacking and eating them. He finds the giant spider asleep, jumps onto the monster's back, and beheads it with a single blow of his paw. When the other beasts find out what has happened, they acknowledge the Cowardly Lion as their King.

Chapter 22. The Country of Quadlings

Beyond the forest, in the twenty-second chapter, the travelers come across the land of the Hammerheads. The Hammerheads have no arms. But their stretchable necks allow them to use their heads to butt anyone who tries to enter their country.

The Scarecrow and the Cowardly Lion both defy the Hammerheads' order to keep out. Both of them are butted down the hill that marks the boundary of the Hammerhead country. So Dorothy uses the Golden Cap to summon the Winged Monkeys, who carry the travelers through the air and far beyond the shooting range of the Hammerheads' heads. The Winged Monkeys point out that this is the last time that Dorothy can call them.

The travelers meet with no further difficulties. Presently they arrive at Glinda's castle. There, they obtain immediate admittance.

Chapter 23. Glinda The Good Witch Grants Dorothy's Wish

Before they went to see Glinda, however, they were taken to a room of the Castle, where Dorothy washed her face and combed her hair, and the Lion shook the dust out of his mane, and the Scarecrow patted himself into his best shape, and the Woodman polished his tin and oiled his joints.

When they were all quite presentable they followed the soldier girl into a big room where the Witch Glinda sat upon a throne of rubies.

She was both beautiful and young to their eyes. Her hair was a rich red in color and fell in flowing ringlets over her shoulders. Her dress was pure white but her eyes were blue, and they looked kindly upon the little girl.

"What can I do for you, my child?" she asked.

Dorothy told the Witch all her story: how the cyclone had brought her to the Land of Oz, how she had found her companions, and of the wonderful adventures they had met with.

"My greatest wish now," she added, "is to get back to Kansas, for Aunt Em will surely think something dreadful has happened to me, and that will make her put on mourning; and unless the crops are better this year than they were last, I am sure Uncle Henry cannot afford it."

Glinda leaned forward and kissed the sweet, upturned face of the loving little girl.

"Bless your dear heart," she said, "I am sure I can tell you of a way to get back to Kansas." Then she added, "But, if I do, you must give me the Golden Cap."

"Willingly!" exclaimed Dorothy; "indeed, it is of no use to me now, and when you have it you can command the Winged Monkeys three times."

"And I think I shall need their service just those three times," answered Glinda, smiling.

Dorothy then gave her the Golden Cap, and the Witch said to the Scarecrow, "What will you do when Dorothy has left us?"

"I will return to the Emerald City," he replied, "for Oz has made me its ruler and the people like me. The only thing that worries me is how to cross the hill of the Hammer-Heads."

"By means of the Golden Cap I shall command the Winged Monkeys to carry you to the gates of the Emerald City," said Glinda, "for it would be a shame to deprive the people of so wonderful a ruler."

"Am I really wonderful?" asked the Scarecrow.

"You are unusual," replied Glinda.

Turning to the Tin Woodman, she asked, "What will become of you when Dorothy leaves this country?"

He leaned on his axe and thought a moment. Then he said, "The Winkies were very kind to me, and wanted me to rule over them after the Wicked Witch died. I am fond of the Winkies, and if I could get back again to the Country of the West, I should like nothing better than to rule over them forever."

"My second command to the Winged Monkeys," said Glinda "will be that they carry you safely to the land of the Winkies. Your brain may not be so large to look at as those of the Scarecrow, but you are really brighter than he is--when you are well polished--and I am sure you will rule the Winkies wisely and well."

Then the Witch looked at the big, shaggy Lion and asked, "When Dorothy has returned to her own home, what will become of you?"

"Over the hill of the Hammer-Heads," he answered, "lies a grand old forest, and all the beasts that live there have made me their King. If I could only get back to this forest, I would pass my life very happily there."

"My third command to the Winged Monkeys," said Glinda, "shall be to carry you to your forest. Then, having used up the powers of the Golden Cap, I shall give it to the King of the Monkeys, that he and his band may thereafter be free for evermore."

The Scarecrow and the Tin Woodman and the Lion now thanked the Good Witch earnestly for her kindness; and Dorothy exclaimed:

"You are certainly as good as you are beautiful! But you have not yet told me how to get back to Kansas."

"Your Silver Shoes will carry you over the desert," replied Glinda. "If you had known their power you could have gone back to your Aunt Em the very first day you came to this country."

"But then I should not have had my wonderful brains!" cried the

Scarecrow. "I might have passed my whole life in the farmer's cornfield."

"And I should not have had my lovely heart," said the Tin Woodman. "I might have stood and rusted in the forest till the end of the world."

"And I should have lived a coward forever," declared the Lion, "and no beast in all the forest would have had a good word to say to me."

"This is all true," said Dorothy, "and I am glad I was of use to these good friends. But now that each of them has had what he most desired, and each is happy in having a kingdom to rule besides, I think I should like to go back to Kansas."

"The Silver Shoes," said the Good Witch, "have wonderful powers. And one of the most curious things about them is that they can carry you to any place in the world in three steps, and each step will be made in the wink of an eye. All you have to do is to knock the heels together three times and command the shoes to carry you wherever you wish to go."

"If that is so," said the child joyfully, "I will ask them to carry me back to Kansas at once."

She threw her arms around the Lion's neck and kissed him, patting his big head tenderly. Then she kissed the Tin Woodman, who was weeping in a way most dangerous to his joints. But she hugged the soft, stuffed body of the Scarecrow in her arms instead of kissing his painted face, and found she was crying herself at this sorrowful parting from her loving comrades.

Glinda the Good stepped down from her ruby throne to give the little girl a good-bye kiss, and Dorothy thanked her for all the kindness she had shown to her friends and herself.

Dorothy now took Toto up solemnly in her arms, and having said one last good-bye she clapped the heels of her shoes together three times, saying:

"Take me home to Aunt Em!"

Instantly she was whirling through the air, so swiftly that all she could see or feel was the wind whistling past her ears.

The Silver Shoes took but three steps, and then she stopped so suddenly that she rolled over upon the grass several times before she knew where she was.

At length, however, she sat up and looked about her.

"Good gracious!" she cried.

For she was sitting on the broad Kansas prairie, and just before her was the new farmhouse Uncle Henry built after the cyclone had carried away the old one. Uncle Henry was milking the cows in the barnyard, and Toto had jumped out of her arms and was running toward the barn, barking furiously.

Dorothy stood up and found she was in her stocking-feet. For the Silver Shoes had fallen off in her flight through the air, and were lost forever in the desert.

Chapter 24. Home Again

Aunt Em had just come out of the house to water the cabbages when she looked up and saw Dorothy running toward her.

"My darling child!" she cried, folding the little girl in her arms and covering her face with kisses. "Where in the world did you come from?"

"From the Land of Oz," said Dorothy gravely. "And here is Toto, too. And oh, Aunt Em! I'm so glad to be at home again!"